Alexander

Alexander
Destiny and Myth

Claude Mossé

translated by
Janet Lloyd

with a Foreword by
Paul Cartledge

The Johns Hopkins University Press
Baltimore, Maryland

Alexandre: La destinée d'un mythe first published in French in 2001 by
Éditions Payot & Rivages
First published in the United Kingdom by Edinburgh University Press, 2004
Published in the United States by The Johns Hopkins University Press, 2004
1 2 3 4 5 6 7 8 9

The Johns Hopkins University Press
2715 North Charles Street
Baltimore, Maryland 21218-4363
www.press.jhu.edu

ISBN 0-8018-7995-7
ISBN 0-8018-7996-5 (pbk.)

Library of Congress Control Number: 2003116212

A catalog record for this book is available from the British Library.

This book is supported by the French Ministry for Foreign Affairs, as part of the
Burgess programme headed for the French Embassy in London by the Institut
Français du Royaume-Uni.

Liberté · Égalité · Fraternité
RÉPUBLIQUE FRANÇAISE

The publishers thank the French Ministry of Culture – National Book Centre – for
kindly granting a translation subvention.

Contents

Part IV: The Legacy of Alexander

Part V: Alexander the Mythical Hero

'Some more talk of Alexander'

Paul Cartledge

Quot auctores, tot Alexandri. Every student has an Alexander of her or his own. Just to canvass in outline the views of some of the leading scholars of the past century, we have had Ulrich Wilcken's reasonable Alexander, the gentlemanly and visionary Alexander of W. W. Tarn, the titanic and Führer-like Alexander of Fritz Schachermeyr, the Homerically heroic Alexander of Robin Lane Fox, and the amoral and ruthlessly pragmatic Alexander of Ernst Badian and Brian Bosworth.

There are three main reasons for this enormous diversity. The first is common to pretty much all historiography or biography: we – whether 'we' are formally paid-up historians or not – make the past in our own image, and all history is, up to a point, contemporary history, in the sense that present concerns and our own self-image inevitably condition or at any rate colour our perception and representation of past figures. Second, there is the specific character of the extant written evidence for Alexander: though ample in quantity, it is poor in historical quality, being mostly non-contemporary and partial in both senses (both incomplete and biased). So far as its dating goes, it is as if, one historian has written, we had to try to recover the history of Tudor England (sixteenth century) only from the essays of T. B. Macaulay (nineteenth century) and the histories of the philosopher David Hume (eighteenth century). So far as the bias is concerned, it is one of the paradoxes of history (and historiography) that this king, who took unusual trouble to secure the preservation of his own desired point of view, should have been handed down finally in history as an enigma. Which in turn leads to the third reason for the diversity of modern estimates of Alexander:

so stupendously mind-boggling were his achievements, however one glosses them morally or in any other way, that we historians inevitably interpret the great drama of his life and career in terms of our own – relatively puny – dreams and experience.

Claude Mossé, the distinguished French historian of ancient Greece from Mycenaean through Hellenistic times, was therefore both historically prudent and historiographically astute in deliberately casting her study of Alexander chiefly as a study of his legacy and above all his perception and reception. Her Alexander, therefore, is in a sense not hers – peculiarly and exclusively – at all, but rather an amalgam of all the most influential previous Alexanders, not excluding that of the recent trilogy of Alexander novels by Valerio Massimo Manfredi, originally in Italian but quickly translated into both French and English, on which one of the two Alexander films in development as I write is being based. This wise approach not only makes her study of inestimable value as a documentary record of the historiography and other kinds of writing about or representations of Alexander. It also gives it an exceptionally contemporary and up-to-the-minute feel.

Mossé divides her book into five parts. The first is a relatively conventional attempt to reconstruct the major stages of Alexander's reign, his *res gestae*, as the Romans would have called them. She first sets the scene at the time of Alexander's accession to the throne of Macedon in 336. By then, Macedon's empire embraced most of northern Greece and the immediately adjacent areas between the Adriatic and the Black Sea, nearly as far north as the Danube, and almost all of mainland Greece to the south – the one major exclusion, Sparta, was deliberately left out in the cold by Alexander's mercurial father, Philip II, whose assassination had opened the way to the throne for his 20-year-old son. She then treats of his initial establishment of his authority both within Macedon and over Greece before embarking on the Asiatic campaign that had been left to him as his principal legacy by Philip and already begun at the time of Philip's assassination.

She divides her account of Alexander's conquest of the Persian Great King Darius III and his Achaemenid empire (334–331) into two, between the western and the eastern satrapies (administrative provinces, ruled by viceroys), then tracks Alexander's conquest of the upper satrapies (roughly modern Afghanistan), his Indian campaign, and his return to Susa in southern Iran (Darius's and now his administrative capital) and to Babylon (capital city of the richest single satrapy), where he died prematurely, aged only 32, on 10 June 323.

Part II explores the different faces or images of Alexander that he presented, or had presented, to the various different groups of his subjects: his fellow-Macedonians, other Greeks, and his new Oriental subjects. Mossé rightly pays special attention to the foundation of new cities, whether for pragmatic or symbolic purposes or both, to the delicate diplomatic mission to the Greeks then celebrating the quintessentially panhellenic festival of the Olympic Games at Olympia with which he entrusted Nicanor in 324, to his partial adoption of Iranian vestiments and regalia, and to the role played by women in his life and rule. But it is the final chapter of Part II, 'The son of Zeus', that brings Mossé to the heart of her own (re)presentation: Alexander as a myth, and myths of Alexander, both as developed or exploited by Alexander himself and as received and enhanced by his Macedonian and Greek subjects.

Alexander as 'invincible god' (*theos anikêtos*) leads Mossé, paradoxically but naturally, into Part III, 'Alexander the Man', inevitably the most elusive of all her quarries. A huge debate still surrounds the question of Alexander's character, even if modern historians like to pretend that they are far from wishing to take a moral stance or adopt a moral tone on the topic. Plutarch and Arrian, two of our most worthwhile extant sources, had no such historiographical qualms, even if they also lacked some of what we like to think of as our post-Freudian finesse.

The final two parts, 'The Legacy of Alexander' and 'Alexander the Mythical Hero', are really two sides of a single coin. The former deals with what Alexander had in his possession to bequeath, the latter with what was made of his bequest in antiquity, and in the medieval and modern worlds. Mossé duly emphasises the fragility and dislocation of Alexander's neo-imperial construction, combining as it did a new type or style of monarchy with the birth of a new economic and social order. But in the end she emphasises, as Alexander – driven ever onwards by one or other gigantic *pothos* (yearning, irresistible desire) – undoubtedly would not have done, the limits of his achievement, particularly as regards the extent or depth of the Hellenisation experienced by his Oriental subjects and their descendants. The case of Judaism, singular no doubt to some degree and in some respects, is used as a yardstick to measure the strength of native cultural resistance to Hellenism.

Finally, images of Alexander as mythical hero are traced from antiquity to the present day by way of ancient, medieval and early modern written texts and visual images. For the new Anglophone readership at which this translation is aimed the chapter on Alexander's image in seventeenth- and eighteenth-century France will come over as especially original and welcome. On the other hand, the chapters on the historical, the pseudo-historical and the frankly fictional representations are remarkable rather for the succinct catholicity of their reach.

She ends her survey with two historical novels, one published in 1929 by Klaus Mann (son of Thomas), the other – already mentioned in my third paragraph – by Valerio Massimo Manfredi in the late 1990s. Manfredi's novel supposedly belongs, as an artful postface finally reveals, to what scholars call the 'official' tradition of Alexander historiography, the one that goes back via the extant Arrian to the lost accounts of Ptolemy (of Macedon and later Egypt) and Aristoboulus, and, through them, ultimately to the equally lost and anyway forcibly interrupted account of Alexander's own official historian, Callisthenes of Olynthus, a relative of his one-time teacher Aristotle. Perhaps Ptolemy, the supposed 'author' of Manfredi's novel, really did overlook or omit to mention any kind of sexual activity by Alexander other than heterosexual encounters with physically mature females. But, as Mossé clearly implies, it beggars the imagination to suppose that in reality Alexander never had sex with anyone of his own gender, or with an immature male, and on Mann's part, as she states, 'the choice of a particular kind of sexuality is definitely made' – his Alexander is a preferred homosexual. Strangely, and in a way sadly, it is the straight Manfredi version, not the countercultural Mann version, that is coming very slowly towards a cinema screen near you, courtesy of Dino de Laurentis and Baz Luhrmann. Those with fond memories of Hollywood's homosexually inclined 'beefcake' movies of the

1950s – when the last major movie of Alexander was made – are in for a bitter disappointment.

Which is very far from being the experience that awaits the reader of this lively, learned but never oppressively so, engaged and engaging book. Not that Claude Mossé has said, or would claim to have said, the last word on any of the many topics she addresses. The debate – or rather the many debates – surrounding Alexander will irresistibly and irrepressibly go on, as long as he is found to speak to our dreams. Hence the provision, for this new English edition, of a dedicated supplementary bibliography. Attention may be drawn specially to the collection edited by Ian Worthington, which conveys a very fair flavour of the current state – or states – of play.

Even Worthington's large and fine-meshed net has failed to trawl my final exhibit, however. As I write, the 'London's Best Sellers' list printed in the capital's main newspaper, the *Standard*, for 12 May 2003 includes under non-fiction the following intriguing item (coming in at no. 5, out of five): Partha Bose's *Alexander the Great's Art of Strategy*. Consulting Amazon's website entry for this presumably popular book reveals that it falls, allegedly, into all the following categories: history, business, finance and law. This is, in fact, a self-help how-to book for business people, the catchline of which is that many of the ideas and concepts associated with the decision-making and strategy used by managers and executives today have their origins in the career of Alexander – promoted here (rather less controversially, it must be said) as arguably the greatest military strategist, tactician and ruler in world history. The *Standard's* laconic one-word comment is 'inspiring' – but surely that should have read 'stranger than fiction'? At all events, books like this (if any other books can be quite like this) – and the Manfredi trilogy, and the Hollywood movies – will together ensure that the myth or mirage of Alexander continues to be alive and well in all the major shrines of modern culture.

Clare College, Cambridge, June 2003

Alexander
Destiny and Myth

Alexander's Asiatic Expedition

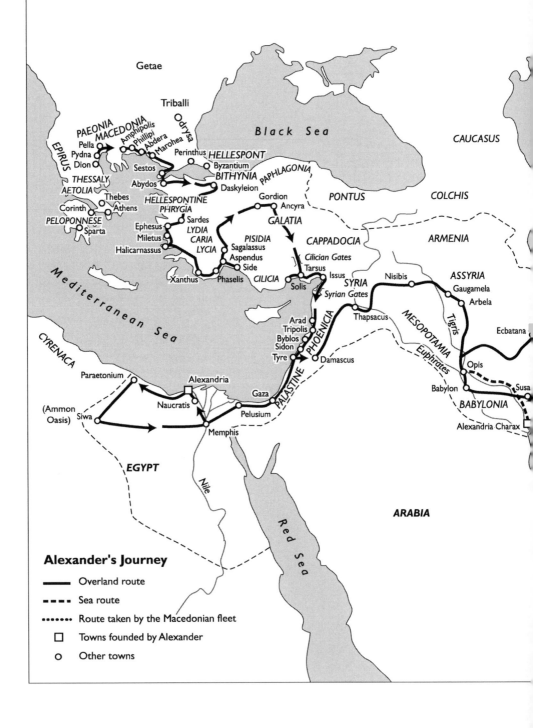

Getae

Triballi

PAEONIA
MACEDONIA
EPIRUS
Pella
Pydna
Dion
THESSALY
AETOLIA
Corinth
PELOPONNESE
Sparta
Thebes
Athens
Amphipolis
Phillipi
Abdera
Marohea
Perinthus
Byzantium
Sestos
Abydos
HELLESPONT
BITHYNIA
Daskyleion
HELLESPONTINE
PHRYGIA
Sardes
Ephesus
Miletus
Halicarnassus
LYDIA
CARIA
LYCIA
Xanthus
Phaselis
PISIDIA
Sagalassus
Aspendus
Side
CILICIA

Odrysa

Black Sea

PAPHLAGONIA
Gordion
Ancyra
GALATIA

PONTUS

CAUCASUS

COLCHIS

CAPPADOCIA
Cilician Gates
Tarsus
Solis
Issus
Syrian Gates

ARMENIA

Nisibis

SYRIA
Thapsacus
ASSYRIA
Gaugamela
Arbela

Mediterranean Sea

Arad
Tripolis
Byblos
Sidon
Tyre
PHOENICIA
Damascus

MESOPOTAMIA
Euphrates
Tigris

Ecbatana

Opis

CYRENACA

Paraetonium

Alexandria
Naucratis
Gaza
Pelusium
Memphis

PALESTINE

Babylon
BABYLONIA
Alexandria Charax

Susa

(Ammon
Oasis)
Siwa

EGYPT

Nile

Red Sea

ARABIA

Alexander's Journey

———	Overland route
- - -	Sea route
·······	Route taken by the Macedonian fleet
□	Towns founded by Alexander
o	Other towns

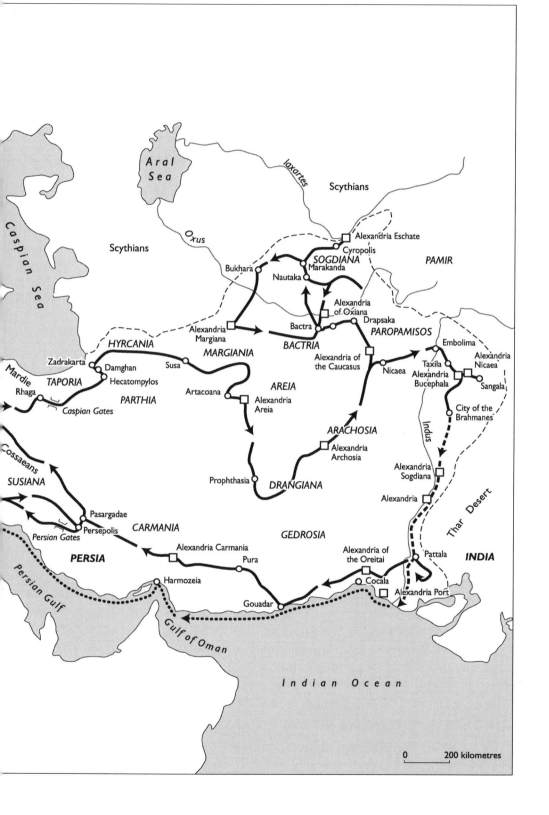

Aral
Sea

Iaxartes

Scythians

Scythians

Oxus

Caspian
Sea

Alexandria Eschate
Cyropolis
SOGDIANA
Bukhara   Marakanda
Nautaka
Alexandria
of Oxiana
Drapsaka
Alexandria
Margiana   Bactra   PAROPAMISOS
BACTRIA

PAMIR

Embolima

Zadrakarta
HYRCANIA   MARGIANIA
Susa
Damghan
Hecatompylos
TAPORIA
Mardie
Rhaga
Caspian Gates
PARTHIA   Artacoana
AREIA
Alexandria
Areia

Alexandria of
the Caucasus
Nicaea

Taxila   Alexandria
Nicaea
Alexandria
Bucephala   Sangala

City of the
Brahmanes

Indus

Cossaeans
SUSIANA

Pasargadae
Persepolis
Persian Gates
PERSIA

CARMANIA

Prophthasia   DRANGIANA

ARACHOSIA
Alexandria
Archosia

Alexandria
Sogdiana

Alexandria

Thar Desert

Alexandria Carmania
Pura

GEDROSIA

Alexandria of
the Oreitai   Pattala   INDIA

Harmozeia

Cocala

Persian Gulf

Gouadar   Alexandria Port

Gulf of Oman

Indian   Ocean

0   200 kilometres

Introduction

Few historical figures can have aroused as much admiration as Alexander the Great, the Macedonian king who, in little over ten years, between 334 and 323 BC, conquered the immense Persian Empire and led his army as far as India. Even in antiquity, he was already a legendary hero, and over the centuries he has remained the model of all good generals, all great conquerors, all those who, at a given point in history, have aspired to supreme power. Yet few of the actors in that history present the historian with as many problems. Paradoxical though it may seem in the case of a contemporary of Demosthenes and Aristotle, whose works fill many shelves in our libraries, we possess only a very little direct evidence on Alexander: just a few allusions in the speeches of the Athenian orators, a few inscriptions from the Greek cities of Asia Minor, a few coins some of whose dates are uncertain, and a few portraits. The extant accounts of his extraordinary epic were written three or more centuries after his time. Not that contemporaries of his who took part in his conquest left no records of its progress; but their works have not been preserved for us, so we know of them only through the references made to them by much later authors, such as the historian Diodorus Siculus, a contemporary of Caesar and Augustus, the moralist Plutarch who, one century later, produced a *Life of Alexander* and two treatises *On the Fortune of Alexander*, the first-century AD Roman Quintus Curtius, and the second-century AD Greek Arrian of Nicomedia. Those four authors constitute our principal sources. Moreover, in the course of the four or five centuries that separate them from their hero, the legend surrounding him had been growing ever richer and the image, or rather images, that they have transmitted to us are clearly marked by that enrichment. On the basis of the evidence that these authors provide it may be possible to reconstruct the various stages of Alexander's conquest of the Persian Empire, but it is more difficult to pass any judgement on the man himself, his behaviour and his aspirations. Nevertheless, the fact remains that after Alexander the world of the eastern Mediterranean was no longer the same as it was before him. It is also undeniable that his brief thirteen-year reign marked the end of not only the vast empire constructed by Cyrus II the Great from the mid-sixth century BC onwards, but also the civilisation of classical Greece or, more precisely, the type of political culture of which Athens had been the 'model' for over a century and a half. Of course, Greek cities continued to exist after the death of Alexander, but they no longer carried any real weight in the determination of Mediterranean politics, which now passed into the hands of the kings who had become the masters of the vast states created out of Alexander's conquest – kings who based their authority on their claims to the conqueror's legacy. It is perhaps that legacy, even more than the great adventure itself, that makes the life of Alexander so interesting, to the extent that it invites the historian to ponder the role that particular individuals play in the evolution of civilisations.

To find answers to the questions that are raised, it is not enough to provide an account of a life which, in the case of Alexander, was particularly brief, since he died at the age of 32. We also need to understand why and how it was that he was led to embark on the conquest that took him all the way to the banks of the River Indus.

It is clear that Alexander was not acting in a purely personal capacity. His conquest was prompted by preoccupations that led him successively or simultaneously to play a number of different roles: that of the king of the Macedonians, but at the same time that of the head of a coalition of Greek states, and, as the successor to the Achaemenids, that of the master of an eastern empire. Then, over and above those three roles, there was another, said to have been attributed to him by the oracle of Ammon, namely the role of the son of Zeus, who had been promised world dominion. Who was the real man hidden behind all these masks? What ambition fuelled his actions? And how did those actions affect the times that followed his early death? It is by no means easy to answer these questions, for again it involves trying to decipher the myth.

Finally, we need to try to reconstruct the genesis and destiny of the myth in all the often contradictory forms in which it appears, both among the historical actors whom it inspired and among the historians who tried to reconstruct it. As can be seen, the task is by no means a simple one. But I hope that it at least justifies this new biography of Alexander the Great.

PART I

The Major Stages of Alexander's Reign

CHAPTER I

The Graeco-Oriental world at Alexander's succession

In 336, when Alexander succeeded his father Philip II, in circumstances to which we shall be returning, the Greek world and the Oriental world, after decades of warfare, were experiencing a period of relative calm. This was the consequence of, on the one hand, the king of Macedon's victory, in 338, over a Greek army at Chaeronea, in Boeotia, which was followed by the constitution of an alliance that united Philip with the principal Greek states; on the other, it resulted from the reconstitution of the unity of the Persian Empire under Artaxerxes III Ochos, who had, in particular, reconquered Egypt, which had been more or less independent since the beginning of the fourth century. But it was a precarious equilibrium, given that the objective of the alliance formed around Philip was to go to war in Asia against the Great King.

Ever since the beginning of the century, the Persian Empire had been continuously involved in the history of the Greek world. In the last years of the Peloponnesian War, in which Sparta and its allies were pitted against the Athenian Empire, the Great King and his satraps were already interfering, by means of subsidies, in the relations between Greek cities. It was thanks to such subsidies that, in 405, the Spartan navarch Lysander had managed to assemble a powerful fleet and, at Aigospotami, overcome the Athenian fleet, up until then the mistress of the seas. It was likewise such Persian subsidies that enabled the Athenian Conon, the *strategos* (admiral) vanquished in 405, to return to Athens a few years later with fifty warships and to finance the rebuilding of the city walls that had been destroyed on the orders of Lysander, after his victory. One reason for this reconciliation between the Great King and the

Athenians was the unease provoked by the policies adopted in Asia Minor first by Lysander and then by the Spartan king Agesilaus. But subsequently the recall of Agesilaus and, above all, the renascent ambitions of the Athenians, now anxious to re-establish their Aegean hegemony, had again brought the Great King closer to the Spartans. It was with the support of the Spartan Antalcidas that, in 386, he imposed the famous King's Peace upon the Greeks. Through this peace, Artaxerxes II Mnemon proclaimed himself the guarantor of the maintenance of order in the Aegean world.

Such interventions by the master of Asia continued throughout the century and explain the violently hostile reaction of the Athenian orator Isocrates. He denounced the role that the 'Barbarian' was assuming and, in his pamphlets, urged the Greeks to unite and undertake the conquest of Asia, that is to say the western provinces of the Persian Empire. In one of his very last pamphlets, Isocrates, who died in the year of the defeat at Chaeronea, appealed to Philip, the king of Macedon, whom he regarded as the only man capable of successfully carrying out such a mission.

But the most influential orator in Athens at that time was Demosthenes. He, on the contrary, regarded Philip as a threat to Greek liberty and never tired of declaring that the Greeks should oppose the schemes of the Macedonian. His efforts were partially successful but could not prevent Philip's victory. And even if Philip was not planning the apocalyptic fate for Athens predicted by Demosthenes, he nevertheless did impose upon the Greeks gathered in Corinth the constitution of an alliance, known as the League of Corinth, the avowed aim of which was the conquest of Asia, the alleged pretext being rightful vengeance for the evils inflicted on the Greeks in the course of the Persian Wars of the early decades of the fifth century. The Greek states that were members of the alliance, consisting of cities and federations, would supply the contingents to take part in this venture, the command of which would be entrusted to Philip, as the *hegemon* or leader of the expedition.

Athens, which up until this point, swayed by Demosthenes, had spearheaded resistance to Philip, had agreed to the plan and was preparing to take part in the expedition when, in 336, it learned of the assassination of the king of Macedon. According to the orator Aeschines, Demosthenes, his political opponent, despite having just lost his daughter, loudly manifested his joy at the news. However, immediate action was out of the question, for as yet nothing was known of his successor and, above all, at this very moment Athens also learned of the assassination of Artaxerxes IV. In the eventuality of a war against the Macedonian power, aid from the new Great King was by no means certain. It was better to wait for more favourable circumstances.

What was the situation in the Aegean world at this point? Philip had managed to involve in his alliance almost all the cities of Balkan Greece, with the notable exception of Sparta, which had refused to join the League of Corinth. Since the defeat suffered in 371 at Leuctra, at the hands of the Theban armies of Epaminondas, Sparta's position on the Greek mainland had considerably weakened. In particular, the loss of Messenia, conquered by Sparta after two lengthy wars in the seventh century, then restored to independence by the dispensation of Epaminondas, had greatly impoverished the citizens of Sparta. They had lost their possessions in that part of the Peloponnese, estates which, thanks to the tribute paid by the helots who cultivated them, had funded their participation in the public meals of Sparta and had, no doubt, also provided the very means of survival for the poorest of them. The philosopher Aristotle, in his great treatise known as the *Politics*, published a few years later, claimed that the city of Sparta could currently call on not even as many as 1,000 fighters, as the land had by then come to be concentrated in so few hands. Not long before, Xenophon, in his *Agesilaus*, had made no secret of the fact that the reason why this Spartan king, at the end of his life, had placed himself at the service of an Egyptian rebelling against the Great King was so as to swell the finances of the city and ensure that he would be able to pay the wages of the soldiers in his army.

The position of Athens was more favourable, both socially and materially. Piraeus was still an active trading centre. The exploitation of the Laurion silver mines, which had slowed down in the years following the Peloponnesian War, had now picked up again, as is testified by inscriptions of the *poletai*, the magistrates who distributed mining concessions. The only dark cloud on the horizon, following its loss of positions in the Aegean, was the threat hanging over supplies of grain to the city. These were now at the mercy of the attacks that pirates or hostile states made against ships that had to pass through the Straits of the Hellespont. It was, in fact, Philip's seizure of merchant ships carrying grain to Athens in 340 that had unleashed the last war. And if the final decision had been made on land, that was only because Philip, in his capacity as a member of the Delphic Amphictyony (the council of representatives of the Greek peoples who administered the sanctuary of Delphi), happened to be at the head of an expedition directed against the Amphissans, who were guilty of cultivating land that belonged to the sanctuary of Apollo. It was, in fact, the outbreak of this fourth sacred war that had provoked the alliance between Athens and Thebes.

Thebes was at this time the most powerful city in the Boeotian Confederacy. This had been dissolved by the terms of the King's Peace of 386, which had proclaimed the autonomy of all cities and hence the dissolution of the *koina*, or confederations of cities; but it had been reconstituted when the democrats, led by the Theban Pelopidas, had ousted the city's pro-Spartan leaders. In 371, according to the terms of a new King's Peace, the Thebans were forbidden to swear an oath in the name of all the Boeotians. This was tantamount to denying the existence of the Confederacy. At this, the Thebans revolted, and it was their victory at Leuctra, under Epaminondas, that marked the end of Sparta's hegemony in the Peloponnese. For the next ten years, the Thebans, led by Pelopidas and Epaminondas, in tandem, dominated mainland Greece. In 362, the battle of Mantinea put an end to their aspirations, which were thereafter limited to central and northern Greece. No doubt this explains the *de facto* alliance between the Boeotian Confederacy and the young king of Macedon, Philip II, an alliance subsequently broken when Philip seized Thessaly and entered the Amphictyonic Council.

Macedon was one of the states situated on the fringes of the Greek world. Today it seems to be agreed that the peoples of this region probably belonged to the last waves of Greek-speaking invaders to arrive in the Balkan peninsula. They seem for a long time to have led a semi-nomadic life as herdsmen, concentrated in the north of the region. Not until the seventh century, apparently, did a centralised power emerge, as is attested by the royal necropolis at Aegae. According to tradition, this resulted from the seizure of

Macedon by a dynasty from Argos, known as the Temenids. However reliable or unreliable the bases for that tradition may be, it appears that from the late seventh century on, royal power was handed down in hereditary fashion within this family. The kings of Macedon declared themselves Greek by origin, and on that ground had been taking part in the Olympic Games, in person, at least since the early fifth century.

This was also the point at which they involved themselves in the affairs of the Greek world, given that numerous Greek cities dotted the Thracian–Macedonian coastline. From the time of the Persian Wars on, it was essentially with Athens, which controlled these cities that had entered into its alliance, that the kings of Macedon maintained both political and commercial relations. The Athenians bought wood from them, to build their fleet. The fifth century was also when coins were first minted, attesting the Macedonian kings' increasing authority in the region. But the most spectacular transformations came in the fourth century: new towns were built, the gold and silver mines of Mount Pangaeum were exploited, and closer relations with the Aegean world developed. At this time, the Macedonian kings were also embellishing their old capital Aegae (Vergina), which was soon to be replaced by Pella. The rich tombs discovered in Vergina testify to both the Hellenism of the culture of these kings and also the considerable resources that they enjoyed – resources that would, in particular, allow them to develop their military forces. The cavalry of the *hetairoi* or 'companions' was always the arm par excellence, but by the late fifth century heavy infantry had made its appearance, consisting of 'foot companions' (*pezhetairoi*), armed with the heavy spear known as a sarissa that was to turn the Macedonian phalanx into a redoubtable fighting force that Philip was to use with great skill.

Up until Philip's accession, the kingdom had known relatively settled periods interspersed with more troubled ones. One of the causes of the disturbances was the constant agitation maintained on the northern and western frontiers of the kingdom by peoples that were theoretically subject to Macedon but frequently attempted to regain their freedom. Another was the dynastic quarrelling between aspiring pretenders to the throne. Thus, after the death of King Archelaus in 399, Macedon was partially overrun by the Illyrians and did not regain its unity until the reign of Perdiccas III, who in 368 succeeded his brother Alexander II, when the latter was assassinated. In the course of his reign, Perdiccas was challenged by various other claimants to the throne, and Athenian *strategoi* (Timotheus, Iphicrates) intervened personally in these clashes. In 359 Perdiccas too was assassinated and, since his son Amyntas was too young to succeed him, it was his second brother Philip who was proclaimed king by the military assembly. As we shall see, this body appears to have wielded a certain political clout.

From his accession, in 359, to his death, in 336, Philip dominated the history of the Aegean world. First he became master of the Thracian–Macedonian coast which, as we have noted, had up until then been controlled by Athens. He did so by seizing, in particular, the fortified city of Amphipolis. Then he exploited the conflicts between the various Thessalian cities, imposed his own authority over them, and reorganised the Thessalian League. His conflict with Athens, briefly interrupted by the peace of 346, which sanctioned his entry into the Delphic Amphictyony, was to culminate, in 338, with his victory at Chaeronea. With his skills as both a tactician and a politician who was able to gain the compliance of a number of the Greek cities, within twenty or so years Philip had managed to impose his hegemony upon the Greek world. By the time he died, the victim of yet another assassination, in 336, despite the ever-present threat of the neighbouring peoples to the north and the west, he left a powerful kingdom to his son Alexander.

To complete this picture of the eastern Mediterranean world at the accession of Alexander, we need some idea of the situation of the Persian Empire. This vast collection of territories, brought together in the sixth century by Cyrus the Great, to which Cambyses subsequently added Egypt, had never been properly unified. The western satrapies, in contact with the Greek coastal cities, had been strongly influenced by Hellenism. Some of their governors, such as the famous Tissaphernes, had even intervened in the Peloponnesian War, lending support to Sparta in order to counter Athenian ambitions in the Aegean. In the fourth century, Egypt had won its independence under the pharaohs of the 28th, 29th and 30th dynasties, either with the aid of certain Athenian *strategoi* or, as we have seen, thanks to the intervention of the Spartan king Agesilaus. The attempts of the

Great King Artaxerxes III to recapture this rich province were at first unsuccessful, and his failure sparked a general revolt by his satraps, led by Ariobarzanes, the satrap of Phrygia. The revolt broke out in 371 and soon spread to the whole of western Asia. The efforts of King Artaxerxes III Ochos to restore order in the empire were at first unsuccessful, as the rebels enjoyed the support of a number of Greek cities. However, thanks to an alliance with the satrap of Caria, Idrieus, the brother of the famous Mausolus, who had turned his satrapy into a veritable independent state, with the Greek city Halicarnassus as its capital, Artaxerxes did eventually manage to overcome the rebels; and in 345 he reconquered Egypt. He allowed terror to reign in the reconquered provinces, particularly in Egypt, which was given over to his mercenaries to pillage. Nevertheless, despite this reconquest and the stricter control imposed on the Greek coastal cities, the empire's lack of unity seemed to justify the ambitions of those in Greece who were encouraging Philip to launch himself into the conquest of Asia. The assassination of Artaxerxes IV at the very time of Philip's death gave rise to hopes of an easy conquest. The fate of the eastern Mediterranean world would now be played out between the two new kings, Alexander and Darius III Codomannus.

CHAPTER 2

The beginning of Alexander's reign: the revolt of Thebes

The assassination of Philip, in 336, ushered in a period of crisis in Macedon. Young Alexander, the son of the king and Queen Olympias, was barely 20 years old. To be sure, Philip, in accordance with tradition, had raised his son in the expectation that he would be called to succeed him. That was probably why he had summoned the philosopher Aristotle to his court and entrusted to him the education of his adolescent son. Furthermore, Alexander had already fought at his father's side at Chaeronea. But shortly before his death Philip had repudiated his Epirote wife, Alexander's mother, in order to marry the young Cleopatra, and Olympias was suspected of having played some part in Philip's assassination. Hence the attempts of some to oppose Alexander by supporting the claims of his cousin Amyntas, the son of Perdiccas III and Philip's nephew. Other claimants to the throne had also appeared, in particular the princes of the family that controlled the Lyncestis region in upper Macedon. To impose his authority, Alexander had to act swiftly. With the help of Antipater, one of Philip's advisers, he managed to get rid of his opponents. First he blamed the assassination of his father on the Lyncestid princes and took his revenge accordingly. Soon after, he ordered the deaths of Amyntas and Cleopatra, and also those of her uncle Attalus and all her family. Then he convened an assembly of the people in arms and had himself proclaimed king.

But he was not yet in the clear. As we have seen, the news of Philip's death had caused a measure of agitation in the Greek world, and meanwhile, on the northern frontiers of Macedon, the subjected peoples were preparing to rise up against him.

Alexander seems to have tackled the Greek problem first. He

entered Thessaly to have reaffirmed the authority that Philip had acquired over the cities of the confederation. Moreover, he got the Amphictyonic Council meeting in Thermopylae to bestow upon himself the title of *hegemon* of the Greeks. Finally, the Council of the League of Corinth confirmed him as leader of the campaign against Asia planned by Philip. In just a few months, he succeeded in establishing his authority over the Greek allies, who realised that they had no hope of regaining their independence.

The second stage began in the spring of 335. Alexander crossed the Danube and subdued the rebellious populations in the north. He then turned his attention to the west to put a stop to the Illyrian incursions into Macedon. During this campaign he received news of the Theban revolt.

As mentioned above, Thebes, at the head of the Boeotian Confederacy, had long practised a policy of alliance with the kings of Macedon. Philip's membership of the Delphic Amphictyony, following his victory over the Phocians, which had brought the third sacred war to a close, had nevertheless been perceived by the Thebans as a threat to their own authority in central Greece. That was why some of them, solicited by Demosthenes, entered into alliance with Athens. Thebes thus found itself affected more than Athens by the defeat that had taken place within the Confederacy's territory. Whereas he had dealt quite leniently with Athens, Philip inflicted upon the Thebans a Macedonian garrison, on the Cadmea, the city's acropolis.

In 335, when Thebes received false news of Alexander's death in the course of his campaign against the Triballi, in northern Thrace, the Thebans revolted, with the intention of ejecting the Macedonian garrison. Had they been encouraged to do so by the new Great King, Darius III, who was said to have sent emissaries equipped with subsidies to Greece, with the purpose of inciting revolt? Had the Athenians, at the instigation of Demosthenes, promised support for the revolt? However that may be, Alexander's riposte struck them with the force of lightning. He led a forced march to Thebes, seized the town, and handed it over to his soldiers to loot. The speeches of Aeschines and Demosthenes on the occasion of the lawsuit concerning the crown, in 330, reflect the strong feelings that the news of the fate suffered by the Boeotian city provoked among the Greeks. Later on, claims were made that it was the Greek allies who insisted that Alexander, who was ready to pardon Thebes, should inflict an exemplary punishment on the city. (That idea resurfaces in Arrian, and others too.) The Greek allies were even said to have raked up their old grudge against Thebes at the time of the Persian Wars. For the Greeks gathered together within the League of Corinth, the enemy was no longer the king of Macedon, but the Barbarian of Asia whose predecessors had won submission from the Thebans.

Whatever the interpretation of the fate inflicted on Thebes, the crushing of the Boeotian city's revolt suited Alexander very well, as it confirmed him in his role as leader of the Greek allies. It was reported that he now demanded that the Athenian orators who had supported the Theban rebellion, chief among them Demosthenes, be handed over to him. The orator himself alludes to such a demand in his speech *On the Crown*, but without explaining how it was that it was never followed up. Aeschines, Demosthenes' opponent, went so far as to declare, in his speech *Against Ctesiphon*, that Demosthenes had secret contacts with the king of Macedon, and Demosthenes certainly never denied this. Most likely, though, partisans among the Athenian orators, partisans who had been close to his father, such as Demades in particular, intervened to persuade Alexander not to press his demands.

Is it true that, at this point, Alexander, as the *hegemon* of the Greeks, took steps to settle a number of local conflicts? One speech, attributed to Demosthenes but in which a number of commentators, even in antiquity, detected a different style from that of the orator, mentions a number of interventions that Alexander made in contravention of the League of Corinth pact: at Messene, at Pellene in Achaea, in Sicyon, and so on. If these did take place, it must have been after the crushing of the Theban revolt. It is indeed reasonable enough to suppose that the Macedonian king would have wished to ensure that, before he left Europe, the Greece that he was leaving was well pacified.

The situation in the Aegean was certainly still alarming. Parmenion, Philip's old Companion, who had been sent to scout out the scene, had suffered severe rebuffs at the hands of Memnon of Rhodes, who had rallied to the service of the Great King. Alexander therefore needed to act without delay, making the most of the relative passivity of his Greek allies. In conformity with the terms of the alliance, the latter had supplied the king of Macedon with contingents of soldiers and ships. But to judge by the Athenian contribution (700 men and 20 ships), the allied forces that were contributed did not amount to very much. There were probably no more than 7,000 Greek infantrymen and 600 Greek horsemen in the army that set out in the spring of 334. As for the fleet put together by the allies, it was to play an altogether secondary role.

In truth, Alexander was depending more on his own Macedonians and on the contingents supplied by the peoples subject to Macedon, chiefly the Thessalian cavalry but also men from Thrace, the Triballi, the Paeonians, and so on, who made up the greater part of his infantry.

He left part of his forces in Macedon, under the command of Antipater, whom he could trust. Their particular task was to keep an eye on the Greeks, but also, in Macedon itself, to maintain Alexander's authority. This was soon to be strengthened by the king's rapid successes, but could still be compromised by the slightest setback.

Now the Asiatic adventure began.

CHAPTER 3

The conquest of the western provinces of the Persian Empire

We have already come across the problem of sources, in connection with the events in Thebes. Concerning the campaign that began in the spring of 334 we have at our disposal two traditions that sometimes overlap. The first is to be found in the account of Diodorus Siculus and that of the Latin historian Quintus Curtius. It stems from the work of Clitarchus of Alexandria. He did not himself take part in the campaign, but used the memoirs of one of Alexander's companions, Aristoboulus of Cassandreia, and also the account provided by one of the Macedonian generals, Ptolemy, the future master of Egypt and the founder of the Ptolemaic dynasty. The other tradition, represented essentially by Arrian, appears to have more direct contacts with the contemporary sources, which obviously include Aristoboulus and Ptolemy, and may therefore be more trustworthy, particularly with respect to the various battles fought by the conqueror and his generals. In the pages that follow, we shall steer clear of the debates and disagreements on this subject between specialists on warfare. For that is not the purpose of the present work.

THE CONQUEST OF ASIA MINOR

In the spring of 334, Alexander landed in Asia, and the first thing he did was visit Troy. He was an assiduous reader of Homer's poems (a subject to which we shall be returning) and so posed as a latter-day

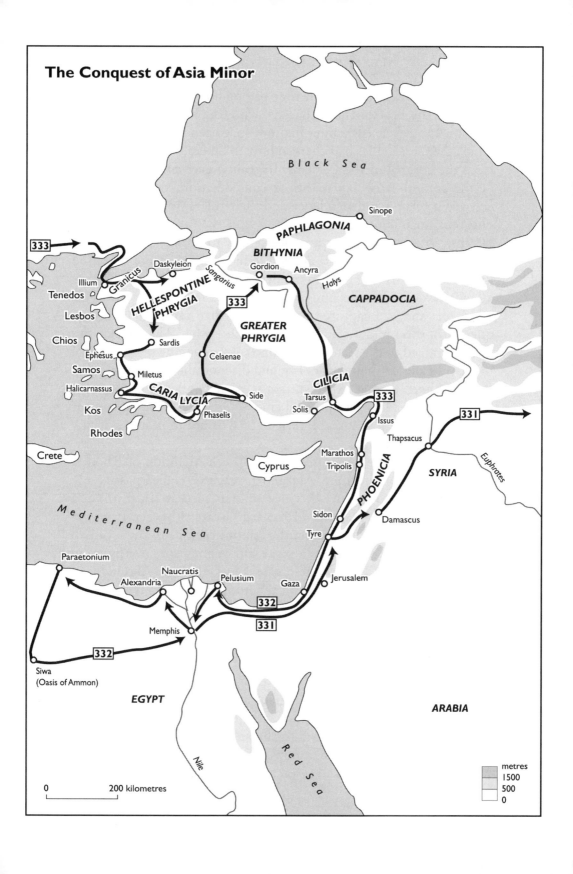

The Conquest of Asia Minor

Black Sea

Mediterranean Sea

Sinope

PAPHLAGONIA

BITHYNIA

333

Daskyleion

Gordion

Ancyra

Halys

CAPPADOCIA

HELLESPONTINE PHRYGIA

Sangarius

333

GREATER PHRYGIA

Illium

Granicus

Tenedos

Lesbos

Chios

Sardis

Ephesus

Celaenae

Samos

Miletus

Halicarnassus

CARIA

LYCIA

Side

CILICIA

Tarsus

Solis

333

Issus

Thapsacus

331

Euphrates

Kos

Phaselis

Rhodes

Crete

Cyprus

Marathos

Tripolis

PHOENICIA

SYRIA

Sidon

Tyre

Damascus

Paraetonium

Naucratis

Alexandria

Pelusium

Gaza

Jerusalem

332

331

Memphis

332

Siwa
(Oasis of Ammon)

EGYPT

ARABIA

Nile

Red Sea

0   200 kilometres

metres
1500
500
0

Agamemnon while at the same time paying homage to his 'ancestor' Achilles, 'the best of the Achaeans' who fought beneath the walls of Troy. However, Alexander had not forgotten the 'mission' with which the Greek allies had charged him: to 'liberate' the Greek cities from the control of the Persians. In reality, ever since the collapse of the second Athenian maritime confederation, these cities had enjoyed a relative independence and their rulers, for the most part oligarchs, maintained good relations with the Great King and his satraps. So Alexander's first concern was to strike a heavy blow against Darius. This he did at the Granicus river, where he pitted his cavalry against the Persian cavalry, which he annihilated. Within a few weeks, he had become the master of Hellespontine Phrygia and Lydia and had captured Sardis, the Lydian capital. The consequences of this rapid success were immediately felt. The Greek cities of Ionia rallied to the victor, who imposed democratic regimes upon them, proclaimed their autonomy, and discontinued the tribute that they had been paying. At least, that is what Diodorus Siculus tells us (XVII, 24, 1). However, the 'liberated' Greek cities do not appear to have been admitted to the League of Corinth (a point to which we shall be returning).

Persian resistance, organised by the Greek Memnon of Rhodes, had stiffened by the time Alexander reached Halicarnassus. He did not manage to capture this city at first (see Part II, p. 56) and decided to push further inland toward Greater Phrygia. It was in the course of this campaign that the famous episode of the Gordian knot is supposed to have taken place, although it does not figure in Diodorus' account. It helped to create the legend of an Alexander so impatient that he preferred to cut the knot rather than try to undo it. The king does not appear to have encountered much resistance during this campaign. By the end of the autumn of 334 he could consider himself the master of Asia and to have attained the objective that Philip had set for himself as *hegemon* of the League of Corinth.

But there was still the threat represented by Memnon, who remained the master of Halicarnassus and who, in the early spring of 333, embarked on a maritime campaign that enabled him to capture Chios and Lesbos and to threaten the region of the Straits (Hellespont). However, Memnon's death stopped the movement from extending to mainland Greece and – in particular – to Athens.

Darius now had to engage in battle on land in order to block Alexander's army's route to Syria. The two sides clashed at Issus. Again the role played by the Macedonian cavalry proved decisive. Darius fled, leaving his camp and part of his family in the hands of the victor (November 333), and retreated to beyond the Euphrates. He then tried to negotiate, but Alexander, from his position of strength, rejected the very idea and, virtually without striking a blow, proceeded to capture the cities along the Syro-Phoenician coast, which were the Great King's main maritime supporters. Only Tyre refused to welcome him and, despite using siege-machines of the highest sophistication, Alexander was obliged to besiege it for seven months before capturing it. The town surrendered in July 332 and after that Alexander soon obtained the submission of the whole coastal region, by capturing Gaza.

Once again, Darius tried to make peace, but without success. Now master of the entire sea-coast of the Persian Empire, Alexander could afford to ignore the more or less sporadic rebellions that continued to shake the Aegean world. Elsewhere, he counted upon the generals he had left in Asia to quell certain satraps' attempts at resistance, and upon Antipater to oppose the disruptive actions of the Spartan king Agis III.

Alexander was thus relatively confident of his rear positions when he entered upon his Egyptian campaign.

ALEXANDER'S TIME IN EGYPT

In the eyes of most commentators, Alexander's stay in Egypt constituted the essential turning point in his reign. Egypt occupied a unique position within the Persian Empire. Conquered by Cambyses II in the last quarter of the sixth century, Egypt had rebelled repeatedly in the course of the following two centuries, frequently with the aid of Greeks serving as mercenaries in the armies of the pharaohs, but also thanks to alliances with certain Greek cities, including both Athens and Sparta. Alexander could thus expect a favourable welcome. After the capture of Gaza, he had little difficulty in obtaining the surrender of the satrap Mazakes.

Seizing Egypt had not been part of the League of Corinth's plan.

So Alexander was careful not to annex it to his empire; in other words, he respected its autonomy by avoiding appointing a new satrap. At the same time, however, he seems to have been determined to exercise his sovereignty not as the Achaemenid ruler but as the successor to the pharaohs. It is not known whether he had himself crowned in accordance with the rituals of the pharaohs, but he did at least adopt some of their traditional titles. Ever practical, he was careful to install garrisons in fortified positions at Pelusium, Memphis and Elephantine, and to entrust the financial administration to a Greek from Naucratis by the name of Cleomenes.

But the importance of Alexander's stay in Egypt really stems from two essential feats: the pilgrimage that he made to the Siwa oasis, and the founding of Alexandria. There is no need to dwell on the question of which came first. The version provided by Plutarch and Arrian seems the most likely one. Alexander's first thought was probably to found a new city, for the idea was in line with a number of his preoccupations, most of them of a military nature. The delta needed to be defended against attacks from the sea. We should remember that at this time (January 331), Agis still presented a threat, and the Persian admiral Pharnabazus still held a number of key positions in the Aegean. If Alexander, who had rebuffed all Darius' peace proposals, was thinking of continuing the conquest of the Achaemenid Empire, it was important for him to have a stronghold from which to defend his rear. Besides, to be seen as the founder of a city fitted in with the heroic aspirations that spurred him on. Whether he had as yet any inkling as to the future of this foundation is more doubtful.

The pilgrimage to the Siwa oasis poses a quite different problem. It was a perilous undertaking, for it involved crossing an inhospitable desert. Does Arrian's explanation suffice to justify it? He suggests that it was Alexander's desire to rival Perseus and Heracles 'because he was of the same race as both of them'. And can we accept the 'miraculous' events said to have enabled the king to find his way to the oasis? These were the beneficial rains that made the sand more compact and the air easier to breathe, and the flights of crows that served to guide Alexander and his companions across the desert. But none of that is what is essential, for the importance of this episode lies in the oracle's reply to Alexander and so also in the question that Alexander put to it. According to Diodorus, Alexander asked the god, 'Do you give me sway over the whole earth?' and the god, through the mouth of his priest, replied that 'the god definitely gave him what he had requested'. The same version reappears in both Arrian and Plutarch. But then Alexander is said to have questioned the god again in order to find out whether his father's murderers had been punished. The priest's reply to this was that the one who had engendered him could not be assassinated because he was the god himself (Diodorus, XVII, 51, 3). Plutarch's account of this second reply is very interesting:

> Some say that the priest of the god, wishing to show his friendliness by addressing him with 'O paidion' or 'O my son', in his foreign pronunciation ended the words with 'sigma' instead of 'nu' and said, 'O paidios', and that Alexander was pleased at the slip in pronunciation, and a story became current that the god had addressed him with 'O pai dios' or 'O son of Zeus'.
>
> (*Alex.*, 27, 9)

Plutarch goes on to say that Alexander refrained from claiming this divine parentage in the presence of his Greek and Macedonian companions. However, very possibly he did allow the reply to be known in Egypt, where a pharaoh was in any case traditionally hailed as 'Son of Re'. More important and more believable is the laconic wording of the statement recorded in our sources, namely that the god 'would grant him what he requested'. It is immediately clear that the question was more important than the answer. That is not to say that the question was as presumptuous as the one recorded in our sources: namely, to return to the wording of Diodorus, would Alexander obtain 'sway over the whole earth?' In 331, when Darius was still the master of most of his empire, Alexander's ambitions were no doubt more moderate.

However that may be, once back in Egypt, he seems to have entrusted those of his companions whom he was leaving on the spot with the task of building this city for which he himself had completed only the foundation rites. His own objective now was to return to Asia and finally have done with Darius.

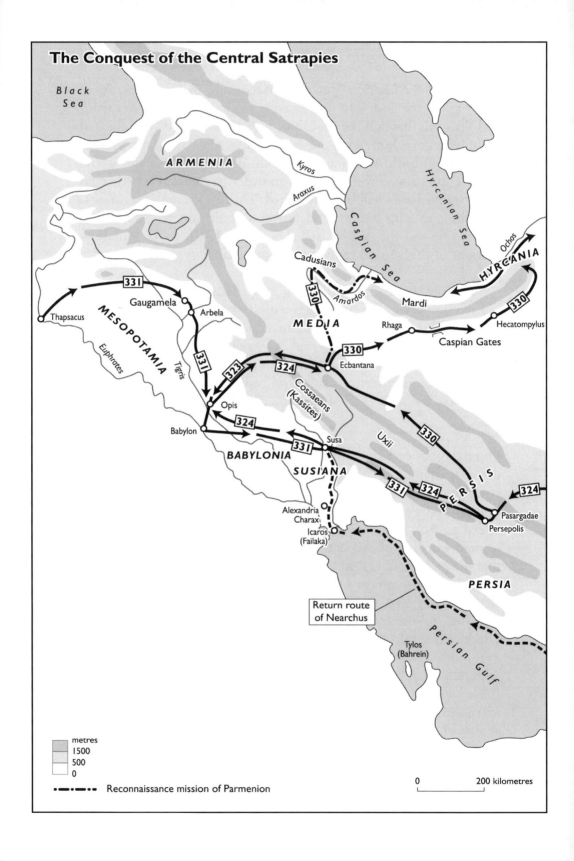

The Conquest of the Central Satrapies

Black Sea

ARMENIA

Kyros

Araxus

Caspian Sea

Hyrcanian Sea

Cadusians

Ochos

HYRCANIA

Amardos

Mardi

330

Hecatompylus

Thapsacus

331

Gaugamela

Arbela

MESOPOTAMIA

Euphrates

Tigris

331

323

324

MEDIA

Ecbantana

330

330

Rhaga

Caspian Gates

Opis

324

324

Cossaeans
(Kassites)

Uxii

330

Babylon

331

Susa

331

324

324

BABYLONIA

SUSIANA

PERSIS

Alexandria
Charax

Icaros
(Failaka)

Pasargadae

Persepolis

PERSIA

Return route
of Nearchus

Tylos
(Bahrein)

Persian Gulf

metres
1500
500
0

0   200 kilometres

•—•—•—•—•   Reconnaissance mission of Parmenion

FROM THE END OF THE ASIAN CAMPAIGN TO THE DEATH OF DARIUS

Alexander had spent barely one year in Egypt. In the spring of 331, he returned to Asia, determined to finish off the Great King. After a brief stop in Tyre, where he began to reorganise his conquered territories, he struck northward and crossed the Euphrates at Thapsacus. He then made for the upland valley of the Tigris. Darius, who had gathered together a powerful army in Babylon, was thus obliged also to move to the north, and established his camp at Arbela. Alexander led his army across the river and took up position opposite his opponent. It was close to Arbela, in the Gaugemela plain, that the third great battle in the conquest of Asia was fought.

The ancient historians' accounts of this battle emphasise Alexander's skill. Diodorus, in particular, gives a very detailed description of the way in which the Macedonian leader deployed his troops, positioning on the right wing the royal squadron under the command of Black Cleitus, the rest of his Companion cavalry under the command of Philotas, and seven cavalry units. Behind these the Macedonian and allied body of infantry was lined up. The greatest danger for this relatively modest army confronting the forces of the Great King was constituted by the latter's famous scythe-chariots. And indeed, when the attack began, 'First the scythed chariots swung into action at full gallop and created great alarm and terror among the Macedonians' (Diodorus, XVII, 58, 2). Further on, Diodorus describes the dreadful damage that these scythes were capable of inflicting upon the enemy soldiers:

> Such were the keenness and force of the scythes ingeniously contrived to do harm that they severed the arms of many, shields and all, and in no small number of cases they cut through necks and sent heads tumbling on the ground with the eyes still open and the expression of the countenance unchanged, and in other cases they sliced through ribs with mortal gashes and inflicted a quick death.
>
> (ibid., 58, 5)

Realising the danger, Alexander ordered his soldiers to open their ranks and allow the chariots to plunge through, and then to surprise them by falling upon them with their javelins. After that charge the real battle commenced, between the two opposed sets of cavalry. Initially, Darius' men, led by Mazaeus, managed to gain control of part of the Macedonian camp, but Parmenion, at the head of the Thessalian cavalry, although at first driven back by Mazaeus, then forced the enemy to beat a retreat. Alexander, for his part, had attacked Darius' cavalry and had once again obliged the Great King to take to flight. His victory was thus complete.

After this the route to all the royal capitals lay open. Babylon was the first to surrender, thanks to Mazaeus, vanquished at Gaugamela, rallying to Alexander. He was immediately appointed satrap of Babylonia. After allowing his army a month's rest, Alexander advanced on Susa, which also surrendered without a fight. Alexander entrusted the government of Susiana to the Persian satrap Aboulites. The policy that he was thereby inaugurating testifies to his pragmatism. He made use of the administrative structures already in place without, *a priori*, ruling out recourse to the Iranians. However, his march on Persepolis turned out to be far more difficult, for Ariobarzanes, the satrap of Persis, had organised resistance there. No doubt that is why, having crushed the Persian army, not without heavy losses to the Macedonian troops, Alexander allowed his soldiers to sack and burn Persepolis.

As a result of the capture of all these royal capitals, large quantities of precious metals fell into the hands of the Macedonian king. The sources refer to 40,000 talents of non-minted gold and silver from Susa (Diodorus, XVII, 66, 1), as well as 9,000 talents of minted gold coins. The capture of Persepolis brought Alexander a treasure valued at 120,000 talents. But the recent victories had been won at the cost of heavy losses. So Alexander needed to recruit new troops. The masses of men who flocked to the recruitment centres seem to have reached upper Asia via Tarsus and the Phoenician ports.

Now Alexander really did have to finish off Darius. The latter found himself in an almost hopeless situation, for the only aid at his disposal was that of the eastern satraps, who had always enjoyed virtually total independence from the royal authorities. But Alexander's position was not secure either. He had reason to fear a revolt on the part of even his most faithful troops, who were now faced with the prospect of a campaign across hostile and unknown regions. As it happened, events spared him a final battle against the Great King. Darius was assassinated in July 330 by Bessus, the satrap of Bactria, who then proclaimed himself king.

The death of Darius constituted a crucial moment in Alexander's adventure. In opposition to the usurper Bessus, he now proclaimed himself Darius' successor, and legend would soon be justifying that claim. Plutarch, who liked to liven up his account with anecdotes, reports that Darius was still alive when his body was discovered by the Macedonian Polystratus and that, when the latter gave him something to drink, Darius told him:

> My man, this is the extremity of all my ill-fortune, that I receive good at thy hands, and am not able to return it; but Alexander will requite thee for thy good offices, and the gods will reward Alexander for his kindness to my mother, wife, and children. To him, through thee, I give this right hand.
>
> (*Alex.*, 43, 4)

By the time Alexander found Darius, he was dead. Alexander gave him a royal funeral.

CHAPTER 4

The conquest of the eastern provinces and the end of the Asian campaign

By capturing the royal Achaemenid capitals, Alexander had already exceeded the goals set by Philip when he set up the League of Corinth. However, the lure of booty and the largesse distributed to the soldiers had retained the loyalty of his troops. But before tackling the difficult campaign leading to the eastern satrapies, Alexander had quickly realised that he might encounter strong resistance, particularly from the allied contingents of his army. He had therefore dismissed them, loading them with presents. He could now afford to do this, as Agis of Sparta had just been beaten and killed in battle by Antipater, at Megalopolis. Greece appeared to be calm and the allied contingents could, without risk, be replaced by mercenaries, who were likely to prove more docile.

However, the problem was quite different where the Macedonians were concerned. When he proclaimed himself successor to the Achaemenids, that is to say to monarchs who wielded a despotic power, Alexander broke with the tradition of the Macedonian monarchy. One of the firmest supporters of that tradition was Parmenion, Philip's old Companion to whom Alexander had, from the very start of the expedition, entrusted the command of his elite troops. When Alexander had set off in pursuit of Darius, Parmenion had remained, with the greater part of the army, in Ecbatana. When, following Darius' death, the king embarked on the pursuit of the usurper Bessus in Bactria, he encountered resistance from the local populations and also from Satibarzanes, the satrap of Areia, who had rallied to Bessus. Alexander had been forced to beat a retreat.

The delay in the arrival of help from Parmenion gave the king a pretext for ridding himself of the old general. What has been called 'the Philotas affair' provided him with the opportunity to do so.

Philotas was Parmenion's son who, according to Plutarch, 'had a high position among the Macedonians, for he was held to be valiant and able to endure hardship and, after Alexander himself, no one was more fond of giving or so fond of his comrades' (*Alex.*, 48, 1). But Plutarch also notes his arrogance and his overbearing ways. At any rate, Philotas was betrayed by his Thessalian mistress, Antigone, who told Alexander of her lover's criticisms of him. Perhaps Alexander himself invented the plot that was to cost Parmenion's son his life. However that may be, Philotas was accused of being part of a plot against Alexander, set on foot by a certain Dimnus (or at least of not having revealed the plot despite knowing of it). The death sentence was, it seems, pronounced by the assembly of the Macedonians after Philotas, under torture, had confessed his participation in the conspiracy. Parmenion, who was in Media at the time and could not possibly have been an accomplice, was nevertheless also condemned and executed.

THE CONQUEST OF THE UPPER SATRAPIES

Once order in his army had been thus brutally established, Alexander was ready to undertake the conquest of Arachosia. When his troops from Media had rejoined him, he first took care to install a military colony at Phrada, soon to be known as Alexandria in Drangiana. Such arrangements were to become customary in the course of Alexander's march towards the eastern provinces of the empire. He had also reorganised the command of his army, for it had been destabilised by the disappearance of Parmenion. Command of the Companions' cavalry was now shared by two of his faithful followers, Hephaistion and Black Cleitus. Craterus was appointed as Parmenion's successor, and important responsibilities were entrusted to Ptolemy and to Perdiccas, another of his Companions.

In Arachosia, Alexander founded a new colony, Alexandria Arachosia (now Kandahar). Uprisings among local satrapies obliged him once again to reorganise his troops, and this slowed down his march towards the Hindu Kush. The winter campaign was extremely tough and was punctuated by the founding of two more colonies, Alexandria of the Caucasus and Nicaea. In the spring of 329, Alexander crossed the Hindu Kush, after restoring order in all the eastern satrapies.

Now began the toughest, most difficult part of the campaign, beginning with the capture of the north-eastern frontier of the empire. Alexander's primary objective was to seize Bessus, who had proclaimed himself king, taking the name Artaxerxes V, and was counting on the support of Spitamenes, the commander of the Sogdian–Bactrian cavalry. Alexander returned to the offensive that he had abandoned in the previous year and this time he was successful. Bessus, abandoned by the Bactrian cavalry, was forced to flee to Sogdiana. This was much more rugged terrain, which enabled him to put up a longer resistance, thanks to support from the local lords. Once he was master of Bactria, Alexander entered Sogdiana, where he finally captured Bessus. Darius' short-lived successor was taken back to Ecbatana, where he was tried and executed. But the disappearance of Bessus from the scene did not produce the hoped-for results. Spitamenes now organised resistance and succeeded in rousing the entire region and in re-establishing a foothold in Bactria. Alexander found himself directing highly tricky operations which involved storming and destroying strongholds that were fiercely defended. He was frequently obliged to resort to the use of siege-machines. Furthermore, winter was harsh in these mountainous regions and the snow made it dangerous for both men and beasts to move around.

Fortunately for Alexander, reinforcements, in the shape of Greek and Thracian mercenaries, now arrived from Europe. Also, he was able to establish amicable relations with a number of local chieftains such as Pharasmenes, the king of the Chorasmians, the people who lived in the Oxus delta. Some of the recently arrived mercenaries were established in key positions, with the task of organising the defence of the conquered regions, whenever the need to do so arose. Those centres of defence eventually turned into cities such as Alexandria Eschate and Alexandria on Oxus.

By the end of the autumn of 328, Alexander had re-established his authority in Bactriana and Sogdiana, the government of which he

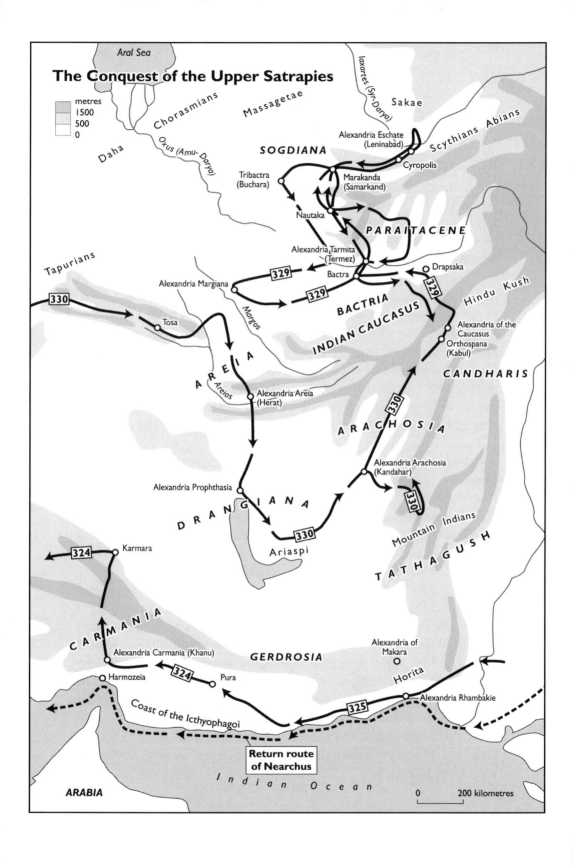

The Conquest of the Upper Satrapies

metres
1500
500
0

Aral Sea

Chorasmians

Massagetae

Sakae

Daha

Oxus (Amu-Darya)

Iaxartes (Syr-Darya)

SOGDIANA

Alexandria Eschate
(Leninabad)

Scythians Abians

Cyropolis

Tribactra
(Buchara)

Marakanda
(Samarkand)

Nautaka

PARAITACENE

Alexandria Tarmita
(Termez)

Bactra

Drapsaka

329

329

329

Alexandria Margiana

Hindu Kush

BACTRIA

INDIAN CAUCASUS

Alexandria of the
Caucasus
Orthospana
(Kabul)

330

Tapurians

Tosa

Margos

A R E I A

Areios

CANDHARIS

Alexandria Areia
(Herat)

A R A C H O S I A

330

Alexandria Prophthasia

Alexandria Arachosia
(Kandahar)

Mountain Indians

330

D R A N G I A N A

Ariaspi

330

T A T H A G U S H

Karmara

324

C A R M A N I A

Alexandria of
Makara

Alexandria Carmania (Khanu)

GERDROSIA

Harmozeia

324

Pura

Horita

325

Alexandria Rhambakie

Coast of the Icthyophagoi

**Return route
of Nearchus**

ARABIA

I n d i a n   O c e a n

0   200 kilometres

entrusted to Cleitus. He had forced Spitamenes to retreat towards
the northern steppes and could even envisage the possibility of
allowing his army to rest during the winter of 328–327. It was during
this interlude that an incident occurred about which our sources
are particularly eloquent: in the course of a drunken quarrel, Cleitus
was murdered. At the time, Alexander was living in Marakanda
(Samarkand), the capital of Sogdiana. According to Plutarch's
account, during a meal following a sacrifice to the Dioscuri, Cleitus
criticised Alexander's manifest preference for the company of
Iranians rather than that of his Macedonian companions. He
accused Alexander of mixing only 'with Barbarians and slaves, who
would do obeisance to his white tunic and Persian girdle' (*Alex.*,
51, 5) and even went so far as to quote some lines from Euripides'
Andromache, in which the poet denounces generals who take all the
glory for victories that are really won by their soldiers. Unable to
control his anger, Alexander apparently ran his spear right through
the body of his unfortunate critic. We shall be returning to consider
this affair at greater length, but it reflects a new atmosphere in the
army, one that was to be aggravated when, following the conquest
of Paraitacene, in the spring, Alexander, on his return to Bactriana,
announced his marriage to Roxane, the daughter of the Iranian
Oxyartes. Soon after this came the 'revelation' of the famous Pages'
Plot, in which Callisthenes, Aristotle's nephew, who had accompanied Alexander in order to keep a record of the conquest, was
compromised. This was followed by the *proskynesis* (obeisance)
affair, when the Macedonians refused to prostrate themselves before
the king. We shall be returning to these matters.

It was quite true that the conquest of the eastern satrapies had
made it increasingly necessary to turn to Iranians, and these were
soon to be integrated into the Macedonian army. The king's authority had certainly not diminished and he could continue to depend
on his faithful supporters. But the incidents mentioned above, just
when he was preparing to set out to conquer India, were signs that
pointed to important changes in both his behaviour and the goals
that he now set for himself.

At the beginning of the summer of 327, he had been rejoined by
Craterus. His army now numbered 12,000 men. A new adventure
was about to begin.

THE INDIAN CAMPAIGN

This was definitely the part of Alexander's adventure that, already in antiquity, most caught people's imagination, for it was now no longer a matter of the remoter provinces of the Persian Empire, but of a world that was practically unknown. It is true that Cyrus the Great and Darius I had extended their conquests as far as India, but it was not long before those distant territories eluded Achaemenid domination, and by now they were largely forgotten. Furthermore the imaginary representations of Greeks were filled with the mythical expeditions of Heracles and Dionysus. As Alexander set out to conquer India, he no doubt felt that he was following in their footsteps. However, it was a risky project and was to prove more difficult than might have been expected, judging by the ambassadorial advances made to Alexander by a number of representatives from beyond the Hindu Kush, in particular those from the king of Taxila. He controlled the land between the valleys of the Indus and the Hydaspes, and was counting on an alliance with Alexander in order to resist the encroachments of Porus, the powerful ruler of the Punjab.

The campaign began in the spring of 326. The army had been divided into two groups. The mission of one, under the command of Hephaistion and Perdiccas, was to reach the valley of the Indus as soon as possible. The second group, which included the elite troops, was to skirt the Himalayan foothills. This was the group that encountered the stiffest resistance. It came from minor local lords, holed up in their strongholds. The campaign was marked in particular by the siege of the Massaka fortress of the Assacenes. Eventually it surrendered and all its defenders were massacred. Another stronghold, Aornos, was only captured thanks to the use of elaborate siege-machines. The two groups met up to cross the Indus and advance into the kingdom of Taxila. Alexander obtained the submission of all the local dynasts and with relative ease established his control over the whole territory bounded by the Indus and the Hydaspes. Now he had to confront the most daunting of the kings, Porus, who had pulled back to the other side of the Hydaspes. Alexander successfully crossed the river, thanks to the technique already used to cross the Indus (a bridge formed of boats), and was able to position his army facing that of the Indian prince, who was relying on his elephants to halt the Macedonian army. The battle against Porus provided Alexander with yet another opportunity to demonstrate his skills as a *strategos*. He attacked with his cavalry, avoiding confronting the elephants, then deployed his phalanx and routed the army of the Indian ruler. In the course of this battle he apparently lost his horse, Bucephalas, whose name he later gave to one of the towns that he founded to commemorate his victory.

The vanquished Porus acknowledged his defeat, whereupon Alexander, who seems to have been planning to make straight for the Indian Ocean, entrusted him with the government of the land beyond the Hydaspes. But when Porus convinced him that the Indian populations were ready to acknowledge him as their overlord, he first moved eastward, possibly with the intention of reaching the Ganges. The campaign was not as easy as he had been led to believe it would be. To capture the fortress of Sangala, he again had to resort to siege-machines. It was therefore not surprising that, having reached the bank of the Hyphasis, a tributary of the Indus, the army manifested its wish to go no further. In the course of two successive assemblies, Alexander endeavoured to persuade his soldiers to continue. But he soon realised that he could not make any more demands of his men who, on top of everything, were now weakened by a particularly trying monsoon. In any case the omens were unfavourable. So Alexander limited himself to erecting twelve monumental altars on the opposite bank of the Hyphasis.

The king could now return to his initial plan to descend the valley of the Hydaspes and the Indus all the way to the ocean. For this he needed a fleet, and the winter of 326–325 was put to good use in the construction of river-worthy ships (800 according to some sources, 2,000 according to others). The huge number of these ships gave the expedition a triumphal air. The fleet was placed under the command of the Cretan Nearchus, while the armies of Craterus and Hephaistion made their way downstream on foot along both banks of the river. Once again the campaign proved more difficult than had been expected and several times Alexander found himself fighting in person in the front line, in particular in the siege of Sangala, a stronghold of the Mallian people. Plutarch tells the story:

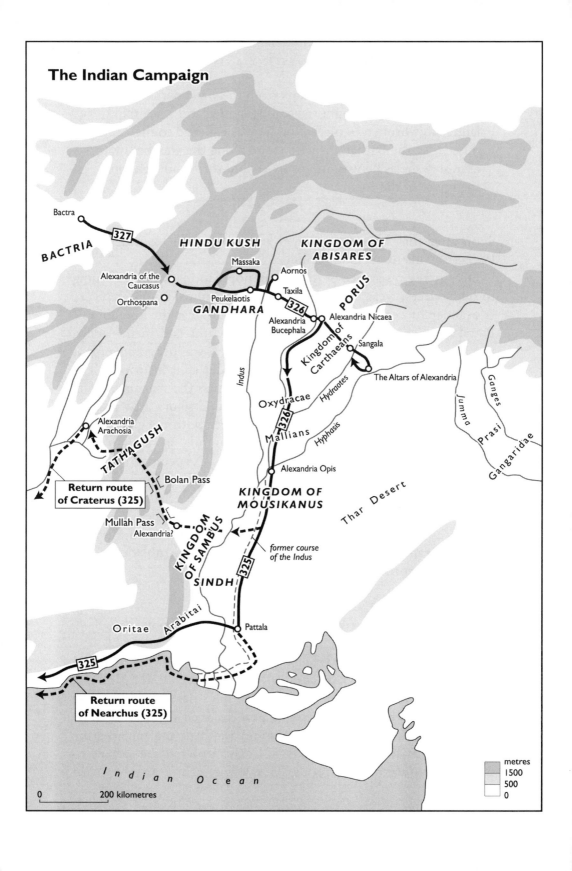

The Indian Campaign

Bactra

BACTRIA

327

HINDU KUSH

KINGDOM OF
ABISARES

Massaka

Aornos

Alexandria of the
Caucasus

Orthospana

Peukelaotis

Taxila

GANDHARA

326

PORUS

Alexandria
Bucephala

Alexandria Nicaea

Kingdom of
Carthaeans

Sangala

The Altars of Alexandria

Indus

Oxydracae

Hydraotes

326

Mallians

Hyphasis

Alexandria
Arachosia

TATHAGUSH

Bolan Pass

**Return route
of Craterus (325)**

Mullah Pass

Alexandria?

KINGDOM
OF SAMBUS

KINGDOM OF
MOUSIKANUS

Alexandria Opis

Thar Desert

Jumna

Ganges

Prasi

Gangaridae

325

*former course
of the Indus*

SINDH

Oritae

Arabitai

Pattala

325

**Return route
of Nearchus (325)**

I n d i a n   O c e a n

metres
1500
500
0

0   200 kilometres

After dispersing the inhabitants from the walls with missiles, he was the first to mount the scaling ladder, and since the ladder was broken to pieces and he was exposed to the missiles of the Barbarians who stood along the wall below, almost alone as he was, he crouched and threw himself into the midst of the enemy.

(*Alex.*, 63, 3)

Soon after this, he was wounded and only saved from death by Peucestas, one of his Companions.

Despite the resistance of the Indian populations, who, according to our sources, were encouraged by the Brahmins, in mid-July 325 Alexander succeeded in imposing his control over the kingdom of Pattala, which was deserted by its inhabitants and their leaders, and at last arrived at the mouth of the Indus. It was becoming urgent to return to the West. Once again, Alexander split his forces. The fleet, under Nearchus' command, was to take the maritime route while part of the army, led by Craterus, would rejoin it by a direct route across inland Carmania, and Alexander, with the greater part of the army, would follow the coastline, counting on supplies from the fleet. Again things went worse than was expected. The food promised by local populations never materialised, and some of them resisted the army's advance. Crossing the Gedrosian desert was a terrible trial, in the course of which many soldiers perished. But once he arrived in Carmania, none of this prevented the king from celebrating the end of his Indian adventure with athletic Games, theatrical performances and 'Dionysiac' banquets.

THE RETURN TO SUSA AND BABYLON

The last month of 325 and the beginning of 324 were marked by a serious crisis. A number of satraps, Macedonian as well as Iranian, hearing that the king was presumed to have perished during the last stages of the Indian campaign, now declared themselves to be independent. Alexander hastened to depose them and replaced the Iranians with loyal Macedonians. He also ordered the satraps to dismiss their mercenary troops. This was clearly a way to guard against further revolts against him. And Alexander may also have regarded it as a chance to reconstitute his own troops, which had been considerably depleted since the horrendous crossing of the Gedrosian desert. But at the same time it was risky, since many of the mercenaries simply wanted a chance to return to Europe or, more precisely, to the region of Cape Taenarum, at the extreme southern tip of the Peloponnese, which had become an assembly point for these professional soldiers.

The repressive measures used against the rebel satraps also gave rise to one particular serious consequence (to which we shall be returning). This was the flight of Harpalus, the king's treasurer, to Europe or, more precisely, Athens, with a troop of mercenaries and funds to the tune of 5,000 talents.

Meanwhile Alexander, after again celebrating his victories, left Carmania and advanced towards Susa, where he arrived at the beginning of the spring of 324. Here the famous 'Susa weddings' took place, in which a number of Iranian princesses were married to some of the king's followers. Alexander himself, who had already set an example by his marriage to Roxane, now solemnly married two Achaemenid princesses, the one a daughter of Artaxerxes III, the other a daughter of Darius III. Hephaistion was married to another of Darius' daughters, Craterus to a niece of the Great King.

Perdiccas, Nearchus, Ptolemy and Eumenes, the secretary of the royal Chancellery, also married Iranian princesses. We shall in due course be returning to consider the significance of these unions. Did they spark off the discontent among the Macedonians? And above all, where did that discontent erupt? There are two traditions here. According to Diodorus, Alexander put down a revolt in Susa. It was said to have been prompted by Alexander's avowed intention not to return to Macedonia. Arrian, on the other hand, tells us that the veterans rebelled at Opis, on the River Tigris, at the announcement of their demobilisation. It is not hard to recognise the contradictions between the two versions, even if both testify to the Macedonians' discontent at seeing new recruits preferred to themselves, starting with the Iranians who had been integrated into the army. They may well also have resented not being associated with the future campaigns that the king was planning. In Arrian's version of this episode, the king managed to calm things down by bringing the two sides together at a fraternal banquet. The veterans being sent back to Macedon were loaded with gifts and each received one talent over and above his regular pay. Craterus was put in command of these men, with orders to lead them back to Macedonia, where he was to take the place of Antipater, who, for his part, was to bring the king fresh troops to fight in his future campaigns.

Alexander then moved to Ecbatana, where there were further festivities, while embassies from all over the Mediterranean world arrived to pay homage to the king. It was during this autumn of 324 that Hephaistion fell ill and died. He had been a loyal companion and very close to Alexander, and was now honoured by an exceptionally lavish funeral, and raised to the rank of hero.

During the winter of 324–323, Alexander campaigned against the Cossaeans, the mountain people of Zagros. Then, in the spring, he reached Babylon, to which more ambassadors flocked from every corner of the Mediterranean world. Alexander apparently gathered from them information likely to be helpful in planning his future campaigns. Essentially, these consisted of an expedition of circumnavigation right round the Arabian peninsula, from the Persian Gulf to Egypt. With this in mind, Alexander had detailed Nearchus to assemble a fleet. Arabia itself was to be annexed to the empire at a later date.

However, these plans never even began to be implemented. In May 323, following a banquet, Alexander felt unwell, and death swiftly followed. It was immediately supposed that this was not a natural death, and suspicion fell on Antipater, who was still in Macedonia but was known to be hostile to the king's policies in the East, and to have supporters among the royal entourage.

Whatever the truth of the matter, Alexander's painful death brought to an end an adventure that had enabled him to gather into his hands an immense territory, a far cry from the kingdom of his Macedonian ancestors. Shortly before his death, he had despatched an embassy led by the Greek Nicanor of Stagira, requiring the Greeks gathered together for the four-yearly Olympic Games to grant him divine honours. In one decade he had progressed from being the king of the Macedonians to *hegemon* of the Greeks, to successor to the Achaemenids; and now he wished to be proclaimed *theos anikêtos*, an unvanquished god. Now we must try to understand how a single person could incorporate so many different images of the power of Alexander.

PART II

The Different 'Faces' of Alexander

CHAPTER 5

The king of the Macedonians

When Alexander succeeded his father in 336, he inherited a monarchy that was hard to integrate into the schemata that had been elaborated by Greek thought ever since the mid-fifth century. In Herodotus' famous 'Persian debate' in book III of the *Histories*, monarchy, whether vilified by the Persian noble Otanes or defended by the future Darius I, was first and foremost an absolute power held by a man who was accountable to no one. Where the defender of *isonomia* saw a threat, holding that supreme power leads to pride and *hubris*, the defender of monarchy on the contrary found a guarantee of efficacy. But both held that monarchical power could not be shared in any fashion. As the Greeks saw it, such absolute power came in only two forms. One was tyranny, such as had existed in certain cities in ancient times and, in the fourth century, still existed in Syracuse. The other was the Persian monarchy. Despotism such as this could only be exerted over Barbarian peoples naturally inclined to servitude. Certainly, in the eyes of a man such as Demosthenes, for whom the Macedonians were indeed 'Barbarians', Philip was close to being an absolute monarch, and it was his absolutism that made his decisions so rapid and effective: unlike the Athenians, who took action only after lengthy deliberations, he decided promptly, on his own, what action to take. However, Demosthenes' testimony on this point was dictated by the urgency for him to win over his fellow-citizens. The orator was well aware that the matter was not as simple as he suggested.

MACEDONIAN KINGSHIP

On this point, it is worth turning to Aristotle. The philosopher had lived for a while at the Macedonian court, to which Philip had summoned him, to take charge of the education of his son and future successor. We shall be returning to this education. What is relevant here is a remark that Aristotle made in the *Politics*, his great work on political systems. Reflecting upon the kingships of his day, in book V (1310b 35–40), the philosopher mentions those that are founded upon 'merit' and cites, as examples, 'the kings of the Spartans, the Macedonians, and the Molossians'. The fascination that the Spartan regime exerted upon the Greeks is well known. Aristotle himself, who, unlike his master Plato, was critical of it, nevertheless pointed out that the Spartan kings were answerable to the city. The history of past decades provided plenty of examples of that control, which was exercised by ephors, officials elected annually by all the citizens. In this respect, the double Spartan kingship bore comparison with the colleges of officials which operated in other cities, except, however, for one difference: the fact that those kings were always drawn from two royal houses, the Agiads and the Eurypontids, whose responsibilities were clearly allotted to them for life. In similar fashion, the king of Macedon belonged to a dynasty that had allegedly hailed from Argos and had placed itself at the head of the country back in the seventh century. Power in Macedon was hereditary.

Another point is also worth emphasising. The Greeks – in this case, the Athenians – had two distinct but undifferentiated ways of referring to the figure who reigned in Macedon. Sometimes they spoke of the *basileus Makedonias*, the king of Macedon, as Thucydides did when referring to Perdiccas II, the son of Alexander I, a king who reigned over Macedon at the beginning of the Peloponnesian War (II, 95, 1), or as Demosthenes did when evoking Philip's predecessors' policies in the northern Aegean (*Second Philippic*, 20). At other times they used the formula *basileus Makedonôn*, king of the Macedonians, which implied that the Macedonians formed a political community. It should be remembered that, whereas we customarily speak of Athens, Sparta or Thebes just as nowadays we speak of France, England or Italy, as the case may be, meaning the state itself, the ancients, in contrast, used to speak of the Athenians, the Spartans, the Thebans and so on, thereby conveying a particular characteristic of classical Greek civilisation: a city was conceived primarily as a community of citizens. Does this mean that the community of Macedonians suggested by the formula *basileus Makedonôn* was also a political community? This is a problem on which historians are divided, particularly as, before the period following Alexander's death, there are no (or very few) references to any Macedonian 'people's assembly'. All the same, it does appear that there existed, if not an assembly of the people, at least an 'army assembly' that acclaimed a new king at his accession and possessed certain judicial powers.

In Arrian's account (*Anabasis*, IV, 11, 6), Callisthenes makes some comments intended to remind Alexander that Macedonian rulers Callisthenes uses the term 'archons', that is to say 'the holders of power (*archè*)' – had never governed by force but always by law (*oude bia alla nomoi*). The existence of a Macedonian *nomos*, a law governing relations between the king and the people, would seem to provide further proof that, in Macedon, there were limits to royal absolutism. As Paul Goukowsky writes (*Essai*, p. 11), the Macedonian monarchy consisted of 'a delegation of sovereignty granted to a leader judged to be efficacious and conveyed by acclamation, which was revocable, divisible and could be transferred to other members of the royal family by an assembly that remained the repository of sovereignty'. To be sure, Philip's reign, as we have seen, had been marked by efforts at centralisation. But it was the force of his personality, rather than any institutional modification, that had made that strengthening of the royal power possible, and it continued to remain constantly liable to be called into question.

We have already noted the situation that faced Alexander immediately after Philip's assassination. This was not the first time that the royal succession had been disputed. And Alexander had reason to fear the claims to Philip's succession made by the entourage of the young queen Cleopatra, who was pregnant and about to produce a child who would have an advantage over Alexander in that he or she would be born from a Macedonian princess rather than a foreigner such as Olympias. Of course, we must be wary of the accounts – all of late date – of the circumstances in which Alexander succeeded in gaining the upper hand. But the fact that he immediately set about ensuring the security of the kingdom's frontiers at least suggests that the army rallied to him – the army that Philip had strengthened and reorganised and that had crushed the Greeks at Chaeronea in a victory to which the young Alexander had made a major contribution. It is certainly reasonable to suppose that the soldiers gathered in assembly confirmed him as the *basileus Makedonôn*.

THE MACEDONIAN ARMY DURING
THE ASIAN CAMPAIGN

It is interesting to reflect upon the role played by the army assemblies during Alexander's expedition of conquest. If we accept the figures suggested by Diodorus, the expeditionary force that he assembled before crossing to Asia consisted of 30,000 foot-soldiers and 4,500 horsemen. The Macedonians represented just over one third of that total of fighting men: 12,000 foot-soldiers and 1,800 horsemen. Diodorus refers to a council that Alexander convoked before the departure of the army (XVII, 16, 1–3). It was made up of men described as army 'leaders' along with the most eminent of his 'friends'. That term *philoi* should not be understood in an affective sense. It was simply used to refer to members of the king's court. But did they constitute a permanent council to which, on this occasion, Alexander added the army leaders? There is no evidence to suggest either that that was the case or that it was not. However that may be, there are two interesting points to note. On the one hand, the convocation of this council implies that the king was bound to justify his plans before his soldiers, just as a *strategos* of a Greek city would. But on the other hand, it is impossible not to be reminded of the council meetings that the leaders of the Achaeans held in the *Iliad*. And the possible consequences that could be drawn from that reminder are not hard to imagine: either it might be deduced that Macedonian kingship was still close to 'Homeric' kingship, or it could be regarded as an effect of 'propaganda' that tended to represent the Asian expedition as a new Trojan War, and the king of the Macedonians, who was a distant descendant of Achilles, as another epic hero.

The first phase of the expedition ended with the capture of the western satrapies of the Persian Empire. The three great victories of the Granicus, Issus and Gaugamela were won as much by the

Macedonians as by their king. The men he placed at the head of the conquered satrapies were Macedonians and it was they who received the greater part of the huge masses of booty taken. Reinforcements from Macedon had joined the army at Susa and at Babylon. As we have noted, this arrival of fresh troops had led to a reorganisation of the posts of command in both the infantry and the cavalry. Among the newcomers were fifty sons of the 'king's friends', who were to serve as Alexander's bodyguard. These were the famous 'pages', whom we shall be considering in due course. The capture of Persepolis and the sacking of the empire's capital were also 'rewards' that the king offered his Macedonians.

But, from that moment on, the relations between the king and his army changed. It was an army from which the Greek allies had disappeared, for Alexander had dismissed them at Ecbatana, even before the death of Darius. Shortly after, the death of the Great King left Alexander as the successor to the Achaemenids. It was in this capacity that he then fought against the usurper Bessus; and also in this capacity that he was to retain in their posts the Iranian satraps who had rallied to him. Now it became necessary to convince the Macedonians in the army that the new campaign that was about to begin was also theirs. Diodorus (XVII, 74, 3) describes the meeting of the Macedonian soldiers in an assembly and, to refer to it, he uses the term *ecclesia* which, in Greek cities, designated an assembly of citizens. In this assembly, Alexander is said to have made a speech, telling his listeners 'that at present they were feared by the Barbarians, but if they should merely throw Asia into confusion and then leave it, they would be attacked by them as if they were women' (*Alex.*, 47, 1). Plutarch adds that Alexander allowed all those who wished to leave to do so. This was the first fissure in the united view shared by the king and his soldiers, the first sign of the discontent of one section of the Macedonians.

THE RIFT BETWEEN THE KING AND
THE MACEDONIANS

Perhaps that discontent was further aggravated by the adoption, by the king and some of those close to him, of what Diodorus (XVII,

77, 4) calls 'Persian luxury and the extravagant display of the kings of Asia'. That is certainly what is suggested by our sources, even though Plutarch is at pains to report that, in order not to alienate the Macedonians, Alexander did not change his lifestyle all at once and 'remained as much as possible attached to his earlier practices, out of a desire not to shock the Macedonians'.

The first serious rift, the Philotas affair, should clearly be placed in this context. Philotas was one of the sons of Parmenion, an old Companion of Philip's and the man to whom Alexander had entrusted the command of part of the army in the Asian campaign. Was Philotas the initiator of a plot against the king or, having been informed of one, did he fail to denounce it? On this point our sources differ, although they do agree that most of the suspicion fell on a certain Dimnus. But what is important here is the manner in which this affair was handled. In Plutarch's account, Philotas was tortured and summarily executed. Diodorus, on the contrary, reports that it was 'the Macedonians' who passed this sentence, the king having abstained from coming to a decision himself. Quintus Curtius, for his part, refers to the Macedonian law that made the assembly of the Macedonians responsible for passing sentence, and in this case that was clearly the assembly of the army. Diodorus also records the speeches allegedly made before any decision was reached. According to this version of Philotas' 'trial', it clearly took place in the presence of an assembly empowered to pass judgements, and the behaviour of an absolute monarch consequently had nothing to do with it.

In his dealings with the Macedonians, Alexander had to respect the law. However, it was not an assembly of soldiers that decided Parmenion's fate, rather assassins sent by the king, who brought about his death as his son's accomplice. In order to justify this expeditious procedure, it has sometimes been suggested that Macedonian law authorised the execution of the parents of anyone judged to be guilty, so Parmenion's death did not result from an arbitrary action. But that seems to be an excessively legalistic argument. Besides, both Diodorus and Quintus Curtius report that, to prevent these discontented elements from corrupting the rest of the Macedonians in the army, Alexander then gathered them into a single, separate unit. Diodorus also alludes to letters that the malcontents had sent back to Macedonia, denouncing the assassination of Parmenion. These events provide us with a glimpse of the complexity of the relations between the king and the Macedonians in his army.

The Philotas affair was the first of a series of clashes that reflect the deepening rift between the king and his Macedonians. Two years after the execution of Parmenion and his son came the murder of Cleitus. He too was a noble Macedonian who was close to the king, who had entrusted to him the satrapy of Bactria–Sogdiana. During a banquet in Marakanda, the capital of this satrapy, Alexander, in a drunken state, allegedly ran Cleitus' body through with his spear. Clearly, this was an entirely different situation from that of Philotas' 'trial'. All the same, it seems unlikely that it was simply a drunken quarrel. For in the course of the violent exchange of words between Alexander and Cleitus, the latter allegedly cited some lines from Euripides' *Andromache*, lines that criticised military leaders who took all the glory for themselves when in reality the credit for victory belonged to the ordinary soldiers. Of course this story may have been invented later. It seems unlikely that the Macedonian soldiers would deny their king's military valour. All the same, it reflects an atmosphere of mistrust where he was concerned. What the Macedonians held against Alexander was that, in adopting Barbarian manners, he was behaving as a despot vis-à-vis them, Macedonians, who were free men.

These were the same Macedonian soldiers who refused to go through the *proskynesis* ceremony that Alexander is supposed to have required of them as well as of his eastern subjects. It consisted in bowing low before the king, holding one's hand at mouth level. It was also they who, upon reaching the banks of the Hyphasis, refused to advance any further and obliged Alexander to retrace his steps.

But the most serious crisis was the one that erupted in Susa in 324, just after the king reorganised the administration of the vast empire that he had acquired. The 'Susa weddings' have been mentioned above, and we shall have occasion to return to this ceremony in which the king's Companions, along with the king himself, were joined in matrimony with Iranian princesses. But apparently it was not those unions that provoked the sedition of a group of veterans.

This was almost certainly caused by the arrival of the young Iranians whom Alexander had had trained with a view to using them as phalanx fighters. Diodorus tells us that 'they were splendidly equipped with the full Macedonian armament' (XVII, 108, 2). These 'epigones' were supposed to replace the Macedonian veterans whom Alexander was preparing to dismiss. The latter numbered about 10,000, and not only was each to receive one talent, but furthermore the king was undertaking to repay all the debts that they had run up during the campaign. According to our sources, despite the king's generosity, these Macedonians were nevertheless refusing to obey. Diodorus notes that 'they burst out with invectives whenever assemblies were held'. Again the term used for these assemblies is *ecclesia*, which, when employed by a Greek, possesses an essentially political connotation. Diodorus, along with the source that inspired him, locates this mutiny in Susa, while other sources mention a similar one in Opis. The incorporation of the young Iranians into the army may have occasioned a number of mutinies. Our sources also differ over Alexander's reactions. According to Arrian, the king managed to calm the rebels down. But Diodorus claims that he reacted violently and had the leaders of the mutiny executed. The rest knuckled under and set off on the return journey to Europe.

As can be seen from the records of these clashes, on the eve of the king's death the rift between him and a section of the Macedonians in his army was very real. But, as we have also seen, it is hard to assess both the weight that the army assemblies carried and also Alexander's behaviour in the face of this real or theoretical limitation of his authority. It is, of course, made all the harder by the fact that our sources, derived from evidence provided by Hellenised circles, and themselves for the most part Greek, are strongly marked by the traditional opposition always drawn between Greek liberty and Barbarian despotism.

This brings us to another 'face' of Alexander, that of the *hegemon* of the Greeks who had come together in the League of Corinth.

CHAPTER 6

The *hegemon* of the Greeks

When Alexander landed in Asia in the early spring of 334, he was leading the campaign in his capacity as *hegemon* of the Greek allies who belonged to the League of Corinth. The first goal of the campaign was to 'liberate' the Greeks of Asia from Persian domination. This was the latest formulation of an already ancient theme, for it had been in order to obtain that very liberation that the Athenians had formed the Delian League in the aftermath of the Persian Wars. When the Delian League collapsed, at the end of the Peloponnesian War, victorious Sparta had taken over the torch with policies pursued first by Lysander, the commander of the fleet, then by the Spartan king, Agesilaus. But conditions were now different, in that the Spartan victory had been won thanks to the gold provided by the Great King. In 386, the Great King had, in fact, recognised the autonomy of the Greek cities of Asia. But a few years later, the Athenians again managed to gather some of those cities together in their second maritime confederation. Even Thebes, under its general, Epaminondas, had tried to intervene in Asia. Eventually, the revolt of Athens' allies, supported by the Great King and Mausolus, the satrap of Caria, had again brought the cities under the more or less firm control of the Persian ruler and his satraps. At the time of the accession of Darius III, in 336, most of those cities were paying tribute to the Great King and supplying him with ships and men for his fleet. The majority of them were governed by oligarchies, headed by men who had been won over to the Persian alliance.

THE LIBERATION OF THE GREEK CITIES OF ASIA

The task therefore looked daunting. Parmenion, who had been sent ahead as a scout, had suffered serious rebuffs from Memnon of Rhodes, whom the Great King had entrusted with the defence of the western shores of his empire. It was only after the victory at the Granicus that Alexander obtained the submission of the Ionian cities. Even then, he was forced to lay siege to Miletus and resort to sophisticated siege-machines before overcoming the garrison's resistance. Diodorus tells us that 'Immediately the Milesians, falling before the king with suppliant olive boughs, put themselves and their city into his hands' (XVII, 22, 2). Similarly, Halicarnassus, which, since the 'reign' of Mausolus, had become a powerful city with a well-fortified port, was only 'liberated' after a siege that involved the destruction of part of the city. Elsewhere resistance was weaker.

Wherever he went, Alexander presented himself as the defender of liberty and imposed more or less democratic regimes. The local leaders accused of favouring the Persians were ejected. This happened most notably at Ephesus, where a democracy was restored, dominated by partisans of the Macedonians. The Greek cities of Asia were strategically important, so Alexander certainly cannot have allowed them total autonomy. He probably established a number of Macedonian garrisons, to ensure security and prevent any disturbances that could be exploited by those serving the Great King.

The matter of tribute raised another problem. In Ephesus, Alexander consecrated the tribute to the great temple dedicated to Artemis. Elsewhere he handed it over to the local populations, in order to encourage their goodwill. We have no precise information on this matter and should treat later reports of Alexander's generosity – reports that date from the Seleucid period – with a measure of circumspection. We are slightly better informed about the city of Priene, thanks to a fragmentary inscription recording how much of the territory was assigned to the city and how much passed directly under the king's control. The city and its inhabitants were exempted from tribute, but the territory that he had conquered had to pay it. Another significant example of Alexander's behaviour is provided by the city of Aspendos, on the Pamphylian coast. The city surrendered to Alexander in return for a promise that it would not be given a Macedonian garrison. Alexander agreed, but in return demanded a contribution of 50 talents for the upkeep of his soldiers and horses (Arrian, I, 26, 3). At first the people of Aspendos refused to pay this, but eventually they agreed to. Now, however, Alexander's demands became more exacting: an annual tribute of 100 talents, with hostages to guarantee the city's compliance. Furthermore, the city passed under the control of the Macedonian governor of the satrapy. A similar fate was inflicted upon Soli, in Cilicia, but subsequently, after the battle of Issus and the seizure of part of Darius' treasure, Alexander returned both the tribute and the hostages to the city.

The statuses of the cities 'liberated' from Persian control thus varied widely. The presence of garrisons, the levying of tribute, and the control of institutions took different forms according to the circumstances. Almost certainly, however, Alexander did not conclude alliances with these cities, so they were not integrated into the League of Corinth.

In his *Life of Alexander*, Plutarch, having described the battle of Gaugamela, concludes as follows:

> The battle having had this issue, the empire of the Persians
> was thought to be utterly dissolved and Alexander,
> proclaimed king of Asia, made magnificent sacrifices to the
> gods and rewarded his friends with wealth, estates, and
> provinces. And being desirous of honour among the Greeks,
> he wrote them that all their tyrannies were abolished and
> they might live under their own laws.
>
> (*Alex.*, 34, 1–2)

Yet in the *Life of Phocion*, the same Plutarch reports that Alexander offered four of the Asian cities to this Athenian *strategos*, who was one of his friends. Clearly, the 'liberation' of the Greeks of Asia was subject to certain limitations.

The conquest of Asia Minor, definitively completed after the battle of Issus, indicated that the goal assigned to the alliance concluded between Philip and the Greeks and subsequently renewed by Alexander had been achieved. Yet it was not until two years later, when Alexander had won control of the Syro-Phoenician coast, Egypt and Mesopotamia, that, upon reaching Ecbatana, Alexander dismissed the Greek contingents from his army. The reason why he delayed so long was that, since 333, mainland Greece and the islands had been gripped by unrest, stirred up by the Spartan king Agis III. Following the defeat and death of Agis at Megalopolis, Antipater became the affirmed master of the situation and only at this point did Alexander release the Greeks from his army. They included the Thessalian cavalry, which had played an essential role in the three great battles that had made Alexander's conquest possible. Some of the Greeks nevertheless remained in his service, but as mercenaries and no longer as representatives of their respective cities.

THE FOUNDATION OF NEW CITIES

Many of these Greek mercenaries were now installed in the cities that the conqueror founded all the way across to central Asia. However, the first of those foundations, Alexandria, holds a special place. Alexander founded this city in an Egypt that had been rapidly conquered once the way in through Gaza had been forced, and where he had been heartened in his ambitions by his consultation of Ammon's oracle. What was his purpose when he founded Alexandria? Again we come up against the problem of the sources and, in this particular case, also that of the future destiny of this city. For under the Ptolemies Alexandria was to become the greatest city in the Hellenistic world and the most important cultural and artistic centre in the eastern Mediterranean. It clearly owed its pre-eminence to the first two Ptolemies, Ptolemy I Soter and his son, Ptolemy II Philadelphus. But had Alexander himself had an intuition of that destiny? Was he intent on being seen by his contemporaries as another of those founding heroes of the more or less distant, more or less mythical past? Or did he simply have in view the creation of a reliable port for his fleet at this moment when he was preparing to penetrate deep into the heart of Asia? It is almost impossible to provide answers to these questions, although the last hypothesis seems the most likely.

Our sources are at odds regarding the date of this foundation. Plutarch (*Alex.*, 26, 6) and Arrian (III, 2, 1) suppose it to have preceded the expedition to the Siwa oasis. Diodorus (XVII, 52, 1) and

Quintus Curtius (IV, 8, 1 f) refer to it only after their accounts of the oracle. According to Diodorus, Alexander himself drew up the city plan, ordered the construction of a palace, and laid the foundations of the city wall. It seems reasonable to doubt this. It is true that Alexander was surrounded by engineers and architects who had already demonstrated their skills at the sieges of Miletus, Halicarnassus and Tyre, and he may well have left them instructions. But we should remember that he spent a relatively short time in Egypt, that he was keen to conquer Darius, and that the urgency of future military efforts made it unlikely that he would have devoted such attention to the appearance of the future city.

Another question also arises. For whom was this city designed? It truly was a *polis*, a city, and we know that, even in the Ptolemaic period, it remained 'apart' from Egypt. Was it populated in the first instance by Greek mercenaries, colonists who were allotted plots of land? Or possibly by Greeks already installed in Egypt, in Naucratis, for example? Most historians stress the political, rather than military, foundation of Alexandria, setting it apart from the other cities strung out along the route taken by the conquest. It seems that, right from the start, under the direction of the architect Deinocrates of Rhodes, a space was reserved for the agora and sanctuaries consecrated to the deities of the Hellenic pantheon. Did Alexander himself decide upon the institutions of the future city? We know that, by the third century, the town counted among its inhabitants not only a large Greek population but also Jews and Egyptians. However the latter, confined to their respective quarters, were not citizens of Alexandria. Only much later, when Egypt became a Roman province, could a man such as the Jewish philosopher Philo claim to be 'an Alexandrian'.

Alexandria thus constitutes a rather special case among the many foundations later to be associated with the name of the conqueror. The earliest of these were established during the campaign leading to the eastern satrapies. After the revolt of Satibarzanes, the satrap of Areia, had been crushed, Alexandria Areia (Herat) and Alexandria Arachosia (Kandahar) were founded. Next came Alexandria of the Caucasus, about which our sources are more explicit. We are told that here Alexander established 3,000 colonists (Macedonian veterans or volunteers recruited among the Greek mercenaries), along with

7,000 natives. It is seems to have been a model that was repeated elsewhere: a military garrison surrounded by an indigenous population, to farm the city territory. The fact is that most of the foundations cited by our sources were situated in strategic positions, so there is reason enough to favour a political interpretation of Alexander's actions, rather than that of a desire to Hellenise the Iranian populations. That applies to Alexandria Eschate, Alexandria on the Oxus, and plenty of other cities too. Some were founded on a pre-existing indigenous site, others, on the contrary, on a completely uninhabited spot. It is hard to say how many such foundations there were. They are to be found in Bactria and Sogdiana as well as in India, where, on either side of the Hydaspes river, Alexander created Nicaea and Bucephala as well as other cities as far-flung as the Indus delta, not to mention all those founded on the return journey.

How many Graeco-Macedonians were installed in the heart of Asia in this way? It is impossible to say. Some of these establishments were short-lived, others prospered. Clearly, their links with the Mediterranean world must, in time, have loosened. But the Greek character of these Alexandrias nevertheless survived, as has been shown by the excavations undertaken by French archaeologists at Ai Khanoum.

But, as we shall be discovering, these foundations were more a consequence of the circumstances than the result of a conscious intention to Hellenise the Barbarian world. Nor were they prompted by a desire to put into operation Isocrates' plan to colonise Asia, with a view to solving the social problems of the Greek world.

Does this mean that, once he became the successor to the Achaemenids, Alexander ceased to see himself as either the *hegemon* of the Greeks or even an epic hero? That is by no means certain, as is suggested by his relations with his Greek entourage.

ALEXANDER'S GREEK ENTOURAGE

We have already noted the presence of Greek soldiers in Alexander's army, soldiers who had either originally belonged to the contingents provided by the allied states of the League of Corinth or were mercenaries recruited in the Aegean world, in which there were swarms of such professional soldiers. But as well as these it is important not to overlook the Greeks in Alexander's immediate entourage, who were distinct from his Companions from the Macedonian aristocracy. The most famous of these Greeks were the historian Callisthenes and Nearchus, who, as commander of the fleet, sailed along the coastline of the Indian Ocean. Also worth a mention are Aristoboulus, who took part in the campaign and left an account of it that was used not only by both Arrian and Plutarch but also by the chamberlain Chares of Mytilene, the philosopher Anaxarchus of Abdera, and the chancellor Eumenes of Cardia.

Callisthenes of Olynthus was related to Aristotle. He was a historian who, before joining the Asian campaign, had produced a work entitled *Hellenica*, covering the period between the King's Peace (386) and the beginning of the third sacred war (356). As official historian, he enjoyed a privileged position, close to Alexander; and the few surviving fragments of his work suggest that his version of events was, to some degree, the 'authorised' one. However, Alexander's affirmation of the absolute nature of his power was to lead to Callisthenes' death.

The most detailed account of this affair is to be found in Plutarch's *Life of Alexander*. Plutarch first recounts an anecdote telling how Callisthenes provoked the hostility of the Macedonians. In the course of a banquet, Alexander asked him to make a speech in praise of the Macedonians, and Callisthenes obliged so brilliantly that the king then invited him to display his talents as an orator by making a speech to the opposite effect, that is to say one that denigrated them. Callisthenes, well versed in the rules of rhetoric, did so equally brilliantly, attributing Philip's victory over the Greeks not to his own merits but to the discord between the latter. Callisthenes was a native of Olynthus and, still according to Plutarch, had followed in Alexander's footsteps in the hope that the king would rebuild his city, which Philip had destroyed in 348. The memory of those past events must have provided him with plenty of arguments for the sophistic exercise that consisted in defending first one, then the other of two opposite points of view (*Alex.*, 53, 3–6).

Although we may credit this anecdote to some degree, it seems more likely that the rift was really caused by Alexander's own behaviour. Plutarch, who throughout this passage draws on a third-century

Peripatetic philosopher by the name of Hermippus of Smyrna, relates that Callisthenes, 'by refusing sturdily and like a philosopher to perform the act [of *proskynesis*]', provoked the displeasure of the king and certain of his Companions, who then spread the rumour that 'the sophist went about with lofty thoughts as if bent upon abolishing a tyranny, and that the young men flocked to him and followed him about as if he were the only free man among many tens of thousands' (*Alex.*, 55, 2).

Those accusations were subsequently strengthened when the famous 'Pages' Plot' came to light. The 'pages' were the youths in the king's service who, seeking to avenge a punishment inflicted on one of their number, decided to make an attempt on Alexander's life. Callisthenes was said to be the accomplice and adviser of Hermolaus, the leader of the conspiracy. However, as Plutarch also reports, even under torture none of the plotters implicated Callisthenes. So it seems to have been Alexander himself who took the decision to get rid of this bothersome Greek. Plutarch records several contradictory accounts of Callisthenes' end:

> As to the death of Callisthenes, some say that he was hanged by Alexander's orders, others that he was bound hand and foot and died of sickness, and Chares [a Greek from Mytilene, who was chamberlain to Alexander from 333 on] says that after his arrest he was kept in fetters seven months, that he might be tried before a full council, when Aristotle was present, but that about the time when Alexander was wounded in India, he died of obesity and the 'disease of lice'.
>
> (*Alex.*, 55, 9)

According to the last of those versions, because Callisthenes was a Greek, Alexander envisaged having him tried before the Council of the League of Corinth.

Alexander's relations with the other Greeks in his entourage seem to have been less strained. Nearchus, in particular, enjoyed his full confidence, as is shown by the mission that Alexander entrusted to him on the return journey: to explore the coast all the way from the Indus delta to the tip of the Persian Gulf. The same applies to Eumenes, who was made responsible for keeping a record of the expedition, and also to Aristoboulus, whose account of the campaign was, as has been noted, one of the sources used by both Plutarch and Arrian. Likewise, the other Greeks – doctors, seers and engineers – who accompanied the expedition seem to have had no problems. Alexander prided himself on his Greek origins and his Greek culture and, even if he no longer commanded an army composed of allied Greek contingents, he was still the *hegemon* of the Greeks.

NICANOR'S MISSION TO OLYMPUS

Evidence of that is provided by the mission that he entrusted to Nicanor of Stagira in 324. Now, however, there was one significant difference: in this case, he was acting as an absolute sovereign, dictating his own law to his Greek allies. Moreover, in this instance he took no account of the Council of the League of Corinth. He took this action on the occasion of the festival at Olympia. To the Greeks gathered there, Nicanor announced the gist of an edict in which Alexander ordered the allied cities to allow those who had been banished to return and resume possession of their properties.

This certainly constituted an interference in the internal affairs of the cities, in contravention of the principles of the treaty of alliance concluded after Chaeronea, which preserved their autonomy and specifically prohibited the return of those exiled and all other actions likely to create unrest within the cities: confiscations, the division of land-plots, the abolition of debts, and any massive liberations of slaves. So much, at least, is suggested by a speech attributed to Demosthenes, allegedly delivered soon after Alexander's accession and the renewal of the alliance (*On the treaty with Alexander*, 15–16).

Sentences of exile and confiscations of property had constituted manifestations of what is somewhat misleadingly known as the 'crisis' of the fourth century. This involved both internal struggles between democrats and oligarchs within the cities and also many conflicts between one city and another. When there was a change of regime, the return of exiles, in particular, gave rise to intractable problems surrounding the restitution of property that had been confiscated and, in many cases, subsequently sold off. When

Alexander made these demands of his, he must have been aware of the risk of stirring up unrest in many quarters. Perhaps that was indeed his intention, so that, in the event of his undertaking the conquest of Arabia, he would have nothing to fear in the way of a concerted Greek revolt. Or was it simply a way of demonstrating that he was now the master and the Greeks must bow to this? It seems likely, at any rate, that the exiles who had taken refuge in Asia and had there taken part in the campaign influenced Alexander's decision, which was probably taken when he returned to Susa, in the early spring of 324.

Whatever the case may be, the reactions of the Greek states were, in general, hostile. The first affected were the Athenians, who, since 365, had installed cleruchs (soldier colonists) in Samos, on the lands confiscated from its banished oligarchs. In Athens, there was no shortage of people ready for a showdown with the Macedonian authorities. Nevertheless, it does appear that the Athenians first made an attempt to negotiate with the king. The chronology of the events that then took place in Athens is uncertain. Alexander's decision to demand the recall of those banished was probably known before Nicanor's arrival in Olympia, in the autumn of 324. Shortly before, in the late spring or early summer, Harpalus, Alexander's treasurer, had arrived in Athens. For reasons that remain obscure, he was ready to place men and money at the disposal of the city if it would resist Alexander's orders. Curiously enough, he was at first rebuffed, and Demosthenes was one of those who refused to welcome him. A few years previously, Harpalus had presented a cargo of wheat to the Athenians and, in return, had been granted Athenian citizenship. He had also had an Athenian mistress, the courtesan Pythionike, with whom he is said to have lived during an earlier stay in Athens. However that may be, leaving some of his soldiers and his money at Cape Taenarum, he now returned to Athens with 700 talents and three ships. This time Harpalus was imprisoned and his money was deposited on the Acropolis. But when the Macedonian managed to escape, no doubt with the aid of accomplices, only half the sum deposited on the Acropolis was to be found.

This sparked off an enquiry that was to lead to the condemnation of Demosthenes and a number of other orators, who were accused of having siphoned off a portion of the funds. However, before this condemnation was pronounced, Demosthenes had been chosen to represent the city at the Olympian festival. There, he is supposed to have negotiated with Nicanor so as to defer the decision concerning those banished from Samos. On the other hand he did accept Alexander's second demand (to which we shall be returning), namely that he be granted divine honours. In a speech made at the trial by the anti-Macedonian orator Hyperides, some fragments of which have come down to us, Demosthenes is openly accused of having agreed to that second demand of Alexander's. A decree passed by the orator Demades then did indeed institute the cult of Alexander in Athens.

Two decrees that have recently been studied attest that, while trying by diplomatic means to limit the effects of the implementation of Alexander's demands concerning the return of the Samian exiles, the Athenians had also been preparing to make a military intervention. When some of the exiles managed to return to the island, the assembly immediately decreed that the Athenian *strategos* in Samos be ordered to arrest them and bring them back to Athens, where they were imprisoned and condemned to death. However, thanks to the intervention of a certain Antileon of Chalcis, who bought them their freedom, that sentence was never carried out. We know of this episode through the decree by which the Samians subsequently honoured this Antileon when, after the Lamian War which, in 323–322, set Macedon in opposition to the Greek cities, the island was taken from the Athenians. This indicates that, even before Alexander's death, most of the *demos* (the assembly of Athenian citizens) was ready to go along with the orators of the anti-Macedonian party, and commence hostilities.

Other Greeks likewise reacted against the decree on the exiles, foremost among them the Aetolians, who seem to have aligned themselves with Athens at the beginning of the Lamian War, as did the Achaeans and the Arcadians.

Alexander's premature death was to confer a quite new dimension upon these latent movements of discontent, which might otherwise have been resolved by local arrangements. The power vacuum in Macedon and also in Asia gave the Greeks hope that the moment to recover their independence had now arrived.

CHAPTER 7

The successor to the Achaemenids

It seemed to Alexander that he had accomplished his
objective, and now held his kingdom without contest, and
he began to imitate the Persian luxury and the extravagant
display of the kings of Asia. [. . .] He put on the Persian
diadem and dressed himself in the white robe and the
Persian sash and everything else except the trousers and the
long-sleeved upper garment. He distributed to his
companions cloaks with purple borders and dressed the horses
in Persian harness. In addition to all this, he added concubines
to his retinue in the manner of Darius, in number not less
than the days of the year and outstanding in beauty, as selected
from all the women of Asia. Each night, these paraded about
the couch of the king so that he might select the one with
whom he would lie that night. Alexander, as a matter of fact,
employed these customs rather sparingly and kept for the
most part to his accustomed routine, not wishing to offend
the Macedonians.

(*Diodorus*, XVIII, 77, 4–7)

The above passage from Diodorus indicates the major change
that took place in Alexander's behaviour following the deaths of
Darius and the usurper Bessus. The successor to the Achaemenids
was now himself. The first manifestation of this new status was
Alexander's 'adoption of the clothing of the Barbarians', as Plutarch
puts it.

THE PARTIAL ADOPTION OF
IRANIAN CLOTHING

As the Greeks saw it, clothing constituted one of the essential features that distinguished a Greek from a Barbarian. As can be seen from pictorial representations, including those of episodes in the Trojan War, one of the most obvious signs of the difference was the wearing of trousers. It is significant that when Alexander adopted the insignia of Achaemenid royalty, he nevertheless drew the line at trousers, and also at the caftan, a sleeved coat. Plutarch also declares that Alexander refused to don the tiara, a lacey type of headgear that is represented in a number of Achaemenid documents, and limited himself to wearing a diadem, the flat ribbon knotted at the back of the head, which was to become the distinctive sign of royalty in the Hellenistic world.

Xenophon, in his *Cyropaedia* (VIII, 3, 13), an imaginary account of Cyrus II the Great, provides a description of the royal Persian costume that helps us to understand the importance of Alexander's adoption of certain pieces of this apparel:

> Cyrus himself upon a chariot appeared in the gates wearing his tiara upright, a purple tunic shot with white (no one but the king may wear such a one), trousers of scarlet dye about his legs, and a mantle all of purple. He had also a fillet about his tiara, and his kinsmen also had the same mark of distinction, and they retain it even now.

So Alexander rejected the tiara, the trousers, and the sleeved robe, but did adopt the diadem and the purple tunic with a white stripe, which were all distinctive signs of royalty. Apparently he also authorised his companions to wear such tunics, whereas he alone bound his head with a diadem. Plutarch adds that Alexander 'carefully devised a fashion which was midway between the Persian and the Median, more modest than the one and more stately than the other' (*Alex.*, 45, 2). There is certainly no way of knowing whether Alexander deliberately made that choice. However, it seems reasonable to suppose that, in order to justify to his companions the serious affront to Macedonian simplicity, he may have drawn attention to the Persian heritage as represented in Xenophon's pedagogic tale, with which he must have been familiar. It was certainly more flattering to be seen as the successor of Cyrus the Great than that of the weak Darius. Plutarch furthermore goes on to say that at first Alexander showed himself dressed in Iranian costume only when dealing with the Barbarians or in the presence of his own companions, not yet daring to appear in such apparel before the army.

WOMEN

Diodorus is clearly at pains to relativise the importance of the harem that Alexander inherited from the Great King. This too was a custom that shocked the Greeks, or at least seemed to them to be characteristic of Barbarians. Greeks and Hellenised Macedonians only took one legitimate wife and, at the most, possibly one concubine, – certainly never a whole harem. At this point, what inevitably comes to mind is Herodotus' account of the deputation sent to the Macedonian Amyntas I on the eve of the Persian Wars, demanding 'earth and water' (V, 18–20). The king received Darius' envoys with great pomp. But when the Persians asked for women, Amyntas' son Alexander, unable to tolerate the idea of the Macedonians' wives, mothers and sisters being offered to the Barbarians, summoned to the hall beardless youths disguised as women and armed with daggers, and these massacred the Persians when they made advances to them. It matters little whether the story is true or false. Either way it testifies to an attitude that Alexander could not ignore.

That story also illuminates the accounts of Alexander's marriage to Roxane. She was the daughter of Oxyartes, a noble Iranian who, after rallying to Alexander, became the governor of Bactria. Plutarch's remarks on the subject of this marriage suggest the light in which Alexander wished this union to be seen:

> His marriage to Roxane, whom he saw in her youthful beauty taking part in a dance at a banquet, was a love affair, and yet it was thought to harmonise well with the matters which he had in hand. For the Barbarians were encouraged by the partnership into which the marriage brought them, and they

were beyond measure fond of Alexander because, the most temperate of all men that he was in these matters, he would not consent to approach even the only woman who ever mastered his affections, without the sanction of the law.

(Alex., 47, 7–8)

In the present context, it matters little whether the king did or did not respect the virginity of his young wife. What is important is that he was anxious to let it be known that he had, for Plutarch did not invent this story. Moreover, the fact that he made the union legal explains how it was that Roxane's son was later accepted as Alexander's legitimate heir by his soldiers.

THE ADMINISTRATION OF THE EMPIRE

However, there can be no doubt that this marriage also served more far-reaching purposes. For Alexander did not limit himself to the partial adoption of the costume of the Great King. As king of the Persians and the Medes as well as of the Macedonians, he was about to take Iranians into the administration and defence of the empire. Did he do so out of conviction, rejecting the traditional opposition between the Greeks and the Barbarians that was so firmly anchored in Greek attitudes? That is a question that has given rise to plenty of controversies and to which we shall be returning. What is certain is that by behaving in this fashion towards the Iranians, Alexander was acting in conformity with neither the principles of his teacher Aristotle, who regarded the Barbarians as slaves 'by nature', nor the advice given to his father Philip by the orator Isocrates, who had suggested that he should turn the Barbarians into 'the Greeks' helots'. However, as some historians have pointed out, Macedon had for a brief period been under Persian domination, so a Macedonian's reaction would not necessarily have been that which was typical of the victors of Marathon and Salamis, who were, moreover, citizens of a democracy, that is to say, the Athenians. In this respect, Aristotle, though not an Athenian himself, thought as an Athenian.

But, more prosaically, Alexander was above all faced with a concrete problem. He needed to ensure the loyalty of the peoples he had conquered and to keep in place the men who governed them; and, over and above all this, faced with the growing reluctance of the Macedonians, he needed to recruit among the Iranians in order to procure fresh, well-trained troops.

Right from the start of the conquest, Alexander had maintained the system of satrapies, but initially he had set Macedonians at the head of these administrative units of the ancient Persian Empire, which, for both strategic and financial reasons, he had in some cases regrouped. For instance, he had combined the ancient satrapies of Lycia and Pamphylia and had later attached these to Phrygia, forming a vast unit which he entrusted to Antigonus Monophthalmus, one of his loyal supporters. The military leaders placed at the head of these satrapies exercised extensive powers, even if they included a few independent enclaves. For example, the Greek cities of Asia Minor were, as we have seen, theoretically autonomous, and the Phoenician cities had, in particular, preserved the right to mint their own money, but they were generally placed under the surveillance of Macedonian garrisons.

After the battle of Gaugamela, Alexander entrusted the government of the newly conquered provinces to Iranian satraps. In these eastern provinces, it was preferable that the governors should be capable of understanding the local languages. Besides, once Alexander had presented himself as the Great King's successor, it was no doubt in his interest to win over the Iranian leaders. He nevertheless took care to place, alongside these satraps, Macedonian garrison commanders, whose mission was to keep an eye on the loyalty of the local populations and their governors. In both Babylon and Susa, the Iranian satrap worked in association with the Macedonian officer in charge of the citadel.

As we have already noted, it was also from this moment on that a number of military colonies were founded, namely the series of Alexandrias established at important points along the routes of communication; although theoretically independent, these nevertheless constituted a relatively tightly knit network capable of putting down any attempts at rebellion on the part of the satraps or the local lords. After he crossed the Hindu Kush, Alexander had left the latter in their positions, once they had acknowledged his supremacy. They included the king of Taxila and the Indian rajah, Porus.

All the same, uprisings did occur, and in 325–324, on his return to Mesopotamia, Alexander ejected a number of Iranian satraps of doubtful loyalty. The only ones to retain their functions were Oxyartes, his father-in-law, and Phrataphernes, in Parthia.

One of the tasks entrusted to these satraps was the levying of tribute from the subject populations, sometimes in the form of money but, in the eastern provinces, more often in kind. Local magistrates were set in charge of raising these levies. From 331 onwards, however, the general administration of finances was entrusted to the Macedonian Harpalus. We have seen what happened when he absconded to Greece with part of the royal treasure. He was replaced by a Greek, Antimenes of Rhodes. Alexander had similarly placed the financial administration of Egypt in the hands of a Greek, Cleomenes of Naucratis. He may also have appointed him governor of this province that remained rather set apart in the organisation of Alexander's empire. The author of book II of the *Economica* (which is attributed to Aristotle), who wrote this treatise during the last quarter of the fourth century, describes Cleomenes as 'the satrap of Egypt' and records the various ways in which he procured resources. These included speculating on both the price of wheat and also that of land in the neighbourhood of Alexandria.

So, despite some of the claims of our sources, it is by no means certain that Iranians played a role of primary importance in the administration of the conquered provinces, where administration was not determined by a preconceived plan, but was devised on the spot, as circumstances dictated.

However, the same does not apply where the army was concerned. Right from the moment of the first signs of resentment on the part of the Macedonians, Alexander planned to offset their diminishing number, which was caused not only by the losses incurred but also by their envisaged return to Macedonia. His idea was to call upon recruits of Iranian origin. By the end of 330, already, Persian cavalry apparently made their appearance and then went on to take part in the Indian campaign, albeit forming separate units. It was their integration into the Macedonian Companion cavalry that seems to have sparked off the sedition that erupted in Susa in 324.

As for the infantry, we know that, as early as 327, Alexander decided to recruit 30,000 young Iranians, who were then trained to fight in the style of Macedonian infantrymen. According to Plutarch, it was the arrival of this Iranian phalanx in Susa, even more than the integration of Iranians into the cavalry, that caused the violent discontent among the Macedonians. Yet these *epigonoi* formed a separate phalanx 'from a single age-group of the Persians which was capable of serving as a counter-balance to the Macedonian phalanx' (Diodorus, XVII, 108, 4). Later, however, shortly before the king's death and just after his return to Babylon, Persians were incorporated into the Macedonian phalanx (Arrian, VII, 23, 1–4), and possibly, even earlier, in Susa, Persian guards were attached to the hypaspists, the members of the royal bodyguard (Plutarch, *Alex.*, 71, 4).

Here again, it was not a matter of obliterating the differences between the Graeco-Macedonians and the Orientals, in the name of a universalist ideal. Rather, it was essential to make good the deficiency of soldiers, for the contingents led by Craterus had still not arrived. All the same, in acting in this fashion, Alexander was betraying the Macedonian law (*nomos*). King Alexander was now no longer concerned about the origins of his soldiers, for he was an 'invincible god', the son of Zeus.

CHAPTER 8

The son of Zeus

O f all the faces of Alexander, this is certainly the one that has given rise to the largest number of commentaries. We have already considered the visit to the Siwa oasis and the oracle's reply there, of which Plutarch, despite his sensitivity to all the mythical accounts that illustrated the legend of the conqueror, provided a totally rational interpretation, suggesting that the priest made a mistake over the last letter of the word for child (*paidion*), substituting a sigma for a nu and thereby making Alexander a 'son of Zeus'.

But it is important to understand how it was that a postulated divine ancestry for Alexander might seem believable to the Greeks and the Macedonians. The dividing line between men and the gods was constituted by the immortality with which the latter were endowed. There were, nevertheless, certain cracks in the Greeks' representation of divinity, the chief of which was the ability of the gods and goddesses to engender mortals. The heroes of Homeric epic claimed a divine genealogy, sometimes direct, sometimes only at the origin of their lineage. The great aristocratic families also claimed such ancestors, although by Alexander's day, most of those were extinct. The kings of Sparta and Macedon did likewise.

THE MYTHICAL ORIGINS OF THE ROYAL MACEDONIAN FAMILY

As we have seen, the kings of Macedon claimed descent from Heracles, who was exactly one of those demi-gods born from a mortal woman and Zeus, who, to the chagrin of his 'legitimate' spouse, Hera, was known as a great seducer. Many famous myths tell of Heracles, perhaps the most complex of heroes, who fell victim to the ire of Hera and was condemned to accomplish those famous 'labours' that were to take him to the very ends of the known world. As is also well known, Heracles was said to have died a horrible death, poisoned after donning the famous tunic presented by the centaur Nessus to his wife Deianira, but then to have been elevated to the status of a deity by the grace of his father, Zeus. In order to understand certain aspects of the 'deification' of Alexander, we should bear in mind this image of the most famous hero of Greek mythology, whose life, death and apotheosis inspired the great Greek fifth-century tragedians.

But Alexander also counted among his ancestors, this time on his mother's side, the goddess Thetis, admittedly a less prestigious figure but one who, from her union with the mortal Peleus, produced a son, Achilles, the epic hero par excellence and 'the best of the Achaeans' who fought beneath the walls of Troy. Unlike Heracles, Achilles was not vouchsafed an apotheosis. The poet of the *Odyssey* even ascribes to him words that belie the ideology of the 'fine death' in battle. He confesses to Odysseus that he would rather be a living wretch than a hero condemned to the torments of the underworld. Despite that confession in the *Odyssey*, which renders the implacable hero of the *Iliad* more human, Achilles, the ancestor of the Aeacid family, which reigned over Epirus and to which Alexander's mother, Olympias, belonged, was recognised to be of divine origin.

So on both his father's side and his mother's, Alexander could believe himself a distant descendant, through Heracles, of Zeus and, through Achilles, of the goddess Thetis. But, at the beginning of his *Life* of Alexander, Plutarch is not content simply to record his doubly divine ancestry. Even before embarking on his account of Alexander's life itself, he recalls a whole set of traditions and legends surrounding the birth of the future conqueror. On the very wedding night of Philip and Olympias, lightning struck the belly of the young queen. Soon after, she turned out to be pregnant. Another story has it that Philip one day saw a snake stretched out alongside the sleeping Olympias. Plutarch, always partial to piquant details, suggests that Philip was spying 'through the keyhole' on his wife, lying beside this snake, and that he was punished for this by the god, who, a few years later, caused him to lose an eye in a battle fought before the city of Methone.

The two tales that attribute Alexander's birth to supernatural interventions rather than to Philip performing his conjugal duties refer to two separate deities. The stroke of lightning clearly evokes Zeus, who did not necessarily need to have physical sexual relations with the mothers of his future offspring – as is shown by the shower of gold by which he made Danae pregnant with Perseus. In this case, the lightning plays that same role in the conception of the future Alexander.

However, where the snake is concerned, the matter is more complicated. In this connection, Plutarch evokes a tradition according to which Olympias was an initiate of the orgiastic rites practised by the local women in honour of Dionysus. When she took part in these orgies, 'she dragged behind her large tamed snakes'. Although the biographer does not pronounce upon the identity of the divine snake sharing the queen's bed, Dionysus inevitably springs to mind. There is another way too in which the image of the god of vegetation and orgiastic frenzy is linked to Alexander. Like Heracles, Dionysus, the son of Zeus and Semele, also aroused Hera's ire. To save him from her anger, Zeus was said to have taken the child to Nysa, a place mentioned in the accounts of Alexander's conquest. But even more significantly, Dionysus, as an adult, was, in the course of his wanderings, taken in by the Nereid Thetis, the mother of Achilles. After this, he travelled to India, which he conquered, and so was able to return in triumph first to Boeotia, then to Argolis, before his apotheosis and elevation to the rank of a god, despite the fact that his mother had been a mortal. Even that brief summary shows how Alexander's destiny must have appeared to be intertwined with that of Dionysus. It seemed that Alexander deliberately followed in the footsteps of the god who, in the form of a snake, had coupled with his mother Olympias.

Needless to say, all these stories are of much later date than Alexander's birth. Plutarch, to whom we must return, as he, far more than the historians of the conquest, had gleaned a certain amount of concrete information from his wide reading, rounds off his survey of the more or less supernatural phenomena that accompanied

Alexander's birth with the following far more 'realistic' conclusion:

> To Philip, however, who had just taken Potidaea, there came
> three messages at the same time: the first that Parmenion had
> conquered the Illyrians in a great battle, the second that his
> race-horse had won a victory in the Olympic Games, while
> the third announced the birth of Alexander.
>
> $\qquad\qquad\qquad\qquad\qquad\qquad\qquad\qquad$ (*Alex.*, 3, 8)

After that digression by way of myth, this returns us brusquely to
reality.

ALEXANDER AND THE MYTHICAL TRADITIONS

The problem for a historian is clearly to assess the impact of those
mythical traditions upon the role that Alexander eventually adopted,
in particular the traditions concerning the origins of the Macedonian
dynasty. At the beginning of his reign, they are virtually absent from
the scene. Alexander's policies remained faithful to those pursued
by Philip, whose example Alexander deliberately followed. These
were to retain the respect of Macedon's neighbours, to maintain
order in Greece, and to prepare for the Asian campaign. The only
intimation of influence exerted by the legends is the fact that, after
landing in the Troad, Alexander paid a visit to 'Achilles' tomb'.
Even then, he seems to have acted more as a reader of the *Iliad*
than as a descendant of Neoptolemus. Plutarch relays information
gleaned from Onesicritus, a philosopher of the Cynic school who
took part in the Asian expedition. He tells us that Alexander
'thought the *Iliad* a viaticum of the military art' and that he kept
the edition produced by his teacher, Aristotle, 'lying with his dagger,
under his pillow' (*Alex.*, 8, 2). We shall have more to say below about
Aristotle's teaching. For the moment, it is simply worth noting that
if Alexander did harbour ambitions to prove himself the equal of, if
not greater than, his father, that father was Philip, not Zeus. That,
at least, is what is implied by his dedication of the 300 shields
that he sent to Athens following his victory at the battle of the
Granicus: 'Alexander, the son of Philip, and all the Greeks except the

Lacedaemonians [took this booty from] the Barbarians who dwell in Asia' (Plutarch, *Alex.*, 16, 18; Arrian I, 16, 7). It was only after the expedition to the Siwa oasis that the problem of Alexander's divine ancestry arose. According to Plutarch, the young king was passionately interested in philosophy, in the sense then given to this term. However, that would not have prevented him from at the same time believing in omens and oracles.

The oracle of Ammon was very famous, and it is certainly conceivable that a young general who had just won a string of brilliant victories and captured a vast territory would have wished to have his ambitions confirmed by the god. The priest's reply may very well have been what Alexander wanted to hear: reassurance that he would prove victorious over Darius. It was probably only later that additions were made to that reply, partly so as to expand its meaning (it was not simply a matter of defeating the Great King, but also of becoming the master of all men), and partly to incorporate a reference to Alexander's divine origins, with the implication that Philip was merely his putative father. It would certainly seem that the oracle's reply was a traditional formula used by the priests of Ammon to reassure the pharaoh, the master of the land of Egypt, that his power was limitless. All our sources are in agreement when they state that the god told Alexander that he was granting him 'what he requested' (Diodorus, XVII, 51, 2). Only later, as his conquests multiplied and possibly to justify the plans that Alexander formed just before his death, was that reply attributed a meaning that it did not have at the point when he consulted the oracle. Alexander had also asked the god whether he had dealt justly with his father's assassins. The reply to this second question is probably a later forgery produced, at the earliest, in 324, when Alexander demanded that the Greeks grant him divine honours. Its veracity seems to have been challenged even in antiquity, to judge by Plutarch's remark about the confusion of a nu and a sigma.

The truth is that even if, once he became Darius' successor, Alexander did adopt certain of the Achaemenid kings' practices, particularly with regard to his clothing, never, in the course of the whole campaign, was there any question of the king being deified, either as the son of Zeus, born from a union between his mother and the master of Olympus, or as a new Dionysus. The Achaemenid kings, for their part, had never laid claim to any divine ancestors; the veneration that they demanded from their subjects stemmed from the despotic nature of their power. That despotism was what the Companions rejected and continued to reject more or less to the very end of the campaign.

The problem of the deification of Alexander should thus be posed in other terms. For there can be no doubt that Alexander really did demand divine honours from the Greeks gathered at Olympia in 324; and it was certainly from the Greeks specifically that he required recognition of that divinity.

HEROIC CULTS IN THE GREEK WORLD

We need to reflect upon what the idea of a mortal's apotheosis represented in the Greek world of the last decades of the fourth century. At the beginning of the present analysis we considered the epic hero, a mortal descended either directly or indirectly from a deity. Heroic cults constituted an important element in the religious practices of the Greeks, and had done so ever since the beginning of the archaic period. They were addressed in particular to the founders, real or mythical, of the cities that the Greeks had established along the shores of the Mediterranean. But they were also addressed to other figures who, in a more or less distant past, had been credited with a civilising role. We even know of heroic cults consecrated to victors in the Olympic Games. These cults consisted of processions, sacrifices and competitions which, apart from their modest scale, are not always easy to distinguish from the celebrations reserved for the great deities of the Olympic pantheon or even from those consecrated to the poliadic (or civic) deities.

The phenomenon of heroisation that accompanied the development of the Greek cities from the eighth century onward survived into the classical period. A particularly striking example is provided by the city of Amphipolis, in the northern Aegean, fought over by Athens and Sparta in the first part of the Peloponnesian War. It was a recent Athenian foundation, which had instituted a heroic cult in honour of its 'founder', the Athenian *strategos* Hagnon.

Thucydides relates that, in 424, the town fell into the hands of the Spartan general Brasidas, and the Athenians' attempts to recapture it were all in vain. A new assault led by the Athenian *strategos* Cleon also ended in failure. Cleon was killed in the battle; but Brasidas, again the victor, was likewise fatally wounded. Thucydides ends his account with a description of the honours that the Amphipolitans now offered the Spartan general:

> After this, all the allies gave Brasidas a public burial in the city at a spot facing what is now the market place, following his body in full armour. And the Amphipolitans fenced in his monument and have ever since made offerings to him as a hero, giving honours and instituting games and yearly sacrifices. They also adopted him as founder of the colony, pulling down the edifices of Hagnon and obliterating whatever was likely, if left standing, to be a reminder of his settlement.
>
> (V, 11)

He then goes on to say that, from that time on, the Amphipolitans ceased to honour Hagnon.

Presumably the heroic cult of Hagnon had been instituted only after his death. It was likewise only when he was dead that Brasidas became the object of a heroic cult, centred on the presence of his tomb in the agora. It is important to underline that point, as it will be relevant to the matter of Alexander's tomb in Alexandria.

A further step in the heroisation of great *strategoi* was taken at the end of the century. Again, its object was a Spartan, the navarch Lysander. Lysander, the victor over the Athenian fleet at Aegospotami in 405, celebrated that victory by erecting a monument in Delphi on which his own statue was placed among the statues of the gods. In his *Life of Lysander*, Plutarch refers to the testimony of the historian Douris of Samos, according to whom Lysander was 'the first Greek to whom cities erected altars and offered sacrifices, as to a god', in his lifetime (*Lys.*, 18, 5). What was new was that such honours were offered to a living man, not a dead one.

The two Spartans, Brasidas and Lysander, thus acceded to quasi-divine honours in the city of the peers, the *homoioi*. Where did

Athens, the city of Thucydides and Plato, stand on matters such as these? Up until the end of the fifth century, only the tyrannicides Harmodius and Aristogiton had been offered exceptional honours. Rituals were performed close to their tomb, with the polemarch, one of the three highest officials, presiding. And only this pair had a statue consecrated to them, the famous group of the *Tyrannicides* which, following its destruction (or theft) by the Persians, had been replaced by a work by the sculptors Critius and Nesiotes, which was erected in the agora. It certainly did sometimes happen that the city instituted honours for a foreign ruler, ambassador or *strategos*, but usually these were limited to the attribution of a crown, occasionally *proedria*. This carried the right to occupy a privileged seat at the dramatic competitions or at the dining table of the *prytaneum*, the public building where the city officials would gather for their meals. As will be remembered, that was the 'punishment' that Socrates requested from his judges! Only deities and heroes rated the erection of statues in their memory. However, after the Peloponnesian War, in the early decades of the fourth century, a statue was for the first time erected in honour of a *strategos*, Conon. He had been in command of the Athenian forces at Aegospotami and after his defeat had taken refuge first in Cyprus, then with the Great King. In 393 he had returned to Athens after winning a victory over the Spartan fleet, off the coast of Cnidus. He had brought with him funds made available by the Great King, enough money to make it possible to rebuild the Long Walls, which had been destroyed in 404, on Lysander's orders. So Conon was honoured as a 'liberator' and, as Demosthenes stressed, he was the first since Harmodius and Aristogiton to be honoured by a statue in the agora.

However, examples of the award of such an honour were to multiply in the course of the fourth century, always to recompense victorious *strategoi*. Iphicrates, Chabrias and Timotheus all saw their statues erected in the agora, to commemorate the important victories that they had won. A passage in *Against Ctesiphon*, a speech made by the orator Aeschines, suggests that other *strategoi* too were honoured by statues of themselves placed in the agora to honour 'many a glorious deed in war' (III, 243).

The erection of a statue was thus a form of heroisation reserved for victorious *strategoi*. It is interesting to note that, after the battle of Chaeronea and the conclusion of the Peace of Demades, the victorious general who was given a statue in the agora was . . . Philip, who was thereby rewarded for having liberated the Athenians taken prisoner in the course of the battle, and for having respected the city's independence.

As can be seen from the double example of Spartan and Athenian *strategoi*, being honoured with a statue raised the victor to the rank of, if not the gods, at least the heroes. For a fourth-century Greek this in no way transgressed the rules of either religious or political life.

ALEXANDER, THEOS ANIKÊTOS

In 324, Alexander, having completed his Asian expedition, was certainly the victorious general par excellence. So the possibility of his being granted exceptional honours was not unthinkable either to the Greeks or to himself. Now we can perhaps understand the attitude of Demosthenes, who, according to Hyperides, was agreeable to Alexander 'being the son of both Zeus and Poseidon, if that was what he wished' (*Against Demosthenes*, frg. 8). The famous orator apparently declared this before the assembly. Hyperides also reports that Demosthenes was proposing that a statue of King Alexander, the invincible god, *theos anikêtos*, should be set up in the agora. These accusations brought by Hyperides were levelled against Demosthenes when the latter was arraigned after the disappearance of part of Harpalus' funds. It is quite clear that what Hyperides was denouncing was not the sacrilege that agreement to the deification of Alexander would constitute (as is shown by the off-hand tone of the orator, who cared little whether or not Alexander wanted to be the son of Zeus or Poseidon). What he was attacking was the connivance between Demosthenes and the friends of Macedon that was now revealed. The criticism from Hyperides was purely political.

But how did Alexander feel? How did he interpret the Greeks' recognition of his divine birth and his quality as a *theos anikêtos*? Clearly it is almost impossible to answer that question, given the lack of testimony from the king himself. We shall be returning later to the problems posed by Alexander's personality. Quite possibly, intoxicated by his victories and the apparent extent of his power, Alexander may have wanted to be recognised as an epic hero by the Greeks, and was on that account claiming to be of divine birth. In his *Life of Alexander*, Plutarch attributes to Eratosthenes of Cyrene, the scholar appointed to head the Library of Alexandria in 246, the revelation of 'confidences' that Olympias vouchsafed to Alexander on the secret of his birth. But Plutarch adds that other authors insisted that Olympias 'repudiated the idea as impious' and claimed that Alexander himself had invented it (*Alex.*, 3, 2); and that seems perfectly believable, as Hyperides' testimony suggests. But the real question is this: at what point did Alexander claim such a birth and which god did he suggest had been involved?

It is possible that, in demanding this recognition from the Greeks, Alexander's intention was primarily to make a show of his authority, which he was determined not to have brought into question. The Harpalus affair and the rumours circulating about Antipater's reluctance to obey his orders may have made him fear a revolt on the part of the Greeks. He may have thought that by making such an uprising look impious he might prevent it. It is likewise possible, of course, that it was really his entourage that was pressing for recognition of an apotheosis. But the essential reason for his insistence was probably his desire to have his absolute authority acknowledged.

There is another dimension to the deification of Alexander that we should also consider, namely his assimilation to Dionysus. The reasons why many commentators have made much of this aspect are well known: on the one hand, the conquest of India that mythical tradition attributed to the god, in whose footsteps Alexander seemed to be following; on the other hand, the various Bacchic festivities with which Alexander was said to have celebrated his victories, first at Persepolis, next at Nysa, where a cult of Dionysus may already have existed, then on the banks of the Hydaspes where, it was said, Dionysia were held, and then again at the end of the hard Gedrosian campaign. The festivities were marked by a *komos* (a festive procession) that went on for several days. All that is needed here is a summary of Paul Goukowsky's totally convincing demonstration of the merits of this interpretation (*Essai*, vol. II). When he held celebrations to honour Dionysus, Alexander was simply conforming with a Macedonian and Greek religious tradition of honouring the god of vegetation with orgies that took the form of joyful parades. From the evidence of the various accounts provided by our sources, which frequently contradict one another, it seems that Dionysus made an appearance only after the conquest of India. The king would quite naturally have wanted to associate the god with his Indian victory, but that is not to say that he saw himself as a new Dionysus. In any case, the Dionysiac celebrations seem to have been of a marginal nature. Significantly enough, the famous Carmanian 'bacchanals' are not mentioned by Arrian, whose inspiration came from the first-hand testimonies of Aristoboulus and Ptolemy. So it seems likely that it was only later, in Alexandrian circles and under the influence of the first two Ptolemies, that the myth of a 'new Dionysus' was developed and that Alexander's conquest of India was insistently compared to Dionysus' 'high deeds' in India.

In 324, shortly before his death, Alexander demanded that the Greeks recognise him as an 'invincible god'. Only later was he represented as the reincarnation of Dionysus, and it was then that the myth of his divine birth was elaborated. Plutarch's closing remarks to his account of the Theban uprising of 335 provide an interesting conclusion to this chapter:

> In later times, moreover, as we are told, the calamity of the Thebans often caused him remorse and made him milder towards many people. And certainly the murder of Cleitus, which he committed in his cups, and the cowardly refusal of the Macedonians to follow him against the Indians, whereby they as it were robbed his expedition and his glory of the consummation, he was wont to attribute to the vengeful wrath of Dionysus.
>
> (*Alex.*, 13, 4)

Far from seeing himself as a new Dionysus, Alexander seems to have feared the vengeance of the son of the Theban Semele. That is an idea that provides considerable food for thought about a complex personality that it is hard to make out clearly through all the layers of legend that separate Alexander from us.

PART III
Alexander the Man

A biography should be more than an account of the great moments in the life of an individual and an analysis of the various functions that he performed in his lifetime. One should try to bring out the diverse aspects of his personality. This may be done working from testimony left by those close to him or, sometimes, if writings survive from his own hand, on the basis of what he himself suggests. In Alexander's case there are certainly letters that are attributed to him and are cited in our sources, but their authenticity has, quite rightly, frequently been questioned. As for people who were close to him, our only way of assessing their feelings for this larger-than-life figure is through the accounts of writers who lived long after him. Plutarch, who in this section of the present book will be our principal guide, specifically declares that, because of his exalted position, Alexander had few friends, with the possible exceptions of Hephaistion and Craterus, neither of whom left us any information, even of an indirect nature.

Why choose Plutarch as a guide? In the first place, because he himself wrote a *Life of Alexander* in which he was careful to explain that he was not writing as a historian. What interested him most were not so much the high deeds of the king as manifestations of his 'character'. The many anecdotes that he uses to enrich his account are certainly not all authentic. Nor are they the only ones produced by the legend elaborated in the course of the four centuries that separated the brief reign of this Macedonian king from the times of the philosopher from Chaeronea. In his account of the conquest, Plutarch is frequently uninformative as to his sources, but when relating the anecdotes upon which he depends when it comes to conveying something of the character of his hero, he often refers to them. It should be added that, as we shall see, Plutarch pays more attention to the evolution of his subject's behaviour in the course of the conquest than he ever does in his other *Lives*.

The two treatises entitled *On the Fortune of Alexander* that are attributed to Plutarch are more heavily marked by legend. They relate many of the same anecdotes and paint a picture all in all comparable to that painted in his *Life*, but an extra dimension is added, that of a visionary philosopher. This was the source of an image of Alexander that was to have a particularly rich future.

So although we take Plutarch as our guide in the pages that follow, we must do so with all the prudence that is necessary when on the track of a figure who, as cannot be overemphasised, very rapidly became a myth.

CHAPTER 9

Youth and upbringing

We need not return to the legends evoked above, which turned the birth of Alexander into a quasi-magical event, surrounded by premonitory indications of his exceptional destiny. We should, in any case, remember that, even if Plutarch enjoyed drawing his readers' attention to those omens, he ascribed no more than a relative importance to them. For him, Alexander was, without question, the son of Philip, and the two treatises *On the Fortune of Alexander* confirm that, in his eyes, the king of Macedon's adventure resulted not from some decision made by Tychè, Chance, but from the personal calibre of the conqueror.

Plutarch provides little information as to Alexander's physical appearance. Like all his contemporaries, he must have seen plenty of statues of Alexander, almost all based on the model produced in Alexander's lifetime by Lysippus, which showed 'the neck bent slightly to the left and the melting glance of his eyes' (*Alex.*, 4, 2). Plutarch even claims that Alexander insisted that only Lysippus should produce representations of him. But in fact the many busts of Alexander that have been found are not based on the model produced by the sculptor from Sicyon. In particular, some show a more virile countenance, with a thicker head of hair. But it is certain that it was truly the young Alexander who inspired the sculptors of the Hellenistic and Roman period, above all in the cities of Asia Minor, which piously preserved the memory of the conqueror who had 'liberated' them from the Barbarians.

Plutarch mentions the 'very white' skin of the young man, who blushed easily. But he had also seen a portrait by the painter Apelles in which the young king had a darker complexion. It is reasonable to suppose that, even if the young adolescent did have a white skin, it must soon have been tanned by the Asian sun. It is also worth remembering that the conventions of Greek painting demanded that women and adolescents all be represented with white skin, in contrast to the tanned skin of adult men living an outdoor life. Unsurprisingly then, in the famous mosaic representing the battle of Issus, Alexander is dark-skinned.

To round off this physical portrait, we should remember that Alexander does not seem to have been very tall. His biographer several times points out that he had to fight men bigger than himself. But the evidence is insufficient to warrant pronouncing further on Alexander's appearance.

In Philip's court, Alexander's education was presumably that of a young prince destined one day to succeed his father. In particular, hunting was a normal occupation for an adolescent boy, and several representations of Alexander out hunting have come down to us. Plutarch also recounts in some detail how the young prince managed to break in a spirited horse that no one else had been able to tame. Philip, who was greatly impressed, gave the horse to his son and Alexander called it Bucephalas. This faithful companion was to accompany him throughout practically the entire campaign, and when Bucephalas was killed the king was heart-broken.

Philip appointed a succession of teachers to oversee his son's education. The first was called Leonidas. According to Plutarch, he was an austere man. Despite his name and his austerity, he was not a Spartan, but a relative of Olympias. He taught his charge to be content with little and to live frugally, a lesson that must have stood him in good stead when he later had to struggle across vast arid regions. The second, Lysimachus, fancied himself as following in the footsteps of the centaur Chiron and supervising the education of a new Achilles.

Thanks to the excavations completed at Vergina, we now know that the Macedonian court was extremely brilliant and much influenced by Hellenic culture. The Macedonian kings prided themselves on their Greek origins, so the Homeric poems, which formed the basis of Greek culture, were naturally taught to the young prince. Alexander was thus familiar with both epics; in fact, he took a copy of the *Iliad* along with him when he set out on his Asian expedition. If, thanks to his ancestry on his mother's side, he saw himself as a new Achilles, he is likely, at first at least, to have regarded the expedition as a new Trojan War.

But the young man's reading does not seem to have been limited to the Homeric poems, for he also appreciated the Greek tragic playwrights. We know that Euripides, the last of the great Greek tragedians, ended his days at the court of king Archelaus. So, as a boy, Alexander may well have learnt the poet's lines. However, Plutarch tells us that it was not until Alexander reached Asia that he asked Harpalus to send him the tragedies of Euripides, Sophocles and Aeschylus, as well as the *Histories* of the Syracusan Philistus and the dithyrambs of two little-known authors, Telestes of Selinus and Philoxenus of Cythera. We know that in about 330, the Athenian politician Lycurgus saw to it that the texts of the three great tragedians were set down definitively in writing. We also know that Harpalus, Alexander's future treasurer, paid a visit to Athens at about this time. It seems quite likely that, hearing of the transcription of the tragic authors, Alexander may have asked Harpalus to procure those texts for him. We cannot be certain, but it is certainly not impossible.

Clearly though, the most important event in Alexander's education must have been Aristotle's arrival in Pella. Aristotle was the son of a doctor from Stagira in Chalcidice, who had himself spent some time at the court of King Amyntas III. Aristotle was born in 384 or 383 and, like many other young men of his time, he moved to Athens in order to attend the lectures of the orators and 'sophists' for which the city was renowned. He appears to have been taught by the Athenian orator Isocrates, echoes of whose ideas are to be found in the treatise entitled *Rhetoric*, which Aristotle produced many years later. But he acquired most of his education at Plato's Academy, where he attended his master's lectures until Plato died, in 347 or 346. Like many other pupils of Plato, he then left Athens. We know that he lived for a while at the court of the tyrant Hermias of Atarneus, and then at Pella, after which, in 335, he returned to Athens, where he taught at the Lyceum until he went into exile, shortly before his death in 322.

Aristotle probably arrived in Pella in about 343, invited there by Philip, who wanted to entrust him with the education of his son and future successor. Aristotle had not yet produced the works that were to make him the greatest thinker in antiquity in every domain – the sciences as well as philosophy. Initially, he probably adopted the dialogue form, as his master Plato had. But he soon abandoned this, preferring the form of a treatise, which allowed him to develop his thought by following a logical construction, while at the same time indicating the problems and aporias that were impossible to resolve. Already, before his visit to Macedon, he had collected a wide range of information concerning plants and animals. But as he pursued his research, after studying under Plato, he became interested not only in every field of knowledge, but also in what we have come to call political science, of which he was, in a sense, the inventor.

In the early days, no doubt, Aristotle, like Plato, had entertained dreams of converting a ruler to the wisdom of a philosopher – possibly his friend Hermias of Atarneus. Did he have such hopes when he was called to educate the young Macedonian prince? Plutarch, for his part, is in no doubt as to Aristotle's influence on Alexander. Not only did he introduce him to Greek poetry and tragedy, but he also stirred his interest in the natural sciences. This would explain how it was that the king of Macedon was careful to surround himself with scholars on his Asian expedition and why he entrusted Nearchus with his mission of geographical reconnaissance on the expedition's return. Did Aristotle also exercise a political and moral influence over the young prince? That is a question to which we shall be returning. Whatever the case may be, neither the *Nicomachean Ethics* nor the *Politics*, both produced after Aristotle's return to Athens, contain the slightest allusion to the man who, as the *hegemon* of the Greeks, had by then embarked on the conquest of Asia.

Some sources of late date suggest that the king remained in correspondence with his old teacher; and Plutarch echoes them when he refers to the reproaches that Alexander addressed to Aristotle for publishing his lectures and thereby making available to all and sundry revelations that should have remained secret (*Alex.*, 7, 5). But perhaps we should remain sceptical as to the existence of such a correspondence. In the *Politics*, Aristotle is guarded in his remarks about absolute monarchy, which he considers to be justified only in the event of there being one individual who possesses *aretè*, or virtue, that is superior to that of all the other members of the community. And that 'virtue', which transforms the king into a 'living law', is not the consequence of any *de facto* domination stemming from his military conquests. It is an intrinsic part of the 'character' of this exceptional man. Did Alexander satisfy such a criterion? It is unlikely that his teacher could have made any judgment so early on.

But let us return to the young Alexander. Plutarch's suggestion that Aristotle prompted his curiosity about medicine, the sciences and possibly also philosophy seems reasonable enough. In this connection, he notes the king's interest in the Indian 'philosophers', the Brahmins with whom he seems to have been eager to converse. He also mentions his relations with Xenocrates of Chalcedon, who became the head of the Academy after the death of Speusippus and is said to have addressed a treatise on royalty, *Peri Basileias* (*Alex.*, 8, 4–5), to Alexander. But we should be wary of such 'information', to the extent that it is itself part of the myth that developed immediately after the conqueror's death. Plutarch likewise echoes that myth of a 'philosopher king' in his two treatises *On the Fortune of Alexander*, to which we shall be returning. But first, with the young prince's education completed, let us try to assess the various aspects of this complex personality on which posterity was to pass such conflicting judgements.

CHAPTER 10

Alexander's personality

et us try to assess Alexander's personality on the basis essentially of the anecdotes related by Plutarch in his *Life of Alexander*, but also taking account of the qualities attributed to the king of Macedon in his two treatises *On the Fortune of Alexander*, the purpose of which is to show that his extraordinary successes owed nothing to chance, but were due solely to his own merit.

Those qualities can be classified under four headings: courage and tenacity, self-control, generosity and kindness, and, finally, the particular property of a 'philosophical' nature: behaviour dictated by reason.

PHYSICAL COURAGE AND TENACITY

Any account of the various stages of the conquest clearly provides many occasions to remark on the king's physical courage and tenacity. From the moment he came to the throne, he was ready to risk losing a kingship that he had obtained only with difficulty. He moved into the attack against the Barbarian peoples threatening the kingdom on the west and the north, and by restoring order in a Greece that had accepted Philip's overlordship only under duress and was obviously ready to take up arms again against him (*Alex.*, 11, 4). That same tenacity and determination to accomplish his mission led Alexander to flout the Macedonian traditions that banned the launching of campaigns in certain months of the year. He crossed the Granicus at the moment he judged to be the most propitious. He also manifested his courage and indifference to danger when, despite the warnings of Parmenion, he quaffed the beverage that Philip, his doctor, had prepared to counter the sickness that he had contracted by bathing in the icy waters of the river Cydnus

(*Alex.*, 19, 5). It was his way of showing his trust in those whom he considered his friends.

That same commitment to friendship and gratitude led him, in Syria, to remain at the side of his Companion Lysimachus when the latter was exhausted and ready to quit. This caused him to be cut off from the rest of his army and to pass a dark night out in the cold. However, he turned this setback to advantage: 'Since he was confident in his own agility and was ever wont to cheer the Macedonians by sharing their toils', he fell upon the enemies and defeated them (*Alex.*, 24, 11–12). In Egypt, when he wanted to consult the oracle of Ammon, he braved the dangers of the Libyan desert in order to do so (*Alex.*, 26, 13–14). And on the eve of the last great battle against Darius, he overrode all the advice of his older Companions, who were urging him to engage battle during the night, slept well and the next morning, refreshed and in fine fettle, prepared for battle. Plutarch concludes, 'And not only before the battle but also in the very thick of the struggle did he show himself great and firm in his confident calculations' (*Alex.*, 32, 4).

He took part personally in these battles and was consequently wounded many times, but would always rise above the pain and never hesitated in the face of danger. At the time of the crossing of the River Oxathres, 'he had recently been shot by an arrow in the leg below the knee, so that splinters of the larger bone came out; and at another time he was smitten in the neck with a stone so severely that his eyesight was clouded and remained so for some time' (*Alex.*, 45, 5). In India, he led the attack on the 'Rock of Simithres' in person and went on to capture the citadel (*Alex.*, 58, 4). He showed the same courage and tenacity in crossing the Hydaspes, to confront Porus and his army. Plutarch tells us that, without the slightest hesitation, the king joined his soldiers crossing the river with the water rising to their chests (*Alex.*, 60, 7). He was not just a great strategist, able to deploy the various units of his army so as to take the enemy by surprise, but himself fought in the battles, fearless of the dangers and putting his own life at risk.

SELF-CONTROL

In Plutarch's eyes, that physical courage was but one aspect of

Alexander's most essential character trait, namely self-control, an eminently 'philosophical' quality since it presupposed his ability to dominate his passions. It found expression first in his frugality: he could do without both food and drink. Plutarch takes pleasure in telling the anecdote about Alexander's relations with Ada, whom he had restored to the throne of Caria:

> When . . . , in the kindness of her heart, she used to send him day by day many viands and sweetmeats, and finally offered him bakers and cooks reputed to be very skilful, he said he wanted none of them, for he had better cooks which had been given him by his tutor Leonidas: for his breakfast, namely, a night march, and for his supper a light repast.
>
> *(Alex.*, 22, 9)

When in pursuit of Bessus, he, like the rest of his horsemen, suffered from the lack of water. Nevertheless, when his Macedonians who had managed to find water for their children offered him some to drink, he refused, not wanting to be treated differently from his men:

> When they beheld his self-control and loftiness of spirit, they shouted out to him to lead them forward boldly and began to goad their horses on, declaring that they would not regard themselves as weary or thirsty, or as mortals at all, so long as they had such a king.
>
> *(Alex.*, 42, 9–10)

His continence and self-control were particularly striking where women were concerned. This, at any rate, is a characteristic that Plutarch emphasises. It was particularly noticeable in his behaviour towards the women of Darius' family. The Great King's mother, wife and two daughters had fallen into Alexander's hands. Ever since Homer, it had been accepted in the Greek world that captives' fates were at the mercy of the victor. Not only did Alexander allow these women 'everything which they used to think their due when Darius was undisputed king' but, despite their beauty, he committed no act of violence against any of them. Plutarch adds the following surprising comment: 'Alexander, as it would seem, considering the mastery of himself a more kingly thing than the conquest of his enemies, neither laid hands upon these women nor did he know any other before marriage, except Barsine' (*Alex.*, 21, 7).

This Barsine was the widow of Memnon and had been captured in Rhodes. She came from the Achaemenid lineage, for her father Artabazus was the son of a daughter of the Great King. In taking her as his sole concubine, Alexander was acting in conformity with the epic model of his ancestor Achilles, who had withdrawn to his tent, refusing to fight, when Agamemnon deprived him of his beloved captive Briseis. No doubt the king made a point of drawing his Companions' attention to this comparison. Plutarch nevertheless goes on to note that Alexander was by no means unaffected by the beauty of his Iranian captives and had acknowledged that they were 'a torment to his eyes'. His abstinence was all the more admirable . . .

According to another anecdote recorded by Plutarch in both the *Life* and *On the Fortune of Alexander*, his abstinence was such that he also rejected two young ephebes put at his disposal by Philoxenus, the governor of the maritime provinces: 'Alexander was incensed and cried out many times to his friends, asking them what shameful thing Philoxenus had ever seen in him that he should spend his time in making such disgraceful proposals' (*Alex.*, 22, 1; *Fortune*, I, 333A).

More evidence of Alexander's respect for women and his continence is provided by his attitude towards Roxane, once he had decided to make her his legitimate wife. In doing so, he was flouting Macedonian law if, that is, as in Greek law, only endogamous unions were regarded as legitimate. Barsine, for her part, although a member of the royal lineage, had only been his mistress, so the son she bore could never have claimed to be his successor. In contrast, the purpose of his union with Roxane was, precisely, to produce a legitimate heir. Once he had become the Achaemenid successor, Alexander was entitled to become the legitimate husband of an Iranian princess. But what Plutarch is at pains to stress is, first, the nature of the link, namely love (*eros*) between the king and the young woman and, secondly and above all, the fact that 'he would not consent to approach [her] without the sanction of the law' (*Alex.*, 47, 8).

All the same, as we know, that did not prevent him from choosing a second wife in the person of Stateira, one of Darius' daughters. However, in the second treatise entitled *On the Fortune of Alexander*, Plutarch, after repeating that Alexander loved only one woman, Roxane, justifies his second marriage on political grounds, 'since the union of the two races was highly advantageous' (*Fortune*, II, 338D).

What should we make of this image of Alexander as a faithful and loving husband, able to control his passions? Of course, it is impossible to say, particularly as Plutarch's Alexander is more complex than may at first appear. But let us continue our review of his qualities.

GENEROSITY

Of all the qualities that he attributes to Alexander, this is the one to which Plutarch returns most often. Alexander showed generosity towards the Greeks as well as to the Macedonians and also, of course, towards the Iranians, once he had become Darius' successor. His generosity took the form of not only indulgence towards his enemies but also, and especially, gifts, which he repeatedly offered to his entourage and his soldiers.

Plutarch cites a number of examples to illustrate the king's generosity. When the Athenians took in the Thebans fleeing from their city after its destruction, Alexander did not hold this against them, but 'even bade [Athens] give good heed to its affairs since, if anything should happen to him, it would have to rule over Greece' (*Alex.*, 13, 2). However, we also learn from Plutarch that Alexander demanded that the Athenian orators hostile to Macedon be handed over to him, and it was only thanks to the intervention of Phocion (or Demades) that he changed his mind.

Alexander demonstrated his kindness and generosity not only – as we have seen – towards the women of Darius' family, but also towards the Great King himself. Although he arrived too late to receive Darius' last instructions, he 'sent the body of Darius, laid out in royal state, to his mother' (*Alex.*, 43, 7).

But it was above all his Companions and his soldiers who

benefited from his generosity. Even before the expedition set out, he made enquiries as to his friends' respective situations and distributed among them 'to one a farm, to another a village, and to another the revenue from some hamlet or harbour. And when at last nearly all of the crown property had been expended or allotted, Perdiccas said to him, "But for thyself, O king, what art thou leaving?", ... the king answered, "My hopes"' (*Alex.*, 15, 3–4).

He was soon to lay his hands on fabulous riches that would enable him to make many more gestures of generosity. After capturing Tyre and Gaza, he sent off much of the booty to Olympias, his sister Cleopatra, and his friends who had stayed behind in Macedonia, along with 500 talents of incense and 100 of myrrh for his teacher Leonidas. In the past, Leonidas had reprimanded him for extravagance when he had burned such precious essences on the altars of the gods. Now there was no longer any need to count the cost, since Alexander had made himself the master of the land that produced them (*Alex.*, 25, 6–7).

After the victory of Gaugamela, which assured Alexander of mastery over the Persian Empire, the king 'offered magnificent sacrifices to the gods and heaped riches, estates, and high offices upon his friends' (*Alex.*, 34, 1).

He also sent some of the booty to the people of Croton, to honour Phayllus, who, at the time of the Persian Wars, had used his own funds to equip a ship and had taken part in the battle of Salamis, which ended in an Athenian naval victory over the Persians. No doubt, Phayllus' compatriots had then set up a heroic cult in his honour. This was a way for Alexander to establish a connection between himself and Xerxes' conquerors (*Alex.*, 34, 3).

After the capture of Susa and Persepolis, Alexander seized large quantities of gold and silver, and his generosity knew no bounds. Plutarch records a whole string of anecdotes designed to illustrate this generosity from which so many benefited – not just his close friends but also the leaders of his armies and his ordinary soldiers. One of the latter, in charge of a mule laden with a sack of gold, seeing that the beast was exhausted, had carried the load himself. Then, when he too was exhausted and was preparing to abandon it, Alexander encouraged him to persevere since the gold would now be his.

This boundless generosity seems to have prompted certain reservations on the part of Olympias, who, according to ancient sources, was in regular correspondence with her son. She thought that, by distributing such largesse among his friends, he somehow made them his equals and, as a result, he found himself ever more isolated. That was also the opinion of the Persian general Mazaeus, who, when the king wished to give him a satrapy, replied, 'O king, formerly there was one Darius, but now there are many Alexanders' (*Alex.*, 39, 9).

Upon his return to Susa, Alexander displayed a different kind of generosity. He paid off the debts contracted by his soldiers in the course of the campaign. Following the sedition of some of them, once the rebels had returned to a better frame of mind, 'he dismissed them, with magnificent gifts' (*Alex.*, 71, 8).

His generosity, which earned him from Plutarch the description of *megalodorotatos*, 'the greatest distributor of gifts', was accompanied by a genuine concern for others. Plutarch mentions the letter that he sent to Peucestas when the latter was bitten by a bear, and also Alexander's anxiety when Craterus was wounded, and the constant concern that he manifested for the health of his close friends, not hesitating to intervene personally, in consultation with the doctors attending them (*Alex.* 41, 3–8).

ALEXANDER THE PHILOSOPHER

But for Plutarch, the explanation for these qualities of Alexander lay above all in the fact that he behaved as a philosopher. This was the source of his self-control, his resistance to pleasures and also his concern to warn his Companions against the love of luxury to which most of them succumbed. He would reproach them 'in gentle and reasonable fashion in order to direct them towards "virtue"' (*Alex.*, 40, 2; 41, 1).

His 'philosophical attitude' also explains what could be called his concern for the truth. Despite all the flatteries and oracles, he apparently never gave way to irrationality. Although convinced of his own superiority and despite his self-esteem, he never claimed any father other than Philip. When wounded, he told the friends gathered at his bedside, 'This, my friends, that flows here is blood and not Ichor such as flows in the veins of the blessed gods' (*Alex.*, 28, 3; *Fortune*, II, 341, A–C). Plutarch draws the following conclusion: 'From what has been said, then, it is clear that Alexander himself was not foolishly affected or puffed up by the belief in his divinity, but used it for the subjugation of others' (*Alex.*, 28, 6).

This *sophrosune*, self-control, was certainly encouraged by Aristotle's teaching. Yet it does not appear to be solely by remaining faithful to that teaching that Alexander proved himself to be, as Plutarch puts it, 'highly philosophical' (*Fortune*, I, 328, D–E). His aim was not to turn Barbarians into Greek 'helots', as Isocrates advised Philip to do. It was to civilise them. In this respect, he proved himself a better educator than Socrates and Plato:

> He educated the Hyrcanians to respect the marriage bond, and taught the Arachosians to till the soil, and persuaded the Sogdians to support their parents, not to kill them, and the Persians to respect their mothers and not to take them in wedlock . . . , and the Scythians to bury their dead and not devour them . . . and the Indians to worship the Greek gods . . . When Alexander was civilising Asia, Homer was commonly read, and the children . . . learned to chant the tragedies of Sophocles and Euripides.
>
> (*Fortune*, I, 238, D–E)

But his greatest 'philosophical' merit was to consider the whole of humanity as a single community, with Greeks and Barbarians intermingled. His aim was to subject the whole earth to the same law of reason, a single *politeia*, turning all men into one single *demos* (*Fortune*, I, 330 D). Plutarch's use of this political vocabulary is significant. What he was attributing to Alexander was not so much a sense of the universality of the human race as a desire, by dint of treating the Barbarians tactfully, and adopting some of their customs (their clothing, for example), to win them over more easily to Hellenism, the supreme form of civilisation, and so to achieve what, in a mythical past, Heracles and Dionysus had both attempted.

As we know, such declarations played an important role in the elaboration of the image of Alexander and in the construction of this dream of a unified world in which Greeks and Barbarians would be indistinguishable. The appointment of Iranians to positions of importance, the education given to young Persian nobles so as to turn them into soldiers fighting in the Macedonian manner, and the famous 'Susa weddings' are all treated as evidence to support such an interpretation of Alexander's actions. However, we should not, as many do, see this desire to bring the Greeks and the Iranians all under the same authority as an expression of an ideal obliteration of all differences between Greeks and Barbarians. In his second treatise *On the Fortune of Alexander*, Plutarch declares that the king wished 'to order all men by one law and to render them submissive to one rule and accustomed to one manner of life' (*Fortune*, II, 342 A–B). That way of life was primarily Greek. As has recently been suggested by J. Ober, perhaps in this respect Alexander, far from betraying Aristotle, behaved as his true disciple. By founding Greek cities (or cities of the Greek type) in the course of his conquest, he to some degree implemented the programme elaborated in the last two books of the *Politics*, for the activities of the citizens of those Alexandrias were limited to political and military pursuits, leaving the indigenous inhabitants of the cities' territory to provide the wherewithal for their material lives. In this respect, Alexander's interest in the Iranians was purely material. In his *Life of Alexander*, Plutarch tells us that, when hosting ambassadors from the Great King, in Pella, in Philip's absence, Alexander had shown great interest in the mores and customs of the Persians. But that may have been above all to learn how best to set about becoming the master of the vast Persian Empire.

Plutarch's analysis of the positive aspects of Alexander's personality is thus more subtle than a hasty reading might suggest. To ignore the shadows that increase in density as the conquest proceeds would be to oversimplify the image that Plutarch seeks to create.

CHAPTER II

Light and shade

It is not possible to ignore the shadows included in the portrait of Alexander painted by Plutarch. Even in his childhood Alexander displayed a violent and touchy temperament. When Attalus, the uncle of Cleopatra, Philip's new wife, proclaimed the birth of a son who, for his part, would be legitimate, implying that Alexander, born from a foreign mother, was a bastard (*nothos*) in the eyes of the law, the young man apparently hurled a cup at the head of his denigrator and would have picked a fight with his father had not the king, who was drunk, conveniently collapsed after drawing his sword (*Alex.*, 9, 8). That same violence, this time attributed to drunkenness, seems to be the explanation for the 'accidental' murder of Cleitus. Plutarch mentions this right at the beginning of his account (*Alex.*, 13, 4) and later returns to comment at length on the episode (*Alex.*, 50–1), calling it a 'savage' act. But drunkenness does not appear to have been the only factor. Plutarch tells us that Cleitus, 'who was already drunk and whose blunt and arrogant nature was inclined to anger', violently criticised the king for having listened complacently to insulting remarks made about the Macedonians. He made the matter worse by citing some lines in which Euripides denounced military leaders who laid claim to all the merit for victories that were in truth won by the ordinary troops. 'And so, at last, Alexander seized a spear from one of his guards, met Cleitus as he was drawing aside the curtain before the door, and ran him through' (*Alex.*, 51, 9). So despite its violence and the drink that had befuddled the king, this was not a gratuitous action but punishment for an insult to his own person. However, Plutarch is at pains to add that, at the sight of Cleitus' corpse, Alexander realised the gravity of what he had done and, had he not been restrained by his bodyguards, would have killed himself.

Plutarch's account also contains other examples of violence on Alexander's part, whether or not caused by drunkenness. When he visited Delphi to consult the oracle and the priestess declined to reply to him because it was an unpropitious time, when it was forbidden to deliver oracles, he had no hesitation in dragging her to the temple and refrained from hitting her only when she told him, 'Thou art invincible, my son.' At these words, Plutarch adds, 'Alexander said he desired no further prophecy, but had from her the oracle which he wanted' (*Alex.*, 16, 4).

Nor could Plutarch pass discreetly over the cruelty that Alexander sometimes displayed towards those whom he had defeated. The first example is that of the fate meted out to the Thebans. As we have already noted, the sources contain contradictory accounts of this event, some of them blaming the Greek allies for the decision that was taken. Plutarch himself does not deny Alexander's responsibility, explaining that he 'expected that the Greeks would be terrified by so great a disaster and cower down in quiet' (*Alex.*, 11, 11). But here too he somewhat plays down the king's cruelty by recounting the episode of Timoclea, the noble Theban woman whom Alexander spared, and by describing Alexander's subsequent remorse: 'In later times, moreover, as we are told, the calamity of the Thebans often gave him remorse and made him milder towards many people' (*Alex.*, 13, 8).

The king was likewise overcome by remorse after the massacre of the population of Persepolis. Here, the intoxication of victory is said to have prompted an action that might have appeared to be the fulfilment of his promise to avenge the Greeks on those who had set fire to Athens in the past. This would explain the part played in Alexander's decision by the courtesan Thaïs, whose comments Plutarch records:

> She said, namely, that for all her hardships in wandering over Asia she was being requited that day by thus revelling luxuriously in the splendid palace of the Persians; but it would be a still greater pleasure to go in revel rout and set fire to the house of the Xerxes who burned Athens, she herself kindling the fire under the eyes of Alexander, in order that a tradition might prevail among men that women in the train

of Alexander inflicted greater punishment upon the Persians on behalf of Hellas than all her famous commanders by sea and land.

Thaïs was the mistress of Ptolemy, who may have been the source for this somewhat 'feminist' account. But, to return to Alexander, we can see that his behaviour is shot through by currents of darkness as well as of brilliance, even in those acts of cruelty which, whether or not caused by intoxication, later fill the king with belated feelings of remorse that restore a measure of humanity to him.

But from the death of Darius onwards, that humanity seems to diminish, as is particularly evident in the punishment inflicted on Bessus: 'He had him rent asunder. Two straight trees were bent together and a part of his body fastened to each. Then, when each was released and sprang vigorously back, the part of the body that was attached to it followed after' (*Alex.*, 43, 6). This execution calls to mind that which Theseus, the legendary king of Athens, was said to have inflicted on the brigand Sinis (Plutarch, *Theseus*, 8, 3). Arrian's version of Alexander's treatment of Bessus is different but indicates comparable cruelty. He reports that Alexander ordered his nose and ears to be cut off, before judging and executing him (*Anabasis*, 4, 7, 3).

But the essential turning point came after the Philotas affair. Alexander's worse side was getting the upper hand. His break with Callisthenes, who, of all the members of the king's entourage, in a way represented Greek wisdom, seems to have contributed to his increasing sense of power and superiority. On the eve of setting out on the Indian campaign, 'he was already greatly feared and inexorable in the chastisement of a transgressor. For instance, when a certain Menander, one of his Companions who had been put in command of a garrison, refused to remain there, he put him to death; and Orsodates, a Barbarian who had revolted from him, he shot down with his own hand' (*Alex.*, 57, 3).

After the capture of the fortress of Massaka, in the territory of the Aracenians, he ordered the massacre of the mercenaries serving the Indians, despite having concluded a treaty with them. He also put to death many Indian 'philosophers' (Brahmins), claiming that they were criticising the kings who had rallied to him, or else were inciting people to rise up against him (*Alex.*, 59, 6–8). Meanwhile, his drinking bouts were no longer occasional but became more or less constant, provoking him to uncontainable acts of violence. He could no longer control his temper and, with his own hands, killed Oathres, the satrap of Paraitacene, because his father, Aboulites, the satrap of Susiana, had failed to prepare fodder for his horses. Aboulites himself was thrown into prison.

At another level, the very Alexander whose self-control Plutarch had praised so highly was unable to master his grief at the death of Hephaistion and indulged in some wild excesses. He had the doctor Glaucus (or Glaucias), who had been unable to cure Hephaistion, crucified and, after destroying the ramparts of several fortified towns, 'he went forth to hunt and track down men, as it were, and overwhelmed the nation of the Cossaeans, slaughtering them all from the youth upwards' (*Alex.*, 72, 3–4).

In the last chapters of his account, Plutarch stresses that the way that Alexander's personality evolved was due not only to his excessive drinking but also to the increasing number of negative omens. 'He began to be low-spirited and was distrustful now of the favour of Heaven and suspicious of his friends' (*Alex.*, 74, 1). The 'philosopher king' had been replaced by a superstitious man who was 'perturbed and apprehensive in his mind' (*Alex.*, 75, 1). That fear and distrust of his entourage led him to commit extraordinary acts of violence. He grabbed Cassander, Antipater's son, by the hair and banged his head against a wall, on the pretext that Cassander had laughed at the sight of Barbarians prostrating themselves before him. We are told that Cassander remembered Alexander's behaviour with such horror that, years later, when he had become king of Macedon, he shuddered at the sight of a statue of Alexander in Delphi (*Alex.*, 74, 6). The story may well be a total fabrication, but it nevertheless indicates the level of fear that Alexander's violence produced among his companions.

Plutarch's picture of the personality of the king of Macedon is thus more nuanced than it may appear, and it is more complex in the *Life* than in the two treatises *On the Fortune of Alexander*. As we have noted, in the first of those, Alexander is essentially presented as a philosopher, an incarnation of Greek culture whose 'virtue' rather than 'fortune' explains the greatness of the exploits that he accomplished during his relatively brief existence. In the second, too, Alexander's 'virtue' is exalted, along with his self-control, his physical courage and his military talent. His fondness for wine is hardly mentioned (*Fortune*, II, 338, A–B) and, when it is, is minimised. The shadows which, in the *Life*, mass increasingly densely as Alexander's power increases are absent from the two treatises.

How much should we believe in the picture of sharp contrasts that Plutarch paints of Alexander, the man? Clearly, no categorical answer to such a question is possible. The strictly black or white judgements to be found in many of Alexander's historians are excessive. He was no doubt neither the political and military genius that some have described nor the sage who derived total self-control from Aristotle's teaching. Nor was he the drunkard incapable of mastering his temper, nor the 'savage' barbarian who razed Thebes and burned down Persepolis. He was a man of his times, no doubt affected by the contradictions implied by a Greek education, the extent of his conquests and the servility of part of his entourage. But perhaps, in the end, that is not what matters most. Should we not rather judge Alexander by his achievements and by the evolution of the empire that he conquered in just over one decade?

Let us now endeavour to do just that.

PART IV

The Legacy of Alexander

A biographer of Alexander needs to do more than simply evoke the debates over the conqueror's personality. The reason why the king of Macedon occupies such an important place in history is not just that he was a great war-leader but also, and even more, that his brief, thirteen-year, reign marks a break in the evolution of the eastern Mediterranean basin. Before him, there was, on the one hand, the vast Persian Empire, on the other, a scattering of Greek states among which a few cities stood out as producing a type of civilisation which, in the eyes of the Greeks, appeared as the precise opposite of 'Barbarian despotism'. It was a civilisation of communities that governed themselves in accordance with norms which differed, to be sure, from one place to another, but which nevertheless endowed the notion of a citizen with an active sense that was highly acclaimed. After him, there were at first a number of huge monarchical states in the hands of kings who claimed to be promoters of Greek culture. In mainland Greece and in the West, there were still independent Greek states, cities and federal states. And in the former, at least, political life preserved the forms that had been acquired over the preceding centuries. To that extent, it is true that the Greek city did not disappear with the Macedonian conquest. But even when they were not part of the huge kingdoms that emerged from the conquest, those cities possessed no more than a relative autonomy so far as external politics went and, despite short-lived eruptions of independence, they remained more or less under the thumbs of the Hellenistic kings until they passed under the domination of Rome.

What was involved, then, truly was a break, to the extent that new forms of thought now developed, along with religious syncretisms and other phenomena of acculturation. Of course, it is worth noting that the classical civilisation did not disappear suddenly, that some changes had been detectable for some time already, and that in some domains transformations did not take place until the end of the third century. All the same, as I shall now try to show, Alexander's brief trajectory did, if not change the face of the world, at least precipitate an evolution that was to give the ancient world its definitive physiognomy.

CHAPTER 12

Alexander's empire: a fragile construction

The thirteen years of Alexander's reign were marked by a succession of almost continuous campaigns. As Paul Goukowsky points out, 'Alexander's empire really existed only in the years 324–323.' We can attempt to reconstitute the various measures that the king took, in accordance with the prevailing circumstances, in order to provide his empire with an administrative organisation. But its immediate dislocation following the conqueror's death testifies to the fragility of that organisation. Let us try to understand both the creation of the empire and its dislocation.

THE ORGANISATION OF THE EMPIRE

First, it is important to distinguish clearly between the two parts of this empire: on the one hand, Macedon and Greece, on the other the territories won from the former Achaemenid empire. We do not know what would have happened in Macedon if Alexander had lived longer or if, as he planned, Craterus had replaced Antipater, who had governed the kingdom in Alexander's absence and in his name. Philip's reign had been marked by profound changes that stemmed from the affirmation of his authority, urban development and, thanks to the exploitation of the mines of Pangaeum, the expansion of financial resources. But the Macedon governed by Antipater does not appear to have been deeply affected by Alexander's campaign of conquest. Only later were the consequences of the veterans' return felt. In the meantime, Antipater had striven to maintain the control that Philip had established over his

Greek allies, but without changing the rules that governed the functioning of the League of Corinth.

We are relatively well informed about Athens during this period. Political life there continued in the traditional manner. There is no evidence of any real will to take action against Macedon, not even when the Spartan King Agis tried to provoke an uprising in the Aegean region. Aeschines and Demosthenes were busy settling old scores in the course of the *Crown* debate (330), but this does not appear to have affected the internal peace of the city, which, with the encouragement of the orator Lycurgus, was enjoying an economic and financial renewal. This partly explains the tepid welcome given to Harpalus when, having absconded with part of Alexander's treasure, he proposed putting both men and money at the disposal of the city. Both in Athens and elsewhere, there were men ready to challenge Alexander's representatives at the slightest hint of weakness on the part of the Macedonian authorities. However, Alexander had little to fear from aspirations to independence. As we have noted, he even felt strong enough to have his ambassador, Nicanor, state his demands at Olympia.

It was therefore essentially the organisation of the conquered territories that he needed to address. The fact was that, even after the authoritarian reign of Artaxerxes III, the Persian Empire certainly did not possess a faultless administrative system. The empire was divided up into satrapies but also included more or less autonomous enclaves such as, on the one hand, the Greek coastal cities, on the other, vassal entities such as certain priestly states and the kingdoms situated along the northern and eastern frontiers of the empire.

As we have seen, Alexander, who, following his victory at the Granicus, became the master of most of Asia Minor, recognised the autonomy of most of the Greek cities, whose liberator he claimed to be. He maintained the system of satrapies, limiting himself to placing Macedonians at the head of the ancient satrapies, some of which he regrouped. Very early on in the campaign, he thus placed the Macedonian Calas at the head of the ancient satrapy of Hellespontine Phrygia. In Lydia, he divided power between Asandrus, Philotas' son, who was appointed satrap, and the commander (also a Macedonian) of a garrison established at Sardis. By entrusting

Caria to the rule of Ada, the last (female) representative of the Hecatomnid dynasty, he respected the autonomy of this satrapy, which, under the government of Mausolus, had become virtually independent. But in Halicarnassus he installed a garrison of 3,200 mercenaries, under Ptolemy's command. He combined Pamphylia with the part of Lycia that was separate from Caria, making them a single satrapy. Later, both these territories were reunited with Phrygia, under the sole command of Antigonus Monophthalmus. As we shall see, this was to lead to momentous consequences. For the time being, Antigonus was given a force of 1,500 mercenaries, who were installed in Celaenae, the capital of the satrapy. But some Anatolian regions, such as Cappadocia and Paphlagonia, remained quasi-independent.

The Syro-Palestinian region posed more complex problems. Cilicia was placed under the control of Nicanor's son, Balacrus, who acted as both satrap and *strategos*. In Syria, the north was entrusted to Menon, while the cities of the Phoenician coast kept their local rulers, with the exception of Tyre, which received a Macedonian garrison. Samaria and Judaea remained theoretically independent but were really controlled by a Macedonian *strategos*, first Andromachus, then – when he was assassinated by Samaritan rebels – Menon. Shortly after this, however, Alexander, worried by Agis' disruptive activities just when he was preparing to cross into Egypt, united Cilicia, Syria and Phoenicia, placing them all under the control of his *hipparch*, Menes. Later, once the danger had passed, Syria and Cilicia reverted to being independent satrapies.

Egypt received rather special treatment. The country was not entrusted to a satrap. Alexander retained the ancient division between Upper and Lower Egypt and placed both under the control of Egyptian nomarchs, who, however, were closely supervised by Macedonian officers. The king also appointed Cleomenes, a Greek from Naucratis, to oversee the taxation system and collect the country's revenue, most of it in kind. Thanks to a speech attributed to Demosthenes, *Against Dionysodorus*, and a passage from the *Economica* attributed to Aristotle, we have a certain amount of information about the economic administration of Egypt. Cleomenes seems to have engaged in profitable speculation on the price of wheat. At any rate, his position became increasingly secure, to the point where he became the veritable satrap of Egypt. His financial skills enabled him to amass large revenues, part of which paid for the construction of Alexandria. When Ptolemy acquired Egypt after Alexander's death, he benefited from the system organised by Cleomenes and proceeded to develop it further.

After Darius' death, Alexander, presenting himself as the successor to the Achaemenids, granted Iranians a greater place in the administration of the empire. This association with Iranians who were loyal to him was made necessary by Alexander's continuing advance into little-known regions and his followers' ignorance of the languages spoken locally. The garrisons that were left in place were, to be sure, always under the control of Macedonian officers. But some important satrapies were entrusted to Persians. Mazaeus was appointed satrap of Babylonia, after surrendering the city of Babylon to Alexander. He controlled the entire administration of the satrapy, apart from the levying of tribute. Furthermore, two Macedonians, Agathon and Apollodorus, were placed in charge of the armed forces of the satrapy and the citadel of Babylon. Alexander wished above all to be able to rely on the loyalty of the Iranian nobles and was even ready to show indulgence to those who had initially supported the usurper Bessus but had then rallied to himself and delivered Bessus up to him. Atropates, for instance, received the satrapy of Media, Phrataphernes the satrapy of Parthia. Elsewhere, however, in less secure regions, Alexander preferred to install Macedonians, and was sometimes obliged to replace an Iranian satrap with one of his Macedonian Companions. For example, after the revolt of 329 in Bactria and Sogdiana, where he had initially installed Iranian satraps, one of whom was Artabazus, he forced the latter to resign and replaced him first with Cleitus, then with Amyntas.

In India, the situation was rather different, since there the system of satrapies had never been established and most territories had been part of the empire only fleetingly. Alexander tried to get the local rulers to recognise his authority; but even in these distant lands he entrusted to Macedonian *strategoi* the task of controlling these unreliable allies. The king of Taxila retained his position at the head of his kingdom, but a garrison kept his capital under surveillance. According to Plutarch, only Porus remained the absolute master of his kingdom and was spared the imposition of a Macedonian garrison. In contrast, the local rulers all along the Indus valley were kept under strict supervision.

However, we should not be misled by all these appointments that Arrian ascribes to Alexander. The Indian territories were never properly annexed to the empire. And the series of revolts that erupted in certain satrapies forced Alexander to concentrate above all upon re-establishing his authority in central Iran. The rebel satraps, Orxines in Persis, Aboulites in Susiana, and Astapes in Carmania, were arrested and replaced by Macedonians. One of these was Peucestas, who, Plutarch tells us, had learned the Iranian language. The rebels also included a number of Macedonians such as Cleander and Sitalces. These were arrested and executed.

All this provides telling insights into Alexander's methods. They were extremely flexible, dictated by the prevailing circumstances of the moment, rather than determined by some preconceived plan. This confirms what has already been suggested: the king had no systematic conquest in mind, nor was it in the name of some vague idealism that he decided to associate Iranians with his power. Where necessary, and provided military garrisons kept the conquered peoples under surveillance, he had no hesitation in entrusting local government to Iranians or even to native rulers in regions that were still restive. But military control always remained in the hands of Macedonian officers.

Possibly the most important aspect of this administration related to the levying of tribute. Usually, this was the responsibility of a satrap. Alexander simply took over the Achaemenid system. The tribute, either in monetary form or in kind, was intended to ensure the running of the satrapal administration and the upkeep of the garrisons. In some cases, however, the levying of tribute was the duty of some special magistrate, such as Cleomenes in Egypt, Nicias in Lydia, and Philoxenus in Caria.

The seizure of royal assets had placed extensive resources at Alexander's disposal. We do not know when the management of this treasure was entrusted to Harpalus, but after his flight in 325, he was succeeded by the Rhodian Antimenes. Harpalus seems to have wielded considerable authority. In particular, he was probably in charge of the minting workshops. Nevertheless, we know that throughout the empire, Alexander allowed local mints to continue to operate alongside the production of his own currency.

These resources were destined primarily for the upkeep of his army. We have on several occasions noted how difficult it is to estimate the total number of soldiers engaged in the conquest, since the information provided by the sources is imprecise or even contradictory. However, it is generally agreed that at the start of operations in Asia, the army comprised about 40,000 infantry and between 4,000 and 5,000 cavalry. The Macedonians made up roughly one third of this force, the rest being composed of contingents supplied by the Greek allies, dependent peoples and mercenaries. The importance of the last two was to increase, especially when the allied contingents were sent home. The seizure of the Achaemenid treasures provided the means to pay them and also to form the Iranian contingents that were associated with the army during the last years of the conquest.

Internal alterations in the composition of the army made it necessary to adapt its organisation and command structure. Among the Macedonians, whose number decreased from about 15,000 at the start to 10,000 after the departure of the veterans on the eve of Alexander's death, the special units still included the phalanx of the *pezhetairoi*, grouped into six or possibly seven regiments (*taxeis*), and the royal guard, the hypaspists. The Companion (*hetairoi*) cavalry was now divided into hipparchies, which replaced the former *ilai* (squadrons). The light infantry was mostly composed of mercenaries. But it was clearly the recourse to Iranians that led to the most important changes in the organisation of the army. It is thought that by the end of 330, there may already have been regiments of Iranian cavalry. And from 328–327 on, the presence of Iranians in the army is attested with certainty. Initially, the Iranian horsemen constituted separate units. It was the integration of some of these into the Macedonian cavalry that is believed to have caused the Susa (or Opis) 'sedition'. Where the infantry was concerned, the crucial factor was the creation of an Iranian phalanx trained to fight in the Macedonian fashion. The arrival of this unit in Susa, in 324, was yet another reason for the Macedonians to manifest their hostility.

The high command was also affected by these internal changes. Following the execution of Parmenion, the responsibilities of the commander-in-chief were split. Also, as circumstances evolved, a number of Alexander's Companions were assigned posts of command. Gradually, the group of men who were to play an important part after the king's death emerged: Craterus, Perdiccas, Ptolemy, Lysimachus, Antigonus . . .

Alexander's army was thus a composite one in which, to be sure, the Macedonian element had a special place, but more because of the role that it might be called upon to play, close to the king, than by reason of its size. That is a fact to be taken into account when trying to understand the behaviour of the military leaders after Alexander's death, and the rapid dislocation of the empire, the structures of which had only just been set in place during the few months following the army's return to Babylon.

THE DISLOCATION OF THE EMPIRE

The dislocation did not happen all at once, but after a series of divisions which initially took place within the context of the theoretical preservation of imperial unity and the dynastic legitimacy of the royal Macedonian family. However, the disappearance of first one, then the other of the two 'kings' put an end to that fiction, an end that was confirmed from 306 onwards, when all the principal protagonists eventually assumed royal titles for themselves.

At the beginning of this biography of Alexander, we considered the practices, if not rules, followed in the designation of a new king. He had to be acclaimed by the assembly of the Macedonians. Much discussion has been devoted to the question of whether this was an assembly of the people (but who, precisely, constituted the 'people' in the territorial state that was Macedon?) or an assembly of the army, an army composed of horsemen recruited from the aristocracy, and foot-soldiers recruited by methods that more or less escape us.

In Babylon, obviously, the problem was not posed in quite those terms. If the new king was to be acclaimed by Macedonians, it would have to be the Macedonians present in Asia. That first difficulty relating to the Macedonian *nomos* was compounded by a second, far more immediately worrying preoccupation: the absence of an undisputed heir. As we know, Alexander had married the Iranian

Roxane with the intention of producing a legitimate heir. The young woman was pregnant but the sex of the unborn child was, of course, unknown and, besides, some of Alexander's companions viewed the prospect of a half-Barbarian king with distaste. There was, as it happened, another possibility in the shape of another of Philip's sons, Arrhidaeus, whose mother had been the king's concubine. But Arrhidaeus was mentally deficient and clearly incapable of succeeding his half-brother and carrying out his plans.

The situation was particularly delicate as Antipater and Craterus, the two most influential men at this time, the one in Macedon and the other in Asia, were both absent from Babylon. Antipater, who was in principle supposed to be on his way, bringing new recruits to strengthen the army, was prevented from doing so by the uprising that had broken out in Greece at the news of Alexander's death. Craterus, meanwhile, was on the point of leaving for Europe, to accompany the veterans whom Alexander had loaded with gifts and ordered back to Macedon. It was thus left to the younger officers in Alexander's entourage to take matters in hand. Understandably, the military leaders were, broadly speaking, in favour of naming Roxane's child as the successor to Alexander. That would allow those who were ambitious to act as *de facto* regents, in something like a repetition of the manoeuvre in 359 by which Philip had had himself acclaimed first as regent, then as king, in place of his nephew, the young Amyntas. Among those ambitious leaders, Perdiccas was particularly prominent, and it was probably he who pushed through the decision to wait for the birth of Roxane's child, while he acted as regent in the name of the future king.

But according to other accounts, particularly that of Quintus Curtius, it would seem that there was a movement of revolt among the men of the phalanx, who, for their part, chose Arrhidaeus as Alexander's successor, naming him Philip III. In the face of this revolt, which was all the more dangerous given that other elements in the army seemed likely to be drawn in, a compromise was eventually reached. Arrhidaeus and Roxane's child were to reign jointly, under the confirmed control of Perdiccas, who, however, would share power with Craterus. Perdiccas was given the rank of chiliarch, a title borrowed from the Persian military hierarchy that had already been given to Hephaistion, while Craterus became the *prostatès* (guardian) of the kings.

Meanwhile the army leaders were redistributing the provinces. Ptolemy received the satrapy of Egypt, Leonnatus Hellespontine Phrygia, Lysimachus Thrace, and Antigonus was confirmed as head of the satrapy composed of Phrygia, Lydia and Pamphylia. So far, Antigonus had won little renown. Alexander had entrusted him with the defence of a region that was vital to the empire, so he had not been involved in the conflicts that had torn the king's entourage apart. In the years to come he was to play an increasingly important role.

However, for the time being, Perdiccas was dominant. He could count on the support of Eumenes, Alexander's head of the chancellery. Perdiccas could also exploit the situation that had developed in the Aegean. The wave of revolt had spread. In particular, Athens, led on by the orator Hyperides and the *strategos* Leosthenes, now headed a coalition that included the Aetolians, the Thessalians and numerous other cities, all gathered into an alliance in the formation of which Demosthenes had played a part on returning from the exile into which he had been sent in the aftermath of the Harpalus affair. Antipater was holed up in Thessaly, in the fortress of Lamia, waiting for the reinforcements that Craterus was bringing him from Asia. Finally, revolts had also erupted on the eastern frontier of the empire, in Bactria in particular.

Perdiccas made the most of this situation by withdrawing from Craterus the title of *prostatès* to the kings and thereby setting himself up as the sole regent. It is not easy to follow the unfolding of events through our frequently contradictory sources. It seems that, in order to strengthen his position, Perdiccas was thinking of marrying Alexander's sister, Cleopatra, possibly urged on by the old queen Olympias whose intrigues the sources enjoyed relating.

In any case, within just a few months the situation had radically changed. The two main rivals, Perdiccas and Craterus, were dead, the former assassinated by his own soldiers, the latter fatally wounded in a clash with Eumenes of Cardia, in Cappadocia.

Shortly before, Antipater had managed to lift the siege of Lamia. The Macedonians won a great victory over the Greek fleet off the coast of Amorgos, and not long after the Greek army was defeated at Crannon. In Athens, Antipater imposed an oligarchic regime and installed a Macedonian garrison in Piraeus. Then, with no immediate worries on the Greek side, he joined the rest of the principal Macedonian leaders in Syria. In 321, they gathered at a conference at Triparadeisus. Antipater was appointed *epimeletès* (protector) of the two kings, Arrhidaeus and Alexander IV, Roxane's son; and once again the satrapies were redistributed. Antigonus became the satrap of Asia, his mission to capture Cappadocia and eliminate Eumenes. Seleucus was appointed satrap of Babylonia, while Lysimachus retained Thrace and Ptolemy kept Egypt.

In 319, Antipater died. To the fury of his son Cassander, who had hoped to succeed him, he left the power with which he had been invested at Triparadeisus to a figure who had, until then, remained in the background, Polyperchon. Cassander immediately set about forming a coalition against him, whereupon Polyperchon turned to the Greeks. He reconstituted the League of Corinth and helped the Athenians to oust the oligarchic regime that Antipater had foisted upon them. In his *Life of Phocion*, Plutarch gives an account of the events that then followed in Athens and which, after a hasty trial, led to the death-sentence passed on the *strategos* Phocion. Two years later, Cassander managed to recapture Athens and entrusted its government to the philosopher Demetrius of Phaleron.

A very disturbed period then followed, in which a series of alliances was formed and then disintegrated. They were centred upon the two hapless kings, who were rulers only in name but symbolised the continuity of Alexander's empire. During this confused period the position of Antigonus grew steadily stronger. After an initial alliance with Polyperchon, he entered into a succession of alliances with the principal Greek states, with the increasingly avowed intention to gain control of Macedon. In opposition to him, Cassander, allied with Seleucus, Ptolemy and Lysimachus, nursed the same ambitions, encouraged by the fact that his sister was the wife of Philip Arrhidaeus, which conferred some sort of legitimacy upon himself. That measure of legitimacy increased when Arrhidaeus was assassinated, probably at the instigation of Olympias. Cassander, by now the master of Macedon, and also of part of Greece, had Olympias tried by the Macedonian assembly, which sentenced the queen to death.

However, the young Alexander IV remained, in the hands of

Polyperchon and Antigonus. A coalition was formed against the latter, and this turned out badly for Antigonus: in 311 his son Demetrius was defeated in Gaza by the members of the coalition. Antigonus then agreed to a general peace treaty with his enemies, although Seleucus, absent on a campaign in Asia, was not a participant in the treaty. This general peace treaty confirmed the existing divisions but strengthened the authority of Cassander, who was appointed *strategos* of Europe and confirmed in his functions as the *epimeletès* of Alexander IV. In the following year, 310, he got rid of the child, thereby bringing to an end the fiction which, since Alexander's death, had maintained the unity of the empire.

In truth, the empire was by now nothing but an illusion. Although Cassander kept a firm hand on Macedon, his opponents Antigonus and his son Demetrius, Ptolemy and Lysimachus were all competing for control in the Aegean. In 307, Demetrius succeeded in capturing Athens, where he reinstalled a democracy in the name of the proclaimed autonomy of the Greek states, ejecting Cassander's protégé, Demetrius of Phaleron. After a stay in Thebes, the former Athenian ruler sought refuge with Ptolemy, in Alexandria. We shall be returning to the role that he played at the side of the founder of the Ptolemaic dynasty.

But the essential event that brought this troubled period to a close, in 306, was the assumption of the royal title by Antigonus and his son Demetrius, following the latter's victory over Ptolemy in a battle on Cyprus. A few months later, Ptolemy, Lysimachus, Seleucus and Cassander all followed suit and proclaimed themselves kings.

Only one, however, Cassander, was the master of Macedon. So he alone could call himself *basileus Makedonias*. But could he also be the only *basileus Makedonôn*? The fact was, of course, that there were also Macedonians in the armies of the other *diadochi*, as Alexander's 'successors' were now called. Obviously, this raised a problem, one to which we shall be returning at greater length. If the Macedonian monarchy that Alexander had inherited from Philip was a power that rested upon a *nomos*, a law of which the Macedonians were guardians, how could several kings coexist? And what did the title *basileus* that they had assumed really mean?

That is the question that we must now try to resolve.

CHAPTER 13

The invention of a new type of monarchy

The assumption of the title of king by the principal protagonists in the conflicts that marked the seventeen years following Alexander's death raises the problem of how those men understood their decision. It was clearly not a matter of imitating the traditional Macedonian monarchy, since only one of them, Cassander, was the master of Macedon. Nor was it simply a matter of claiming to be a successor to Alexander, since, by common agreement, the empire had been dislocated, as was clear from the successive territorial divisions that they had made. Even if some of them, in particular Antigonus and his son Demetrius, still nursed an ambition to restore the unity of the empire, Ptolemy, Seleucus and no doubt Cassander too had each decided to rule over only a fraction of the vast territory conquered by Alexander.

We therefore need to return to what was to prove one of the major aspects of Alexander's legacy, namely Hellenistic monarchy.

THE DEVELOPMENT OF A 'ROYAL' IDEOLOGY IN THE FOURTH CENTURY

The first eulogy of kingship passed down to us by the Greek tradition was pronounced, paradoxically enough, by the man whom the Greeks regarded as the very embodiment of despotism: the king of the Persians. In the famous dialogue in which Herodotus presents three Persian nobles discussing the respective merits of the three principal forms of political regime (that in which decision belongs to the people, that in which 'the few' govern and, finally, monarchy), Herodotus has Darius declare:

> Nothing can be found better than the rule of the one best man; his judgement being like to himself, he will govern the multitude with perfect wisdom, and best conceal plans made for the defeat of enemies.
>
> (*Histories*, III, 82)

The second (implicit) eulogy is to be found, no less paradoxically, in the image that Thucydides produces of Pericles, the man who was the true founder of Athenian democracy and its ardent defender. The Athenian historian emphasises that, instead of being led by the people, it was he who led them and so, 'Athens, though in name a democracy, gradually became in fact a government ruled by its foremost citizen' (II, 65, 9).

To be sure, the Greeks still treasured the memory of the kings of epic. But they were heroes of a long-gone past known mainly through the characters elaborated by the tragic poets, characters that could not be not contained within the framework of a city.

It was above all from the fourth century on, in the writings of philosophers, orators and historians, that there developed a current of thought that may be described as 'monarchist'. In opposition to the excesses of democracy and also to the iniquities of oligarchy, it defended the benefits of power placed in the hands of a single man, the very best. Of course this praise of the 'good king' was also set in opposition to other forms of monarchical power such as tyranny or the despotic authority of the king of the Persians. A tyrant like the Great King reigned over enslaved peoples, whereas a man endowed with 'royal' qualities governed men who were free. Accordingly, one of the very conditions of the authority that he held was that it be freely accepted. Xenophon tells us that that was indeed the opinion of his teacher, Socrates:

> Kingship and despotism, in his judgement, were both forms of government, but he held that they differed. For government of men with their consent and in accordance

with the laws of the State was kingship; while government of unwilling subjects and not controlled by laws, but imposed by the will of the ruler, was despotism.

(*Memorabilia*, IV, 6, 12)

That free consent depended primarily on the qualities possessed by the man to whom authority was freely given. Naturally, those qualities are not identical for Xenophon's and Isocrates' ideal kings and the king whose character Plato endeavoured to define in his dialogues. For Isocrates, who declares in his speech *To Nicocles* that kingship 'is the most important of human functions and demands the greatest wisdom' (para. 6), a king's first duty is 'to train his soul' (para. 11), to exercise his reason (para. 14), and thereby to improve his subjects (para. 15). 'In the worship of the gods, follow the example of your ancestors, but believe that the noblest sacrifice and the greatest devotion is to show yourself in the highest degree a good and just man' (para. 20), Isocrates tells the Cypriot king, and goes on to say, 'Govern yourself no less than your subjects, and consider that you are in the highest sense a king when you are a slave to no pleasure but rule over your desires more firmly than over your people' (para. 29).

But Isocrates is not content with these relatively banal moral sentiments. In the speech that that same Nicocles is supposed to have delivered in praise of his own government, the advantages of monarchy are presented in a much more 'realistic' fashion, particularly in relation to warfare and how it should be waged:

Prepare your military forces and use them in such a way as to uncover the enemy's movements and forestall him. Use persuasion on some, force others by means of violence, buy some individuals, and lead them on using many, many means of seduction: these are the methods that absolute governments are more capable than others of adopting.

(*Nicocles*, 22)

But again, the 'virtues' of the king are self-control and a sense of justice (para. 29). And those are the very virtues that characterised the power of Nicocles' father, Evagoras, to whom Isocrates devoted a eulogy, a literary genre that was to become very popular in the Hellenistic period. It was also those same virtues that justified Isocrates' wish to charge Philip with the task of leading the united Greeks in battle against the Barbarians, thereby emulating Philip's ancestor Heracles.

Xenophon is every bit as open as Isocrates about his preferences for a monarchical regime. He expresses them both in the *Cyropaedia*, the 'pedagogic' story devoted to the founder of the Persian Empire, and in the remarks that he ascribes to Socrates in his *Memorabilia*, in the *Oeconomicus*, and in his eulogy of his friend, the Spartan king Agesilaus. On the face of it, it seems surprising that the ideal king can be personified just as well by the king of the Persians, an absolute monarch, as by the Spartan king, a kind of official, strictly controlled by the Gerousia (Council of Elders) and the ephors. And it is perhaps even more surprising that the image of the ideal leader should be based on the example provided by a large-scale Athenian landowner (Ischomachus in the *Oeconomicus*). But all these texts are concerned to define what Socrates, in the *Memorabilia*, calls 'the kingly art' (IV, 2, 11), that is to say the art of commanding others and making them better people. The *Oeconomicus* contains a passage that seems particularly prophetic. Ischomachus, the great landowner who is Socrates' interlocutor, defines the art of government as being always of the same nature, whether it is a matter of agriculture, politics, the economy or warfare. On that last point, he remarks:

> Contrast the genius, the brave and scientific leader: let him take over the command of these same troops, or of others if you like. What effect has he on them? They are ashamed to do a disgraceful act, think it better to obey, and take a pride in obedience, working cheerfully, every man and all together, when it is necessary to work ... Him you may justly call high-minded who has many followers of like mind; and with reason may he be said to march 'with a strong arm' whose will many an arm is ready to serve; and truly great is he who can do great deeds by his will rather than his strength.
>
> (XXI. 5, 8)

It is as if Xenophon were describing in advance the qualities that posterity was to ascribe to Alexander. His portrait of Agesilaus, also – if on a smaller scale – a conqueror of Asia, likewise concludes with a passage in praise of his 'virtue' – virtue that was manifested by the respect that he showed the gods, a generosity expressed in the many benefits that he showered upon those who were attached to him, his apparent indifference to all forms of wealth, his control over his desires, a continence that enabled him to resist the advances of a certain Megabates, with whom he was smitten, and, finally, great physical courage in the face of all dangers. But for Xenophon, the greatest of all Agesilaus' merits was that he submitted himself to his country's laws. Sparta was his fatherland, and a Spartan king, even one superior to all others, could not afford to scorn the laws that had made his city the greatest of all Greek cities. In this very respect, he was the polar opposite of his enemy, the king of the Persians. But even if Agesilaus, through the 'virtues' that Xenophon ascribes to him, seems a prefiguration of Alexander, he would never have adopted the luxurious lifestyle of an Achaemenid ruler. Agesilaus certainly represents one of the figures of the ideal king elaborated by fourth-century Greek thought, but his is a figure which, because it belonged to the context of Sparta, remains distinct from the absolute monarchs that the Hellenistic kings were to become.

A different image of the ideal king emerges from some of Plato's dialogues, such as *The Republic* and *The Statesman*. Plato takes as his starting point the observation that 'None whatever of the existing constitutions is suitable for philosophy' (*Republic*, 497 b). He suggests that the solution to the city's problems is not to be found

> until some chance compels this uncorrupted remnant of philosophers, who now bear the stigma of weakness, to take charge of the State, whether they wish it or not, and constrains the citizens to obey them, or else until by some divine inspiration a genuine passion for true philosophy takes possession either of the sons of the men now in power and sovereignty or of themselves.
>
> (*Republic*, 499 b–c)

We know, from his own testimony (if, that is, *Letter VII* is authentic), that he tried to convert the tyrants of Syracuse, first Dionysius the Elder, then Dionysius the Younger – without success, however. He then went on to pin his hopes on Dion. But rather than attempt to convert living kings, it was really better to envisage an ideal city in which the power would be held by philosophers. Plato was well aware that the realisation of a perfect city was fraught with difficulties, but he nevertheless concluded:

> It is in a way possible, and in no other way than that
> described – when genuine philosophers, many or one,
> becoming masters of the State, scorn the present honours,
> regarding them as illiberal and worthless, but prize the right
> and the honours that come from that above all, and, regarding
> justice as the chief and the one indispensable thing, in service
> and maintenance of that reorganise and administer their city.
>
> (*Republic*, 540 d–e)

Earlier, Socrates had enumerated the qualities of a true philosopher: a love of knowledge, temperance, and courage in the face of death.

All the same, in the *Republic*, Plato does not really recommend power for a single person. It is in another dialogue, *The Statesman*, that he affirms the need for a 'kingly' man at the head of the city, and defines his powers. Such a man could, in extreme circumstances, place himself above the city's laws if the laws turned out to be contrary to justice. And his primary mission would be to make his fellow-citizens better, and consequently happier, people. But Plato is forced to admit that men endowed with these 'kingly' qualities are hard to come by, and he concludes:

> As the case now stands since, as we claim, no king is
> produced in our States who is, like the ruler of the bees
> in their hives, by birth pre-eminently fitted from the
> beginning in body and mind, we are obliged, as it seems,
> to follow in the track of the perfect and true form of
> government by coming together and making written laws.
>
> (*Statesman*, 301 e)

That is exactly what he then endeavoured to do in the *Laws*, but not without repeating that the ideal solution would be for a man holding 'tyrannical' power and endowed with youth, a good memory, an open mind, courage and magnanimity to be so lucky as to meet with an eminent legislator *(Laws, 709e–710d)*.

What Plato desires, in order to save the city from the evils that beset it, is not strictly speaking the establishment of a monarchical regime. But when he defines the qualities of a 'kingly' man, he does elaborate a concept of *basileia* that is more exacting than that of his contemporaries, even if it expresses a state of mind that is limited to a particular, Athenian, intelligentsia. However, it does reflect new aspirations.

We have already considered the problem of Alexander's relations with Aristotle, and we have mentioned traditions according to which a correspondence, attested by more or less authentic reports, was maintained between them. We have also considered the criticisms that the philosopher is supposed to have expressed regarding Alexander's policy of taking Barbarians into the government and defence of the empire. But the point that is interesting here is what Aristotle had to say about kingship in his writings. His simplest definition appears in the *Rhetoric*: 'In a monarchy, as its name indicates, one man alone is supreme over all; if it is subject to certain regulations, it is called a kingship; if it is unlimited, a tyranny' (*Rhetoric*, 1366a). In the *Politics*, he distinguishes five kinds of kingship:

> One belonging to the heroic times, which was exercised over willing subjects but in certain limited fields, for the king was general and judge and master of religious ceremonies; second, the barbarian monarchy, which is an hereditary despotism governing in conformity with law; third, the rule of the functionary called an *aesymnetès*, which is an elective tyranny; and fourth among these is the Spartan kingship, which may be described simply as an hereditary generalship held for life ... But a fifth kind of kingship is when a single ruler is sovereign over all matters.
>
> (1285b, 20–30)

Aristotle devotes some particularly interesting comments to that last form of kingship. Pondering the question of whether it is better to be governed by the best of men or by the best of laws, he decides, after weighing up the advantages and disadvantages of both systems, that the law is to be preferred to the power of a single individual. Among the arguments that he invokes, he seems to rate the problem of the heredity of royal power as important: what guarantee is there that the children of the best of men will have their father's qualities (1286b, 22–7)?

However, Aristotle is not absolutely convinced that his first conclusion is suitable for all human societies. 'A fit subject for royal government is a populace of such a sort as to be naturally capable of producing a family of outstanding excellence for political leadership' (1288a, 8–9). Accordingly,

> When therefore it comes about that there is either a whole family or even some one individual that differs from the other citizens in virtue so greatly that his virtue exceeds that of all others, then it is just for this family to be the royal family or this individual king, and sovereign over all matters ... Hence it only remains for the community to obey such a man and for him to be sovereign not in turn but absolutely.
>
> (1288a, 15–19; 28–9)

Earlier, he had made two remarks about such an exceptional individual which it is worth underlining: his superiority makes him seem 'like a god among men' (1284a, 10–11); and for him there can be no law, for he himself is the law (1284a, 13–14). Those are two essential aspects of Hellenistic royalty.

In fourth-century Athens, that hub of Greek intellectual life, the question of kingship, *basileia*, was clearly one of the foremost preoccupations of those who frequented the schools of rhetoric and philosophy and who aspired to be the educators of future leaders. They lived and taught in a city where decisions were taken by the assembled people; but it seemed to them that only monarchical power could put an end to the disorders and weaknesses that they denounced as being characteristic of democracy. So far as we can judge, the mass of Athenians were still attached to the regime that had made their city great. But they were also inclined to show enthusiasm for a victorious general and to vote that he should receive exceptional honours. However, they were not yet ready to rally to such a man if he was not a member of the civic community. Although the vanquished Athenians had granted exceptional honours to Philip and Alexander, that did not prevent them from rising in revolt when they learnt of the conqueror's death. Athens was not Greece as a whole. But it is in Athens that we have the greatest chance of understanding how what was pure speculation on the part of philosophers and orators was soon to become a reality. Fifteen years after Alexander's death, the Athenian people would be giving a saviour's welcome to Demetrius, the son of Antigonus.

BASILEUS ALEXANDROS

Did the brief reign of Alexander help to enrich the image of the ideal king that the Greek thinkers had elaborated? We have noted the different figures that Alexander embodied: king of the Macedonians, *hegemon* of the Greeks, successor to the Achaemenids, and – finally – the son of Zeus. He had played each of the roles implied by those images, not successively but all at once. However, it was only after his return to Babylon that Alexander demanded that his divinity be recognised by the Greeks – the Greeks whose leader he claimed to be but whom he had in effect distanced from the conquest, even though they remained present as mercenaries or, on personal grounds, within the circle of the king's friends. It is accordingly only in connection with two of those roles, those of the king of the Macedonians and successor to the Achaemenids, that we should address the question of the extent to which Alexander contributed to the elaboration of a new concept of kingship.

We need not return to what has been said above about the relations between the king and the Macedonians in his army, relations which deteriorated in proportion as the personal power of Alexander was affirmed. What chiefly makes it difficult to gauge the evolution of Alexander's authority vis-à-vis the Macedonians, and, consequently, the authority which, at his death, still stemmed from the traditional Macedonian monarchy, are the circumstances themselves. During the greater part of his reign, Alexander lived and exercised his authority outside Macedon, which was governed, in Alexander's name, by Antipater. Consequently, the Macedonian *nomos* that regulated the relations between the king and his people did not command full respect. We have noted, in connection with the Philotas affair in particular, the disagreement among our sources as to the role that the army assembly, as the holder of judicial power, may have played.

We have also noted the incidents that erupted in India, which forced Alexander to give up the idea of advancing further into the territory situated beyond the Hyphasis river, and then again after the army's return westward, at either Susa or Opis. Was it still possible to isolate the Macedonians within an army that contained increasing numbers of Greek mercenaries? When Alexander made speeches before his soldiers gathered into an *ecclesia* (to borrow the term used by Diodorus), was he addressing solely Macedonians? In other words, through our frequently divergent sources we may be able to discern tensions between Alexander and his army, but those tensions may not always have stemmed from the expression of the Macedonian *nomos*. Whenever it was a matter of deciding upon the right moment to engage battle, to negotiate with the enemy, to choose one route rather than another, it always seems to be the case that Alexander decided on his own. In the account of his biographer, Plutarch, the reason for this is the manner in which Alexander's character evolved, but in effect it reflects his growing personal power. The circumstances on their own suffice amply to justify that reinforcement of power: an army on the move in enemy territory needs above all to obey its commander.

Elsewhere in our sources' accounts, we can see the increasingly important role that some of the king's 'friends' came to play. To refer to this group, the Greek sources sometimes use the term *synedrion*, but it seems unlikely that this 'council' possessed any precise juridical status. Besides, as we have seen, some of the king's 'friends' became the victims of his anger or hostility: prime examples are provided by Cleitus' sudden disgrace and also by that of Callisthenes. The example of Callisthenes also shows that this entourage of Alexander's was not composed exclusively of Macedonians, and so could not have held any place at all in the extremely fluid structures of the Macedonian monarchy. Moreover, the absorption of Iranian elements into even the most prestigious corps of the army must have rendered the survival of the traditional Macedonian kingship even more uncertain.

However, that does not mean that Alexander's power was altogether orientalised. He may have demanded from his Iranian subjects the marks of respect due to an Achaemenid sovereign; he may have partially adopted the costume of such a sovereign, in particular the diadem; and he may furthermore have been tempted by a certain level of luxury; but we should remember that he became the successor to the Great King solely in the eyes of the Iranians. For obvious reasons of efficiency, he maintained the satrapy system and the levies imposed on subjects of the Achaemenid Empire. But he spent very little time in its royal capitals.

So what was the real nature of Alexander's authority? The closest we can get to the reality would appear to be to consider his authority as that of a victorious general. It was, after all, his repeated victories that made him the master of a vast empire, and it was by constantly campaigning that he strengthened his power. If it is true that, on the eve of his death, he was elaborating new plans for conquest, it would indicate the importance played by the ideology of victory in the recognition, in the eyes of his soldiers and the subjects, of his empire – in other words, recognition of the superiority that justified his limitless authority.

It is pointless to wonder what would have become of Alexander's kingship if he had eventually returned to Macedon. Let us simply recognise that his was a somehow 'itinerant kingship', that his authority was linked to his personality and, for that very reason, was neither solely Macedonian nor solely Oriental. It was a personal creation which, while incorporating both those elements, went beyond both.

In this respect, the title to be found on coins, the date of which is uncertain but which nevertheless reflect the new situation, is altogether characteristic. Alexander is no longer simply the *basileus Makedonôn*, nor is he the unqualified *Basileus* that the king of the Persians was. He is *basileus Alexandros*: his own name is all that qualifies his authority. He is somehow the incarnation of the ideal monarch whose image was constructed by the fourth-century Greek thinkers. But the question that now inevitably arises is the following: is this 'royal' Alexander simply the product of an image that his contemporaries wished to present, or did he himself knowingly construct that image, influenced by the education he had received from Aristotle and Callisthenes? Without wishing to belittle the difficulties attendant upon any attempt to get through to the real Alexander, who is obscured by all the superimposed images of him, we are bound to recognise that some of his actions during the last few months of his life do suggest that he may consciously have fine-tuned his image as a predestined leader. The plans that he was nurturing, the demand made at Olympia for recognition of his divinity, and his concern to ensure the future of his dynasty by marrying Roxane all reveal not just an evolution in his character, but his sense of an exceptional destiny. It was not purely by chance that he wished to be honoured as a *theos anikêtos*, an invincible god.

He left Europe as king of the Macedonians; after Darius' death, he became the successor to the Achaemenids. But the authority possessed by King Alexander was greater than the sum of those two powers. His royalty was a new construction, elaborated in the last years of the conquest, and it was to be a determining factor in the formation of a new type of power, Hellenistic monarchy.

HELLENISTIC MONARCHY

We have already noted the events that immediately followed Alexander's death, the successive divisions of his empire's territory, and the disappearance of first Philip Arrhidaeus, then the young Alexander IV. The fiction of the survival of the Argead monarchy faded away in 310. Four years later, Antigonus took the title of king.

One might have expected that, after Alexander's sudden death, the Macedonian *nomos* would find expression through the role played by the army. Yet in the course of the years that preceded the *diadochi*'s assumption of the royal title, the Macedonian army seldom expressed itself as a constituted body. It is true that in Babylon it did intervene, and even imposed the final compromise. But after that, in the conflicts between the *diadochi*, not one of them was supported by more than a fraction of that army in which, in any case, the Macedonians were no doubt only a minority. The only one who was in a position to respect the Macedonian *nomos* was presumably Cassander, who, once he became the ruler of Macedon, had the queen Olympias tried by the assembly, on the charge of having organised the assassination of Philip Arrhidaeus. Of course, outside Macedon, any one of the *diadochi* might well, in certain circumstances, have assembled the army under his command to sanction some decision or alliance.

In this connection, Plutarch's *Life of Eumenes* contains an interesting passage. After hearing the news of Antipater's death, Antigonus, wishing to ensure the support of Eumenes, apparently entered into negotiations with Alexander's former chancellor, whom he had shut up in the town of Nora, in Cappadocia. Eumenes then put Antigonus' proposals before the soldiers of his enemy, who were besieging him. He demanded that the oath supposed to unite them should also mention the two kings and Olympias. In this text (*Eumenes*, 12, 4), Plutarch only mentions Macedonians, which may be understandable in this period so close to Alexander's death. This incident seems to provide an example of the political as well as judicial role played by the Macedonian army when engaged in campaigning. But, as was to be expected, very soon the only armies that would count for anything would be those controlled by their respective *diadochi*, armies in the service of the leader in command of them, the composition of which became increasingly heterogeneous. A striking example is provided by the army assembled by Antigonus in Tyre, in 315, which judged and sentenced Cassander... for the murder of Olympias!

The assumption of the royal title by Antigonus, who had throughout this period shown himself to be by far the most ambitious of all the *diadochi*, was particularly significant in one respect. Although Antigonus dreamed of reconstituting the unity of the empire, with himself at its head, he proclaimed himself to be, not *basileus Makedonôn*, but *basileus Antigonos*. Like Alexander, he claimed to possess royal qualities on personal grounds. The occasion of his proclamation was a victory won in Cyprus by his son Demetrius, whom he forthwith associated in this *basileia*, thereby laying claim to 'royal' qualities not only for himself but also for his family.

Soon the other *diadochi*, in their turn, also laid claim to royal titles, and although their ambitions were without a doubt more limited than those of Antigonus, no more than he did they include an ethnic in the titulature. The only one for whom this question arose was, once again, Cassander, for although he appears on his coins simply as *basileus Kassandros*, one inscription refers to him as *basileus Makedonôn*. In this respect, Cassander is representative of what the monarchy was to be in the Hellenistic period, namely a 'national' monarchy. As André Aymard has shown in a number of articles, although Hellenistic monarchy was a unique phenomenon, it nevertheless took two distinct forms. Its cultural unity stemmed from the fact that a Hellenistic king claimed to be an heir to Alexander. Concretely, this was expressed by the diadem, the ribbon tied at the nape of the neck that Alexander had taken to wearing after the death of Darius. It was also expressed by the presence of a court of friends surrounding the king, a more or less hierarchised court within which intrigues developed as soon as any problems of succession arose. Finally, the last characteristic common to them all was that each of these sovereigns founded a dynasty.

However, those common features should not mask the two different forms taken by Hellenistic monarchy. In Macedon, after a series of conflicts between various claimants to the throne (Lysimachus, Antigonus' son Demetrius, and Pyrrhus, the king of Epirus), Demetrius' son, Antigonus Gonatas, eventually became the definitive master of the country; and at this point the monarchy preserved the 'national' character that it had possessed at the time of the Argeads. In inscriptions, the Macedonians are mentioned alongside the king, and there are also other signs that indicate the role played by the Macedonian assembly. It would acclaim a new king and also, in the event of a successor being a minor, it would appoint an *epitropos* or regent. It also performed a judicial function in trials of high treason.

In contrast, there was nothing of this kind in the 'personal' monarchies, those of the Seleucids and the Ptolemies, and likewise those of all the dynasts who seized the opportunity of the decomposition of the Seleucid Empire in Asia to proclaim themselves kings. Here, a king did not need to take account of any community at his side. He alone personified the state and the law. The territory that he governed, 'won by the spear', was the fruit of victory. There were no assemblies of soldiers with the right to oversee justice or the designation of a new king. The eastern sovereigns may sometimes have had their soldiers acclaim them, but that did not imply the existence of any *nomos* which limited their power. What they preserved from the legacy of Alexander was the personal aspect of kingship, and they did so the more naturally given that the peoples over whom they reigned had long been accustomed to absolute submission. The land that they controlled was their own property and they could dispose of it however they pleased, possibly giving it away to their friends and thereby reinforcing the gratitude of their entourage.

But the feature that is perhaps the most distinctive of the monarchies born from the conquests of the Macedonian monarch, even in the new form of the latter, was the cult of the person of the king. We have seen how Alexander eventually came to demand that the Greeks should recognise his divine nature. And we have noted the elements in the Greek tradition that could explain, or even justify, such a claim. Initially, Alexander's successors hesitated to claim such qualities. However, Demetrius and Antigonus, even before assuming the title of king, had been granted divine honours in Athens. Ptolemy had been proclaimed *soter* (saviour) by the Rhodians. Lysimachus, Seleucus and Antiochus (the latter's successor) were the objects of similar cults. What is immediately striking here is that these cults were offered them by the Greek cities that had passed more or less directly under their control so, once again, they found a place within a tradition that originated within the Greek world.

But with the advent of the second generation, a cult of the deceased sovereign was set up before devoting one to his living successor. For instance, Ptolemy II first instituted the cult of his father and mother as 'saviour gods' (*theoi soteres*), and only then a cult of his sister (and wife) Arsinoe and himself as 'sibling gods' (*theoi adelphoi*). This practice became increasingly common in the course of the third century.

In the Seleucid kingdom, the history of the development of the royal cult is less clear. It seems to have gathered pace in the Greek cities integrated into the empire. Here too, the divinity of the king was affirmed by the addition of religious epithets to his name. Thus

Seleucus I was raised to the status of a god by his son Antiochus I, with the assignation of the epithet *nikator* (victor). It was only at the beginning of the following century that Antiochus III imposed upon the entire kingdom the cult of both his ancestors and his own person.

A twofold observation seems called for at this point. In the first place, as Edouard Will points out, the royal authority of these monarchs did not depend upon their divinity. It was their very kingship, the sign of the gods' protection that they enjoyed, that was the foundation of their divinity. The second point is one that applies to all that has been said above about both the nature of royal power and the bases for the kings' authority. We must remember that it was primarily the Greeks (and the Hellenised Macedonians) who were affected by this new type of kingship. As André Aymard remarked, Hellenistic monarchy 'was a Greek achievement, realised by sovereigns who were either truly Greek or else genuinely or apparently Hellenised, and always intended to affect the equally more or less authentic Greeks who constituted their courts, and the obedience of these' (*Etudes d'histoire ancienne*, p. 125).

This brings us to the third aspect of Alexander's legacy: the birth of a 'new Hellenistic world'.

CHAPTER 14

The birth of a 'new world'

Alexander had undertaken his Asian campaign as the *hegemon* of the Greeks. The aim was to realise a plan of Philip's that may have been inspired by the Athenian orator Isocrates. In the speeches that Isocrates proposed as models for his students and in a letter addressed to Philip, he had urged the king of the Macedonians to lead a war against the Barbarians. The principal objective of this war would be to free the Greek cities of Asia from the Persian yoke and obtain revenge for the past injuries that Xerxes had inflicted upon the Greeks, in particular Athens. It would also make it possible to settle in Asia the mercenaries who were swarming all over the Aegean world and who represented a growing threat to peace and social order. Whether Isocrates' advice was really the origin of Philip's plan, or whether, more simply, having established his authority over the many Greek states gathered into the confederation of the League of Corinth, Philip feared an alliance between some of them and the Great King, the expedition of which Alexander assumed command after his father's death certainly had originally been a Greek project.

As we have seen, its nature changed when Alexander proclaimed himself Darius' successor and began to take Iranians into the administration and the defence of the conquered territories. But the fact remains that he himself and his closest Companions had been nurtured by Greek culture, and Greeks and Macedonians constituted a majority of his army. Although a few Iranians remained invested with administrative functions even after the return to Babylon, the organisation of the empire remained predominantly Greek. The many cities founded by the conqueror along the routes that the armies followed established a Greek presence in both Asia and Egypt.

Alexander thus bequeathed to his successors an immeasurably extended Greek world. And although, as we have seen, the unity of that empire was not to survive the conqueror's death, the vast territorial states born from the conquest, along with the rest of the Greek world, were, as a result, sooner or later to present a new face. It is important to distinguish the various aspects of this new world in order to assess the importance of Alexander's legacy in the evolution of the societies of the eastern Mediterranean basin.

CHANGES IN ECONOMIC LIFE

These changes are the subject of one of the most monumental works of recent historiography, Mikhail Rostovtzeff's *The Social and Economic History of the Hellenistic World*, first published in Oxford in 1941. Rostovtzeff's analysis, based on a study of literary, archaeological and papyrological sources, presents the world born from Alexander's conquest as a 'new world' that made it possible for the Greeks to move on from a still primitive economy to far more 'rational' and 'modern' forms of economic development. Many of Rostovtzeff's analyses are still relevant, but we now take a more circumspect view of his conclusions. The installation of Greeks in Asia and in Egypt inevitably resulted in the geographical expansion of the Greek world, and this was reflected in wider commercial exchange. Regions that had until then remained outside the sphere of Mediterranean commerce were now integrated into it. But the two most significant changes were, on the one hand, a shift in the axes of commercial trade, and, on the other, the development of a coined money economy.

In the fifth century and even in the fourth, the Piraeus had been the principal trading centre in the eastern Mediterranean, and this favoured Athens' hegemony in the Aegean. Merchants flocked there from all over the East and also from the far West, and the taxes that the city levied on incoming and outgoing merchandise constituted a major source of revenue, as is attested by the treatise that Xenophon produced around the mid-fourth century, the purpose of which was to review the means of increasing that revenue, in particular by encouraging foreign traders to settle in Athens. In the third century, the Piraeus was still an active trading centre. But with respect to the volume of trade, two other poles now began to replace Athens. The first to do so was Rhodes, an almost obligatory stopover on the journey from Egypt to the Aegean world, and one whose prudent neutrality in the midst of the conflicts between the *diadochi* and those who came after them further strengthened its position. Merchant ships were sure of finding a welcome there, along with all the facilities necessary for trading.

The other pole was, of course, Alexandria, essentially for two reasons. In the first place, Egypt had always been a centre that supplied grain to a Greek world that could not produce enough cereals to feed its population. Secondly, the agents of the royal authority exercised control over the sale of wheat. There is no need to resort to terms like 'interventionism' or long-term 'planning' that are often bandied about. However, to the extent that the land of Egypt was the property of the king, as a prize of conquest, the levying of taxes brought into his hands huge quantities of cereals, the sales of which, abroad, fed the royal treasury. There may have been a measure of control over production, but we do not know that it was particularly effective.

Besides, Alexandria was the normal outlet for products coming from the Indian Ocean, the Arabian peninsula and the African continent. Unfortunately, considerable obscurity still surrounds the organisation of this trade and also the identities of the merchants who frequented the port. They were probably mostly Syrians and Phoenicians, as in Rhodes. It is doubtful whether the Ptolemies controlled this trade. They were really interested only in the fiscal revenue that it brought them.

The expansion of trade and the displacement of the axes of Mediterranean commerce were favoured by (and in their turn favoured) the increasingly general use of coined money. We have already noted the large quantities of precious metals seized by Alexander. The king had coins minted, to be used primarily to pay his mercenaries and also to buy supplies for his army. In the years that followed the conquest, the mass of money in circulation thus increased considerably, and the effect of this must have been to reduce the value of gold and silver. The Persian kings used to mint mainly gold coins, and in addition a few silver ones. But the use of both metals, which Alexander had preserved, was soon replaced by the sole use of silver, as was traditional in the Greek world. The most important thing to note is that, not only did the use of coined money spread to regions where it was almost unknown before, but furthermore Alexander's successors, imitating him, adopted the Attic weight standard. As a result, this became general virtually everywhere, with the exception of Rhodes, which remained idiosyncratic, and Egypt, where the Ptolemies soon chose a lighter standard, no doubt because metal ore was harder to come by there.

The corollary to this increase in the circulation of money was the development of banking activities. Most of the banks, like those in Athens, were private establishments. But certain large sanctuaries (such as Delos) also engaged in money-lending operations, as did some public banks in the Greek cities of Asia and in Ptolemaic Egypt.

However, we should not forget that this monetary economy did not extend to all the conquered regions. Many territories continued with a 'natural' economy, in countrysides far from the trading routes and in provinces where the taxes were levied in kind, with no need to resort to coinage.

It was essentially the urban centres that the new features of the economy affected. In fact, the development of towns was the principal characteristic of this 'new world' engendered by the conquest.

URBAN DEVELOPMENT

The Greek world was an urbanised world. Even though many regions remained unaffected by this urbanisation, it was around towns that the city (polis), the type of state most characteristic of classical Greece, had been constructed. To be sure, even in the most important cities, such as Athens, the town, which was the centre of political and religious life, controlled a more or less extensive rural territory that belonged to the citizens. In fact, in many cities, possession of a plot of land in the civic territory was the primary condition for membership of the civic body. Even in Athens, where it was possible to be a citizen without owning any land, the greater part of the citizen population was composed of people who lived off the income from their plots of land. All the same, urban life, with all the political, religious and also artisanal and commercial activities that were centred upon it, remained the distinctive feature of this civilisation. In the fourth century, a number of the coastal cities of Asia Minor had even become the hub of the development of town planning, inherited from the model elaborated in the fifth century by Hippodamus, the famous architect of Miletus. Priene, Miletus and Ephesus, among others, had all benefited from this architectural and urban impetus.

These were the urban models from which Alexander drew his inspiration when he decided to found a town bearing his name in Egypt. Diodorus relates that, after choosing the site, Alexander drew up the plan of the future town, dividing it into a number of different quarters, 'in accordance with the rules of the art'. The historian goes on to say, 'In shape, it is similar to a *chlamys* (cloak), and it is approximately bisected by an avenue remarkable for its size and its beauty' (XVII, 52, 2–3).

When he founded such a city in such a place, Alexander probably saw himself as the equal of the founding heroes of the cities of the past. But at the same time, he was taking care to defend his rear, at a time when the Spartan king Agis was trying to foment an uprising in Crete. At the time he probably had no idea of the future of this town, which, within a few decades, was to become the richest and most populous in the Mediterranean world.

It also seems reasonable to suppose that, whatever his desire may have been to perpetuate his name by attaching it to new towns, it was on strategic grounds too that he multiplied such foundations as his conquest proceeded. Even the location of these new towns, at the points where major routes crossed or along the northern borders of the empire, clearly indicates that it was partly a matter of ensuring the defence of the conquered provinces. The towns were, in effect, initially military colonies. Unfortunately, we do not know how the colonists were chosen, whether they were given land worked by the natives inhabiting the territory allocated to the city, or whether they simply constituted garrisons. Nor do we know whether, from the outset, these cities established institutions modelled on those of the classical Greek city. Only the period of Alexander's successors affords us glimpses of the modalities of the settlement of the colonists. The inscriptions found in some of these cities, also of late date, attest the presence everywhere of assemblies, councils and elected officials.

The colonists were essentially Greeks and Macedonians. Right from the start, indigenous elements were seldom involved in the populations of these new towns. But that does not necessarily mean that, either for Alexander or for his successors, military considerations were accompanied by a clear intention to diffuse the Greek culture and way of life.

It was above all the Seleucids who developed policies of urbanisation. So it is in Seleucid Asia that, thanks in particular to the archaeological evidence, we can best form an idea of what these cities must have been like. In the wake of first Alexander, then Antigonus, who was the master of Asia up until his death, the first two Seleucids, Seleucus I and his son Antiochus I, founded new towns, among them the kingdom's four greatest, Antioch and Apamea inland, on the Orontes river, and Seleucia and Laodicea on the coast.

As Greek cities, in theory these towns were autonomous but, included as they were within the royal territory, the *chora basilikè*, 'conquered by the spear', they were in fact dependent on the central power. Even though their institutions appeared to function 'freely', their political life was more formal than real. And just as Antioch, theoretically an autonomous Greek city, was *de facto* the capital of the Seleucid kingdom, so Alexandria, 'alongside Egypt', was the capital of the Ptolemaic kingdom.

Apart from their closer dependence, what distinguished these new cities from the ancient cities of Asia 'liberated' by Alexander was the nature of their populations. All their 'citizens' were certainly Greeks or Hellenised Macedonians. But the Greeks among them were natives of a wide range of regions of old Greece, and the inscriptions sometimes commemorate their ethnic origin by attaching it to an individual's name. That is particularly true of the Greek emigrants to Egypt. Unlike the Seleucids, the Ptolemies founded few cities either in Egypt or in their external possessions. The mercenaries whom they recruited formed separate communities that did not have city status. They were known as *politeumata*. The mercenaries received plots of land in the *chora* and contented themselves with the income that these provided.

Alexandria was something of a special case. Whereas most of the cities founded by Alexander in Asia were originally populated exclusively by Hellenes (Greeks and Macedonians), already by the fourth century Alexandria included a large foreign population. The best-known ethnic group was made up of diaspora Jews. The presence of Jews in the city is given different explanations by two traditions. The first, reported by Hecataeus of Abdera, connects it with the first Ptolemy, whose personal 'benevolence' is said to have encouraged Jewish immigration to Alexandria. According to a later tradition, of Alexandrian and Jewish origin, the first immigrants were prisoners captured by that same Ptolemy in the course of the campaign in Syria and then given their freedom. Whatever the truth of the matter, Alexandria was one of the principal centres of the Jewish diaspora. Of course, those Jews did not qualify for Alexandrian citizenship. But the Ptolemaic king (either Ptolemy I or Ptolemy II) had granted them the right to practise their religion and to preserve their law. Other indigenous communities probably obtained similar privileges.

Most of these new towns presented the aspect of a traditional Greek city: a central agora, surrounded by the main public edifices and sanctuaries. There would also be a theatre and a gymnasium. The gymnasium would be where the young men of the city fore-gathered. It symbolised the characteristic elements of the Greek education or *paideia*: athleticism and poetry; but it was a 'democratised' education to the extent that all Hellenes had access to it. Only a very few (privileged) natives could claim to be 'of the gymnasium'.

There can be no doubt that these foundations were the centres that diffused the Greek way of life, but it was a way embraced by no more than a minority among the populations of Asia and Egypt. They were made up of the Greeks who had followed Alexander, later joined by those who emigrated en masse over the last two decades of the fourth century and the early decades of the third.

We have no means of calculating how many people this emigration involved. The first colonists were essentially mercenaries but later, as the new towns developed into trading centres, no doubt others flocked to them: artisans, merchants, various 'technicians', doctors, jurists, and actors too, such as those known as 'the craftsmen of Dionysus', itinerant troupes who performed in the theatres that were a feature of all Greek towns of any importance.

The next question that arises is the extent to which that Greek presence affected the structures of the eastern societies. The Greek emigration to the East has often been compared to a 'colonial' phenomenon. It is true that in the Seleucid kingdom and in Ptolemaic Egypt, and subsequently in the states that emerged from the decomposition of the former, the Greeks occupied a dominant position in the central administration at a local level and in the new cities. The effects of Alexander's efforts to take Iranians into the administration of the empire were short lived. His successors, in the conflicts that opposed them to one another after his death, sought support from the Greek states rather than from the indigenous populations, fearing that these might make the most of the disorders in order to win back their independence.

The Greeks who settled in the East thus formed a privileged group, united by a common language (the *koinè* derived from the Attic dialect, which was eventually adopted universally), by convergent interests, and by a way of life and social practices that tended to become increasingly uniform in the face of an eastern world that had preserved its diversity.

THE EASTERN SOCIETIES

We should not overlook the extreme diversity of these eastern societies. They had preserved their original character within the Achaemenid Empire and thus simply passed from one kind of domination to another. Of course, contacts were made between the Greek immigrants and the indigenous communities, but they seldom affected the structures of the indigenous societies. The great mass of the eastern populations was made up of peasants. These were compelled to make payments to the owners of the land that they cultivated, or else to work for them. Some of that land was 'royal', some was sacred and belonged to sanctuaries, some was land that the king had given to his friends. In Mesopotamia and Syria, there were also peasant communities that were more or less free, but even these had to pay tribute, either in the form of one tenth of the produce from the land or else as a fixed tax.

In Ptolemaic Egypt, the far richer documentation allows us to glimpse more clearly how the Greek presence affected the evolution of the indigenous society. An ancient bureaucratic tradition already existed here, and the Ptolemies simply took it over, setting new cadres, recruited from amongst the Graeco-Macedonians, above the old cadres of the local units of administration: nomes, toparchies and *komai* (provinces, districts and villages). Graeco-Macedonians also filled the top civil and military posts in the central government.

As in Asia, part of the territory 'conquered by the spear' was 'royal land', populated by 'royal peasants' who had to pay heavy dues; part was 'sacred land' in the hands of an indigenous priesthood, some of the revenue from which was used to fund the cult; part was 'cleruch land', formed of smallholdings presented, as remuneration, to the soldiers of the royal army; the rest was land distributed in the form of a gift by the king. One of these *doreai* was assigned to Apollonius, the *de facto* minister of finance of Ptolemy II. The correspondence of this man's steward, Zenon, provides plenty of information about it. The peasants who worked on this land that was more or less independent of the royal authority had to pay the same dues in kind as the royal peasants. Nowadays doubts are expressed about the 'master planning' formerly believed to have subjected the peasant masses to harsher exploitation in Egypt than in Seleucid Asia. However, it does seem that peasant revolts were more common in Egypt than in Asia (although that impression may simply result from the unevenness of the information available to us). Some authors suggest that the indigenous priesthood had a hand in the revolts. Others stress the fact that, from the third century on, Egyptians were called upon to serve in the royal army. But that is a separate problem.

At any rate, in Asia as in Egypt, the peasant masses were for the most part affected by the Greek presence only to the extent that that presence increased the level of their exploitation. We should, however, remember that, after the period of disturbances that followed Alexander's death, in all these societies local leaders, either appointed to minor posts or living in indigenous towns that obtained city status together with the autonomy that went with it, emerged as soon as stability was restored in the Hellenistic states. Let us pick out one example, about which rather more than usual is known and which is particularly interesting as it concerns a community that, on the face of it, might be expected to be particularly refractory to Hellenism: the community of Judaea.

At the end of the fourth century, Judaea was part of the Ptolemaic kingdom. It was a semi-autonomous vassal state that was obliged to pay tribute. What was distinctive about it was that authority there was exercised by a high priest, yet it was not a priestly state. The relevant documents refer to the *ethnos tôn Ioudaiôn*, the Jewish people, so the land was not the property of the Temple of Jerusalem, as was the case in the priestly states that were part of the Seleucid kingdom. The high priests of Judaea were recruited from the priestly Oniad dynasty. They possessed property not only in Jerusalem but also beyond the river Jordan. We find them mentioned in the correspondence of Zenon, the steward employed by Ptolemy II's minister, Apollonius. They appear in a passage devoted to a 'property belonging to Toubias', which Zeno seems to have visited in the course of one of his tours of inspection in the external possessions of the Ptolemaic kings. We even possess two letters, written in Greek, from this Toubias. One is addressed to Apollonius, the other to the king himself. In his *Jewish Antiquities*, the historian Flavius Josephus, a Hellenised Jew and Roman citizen, who was writing in the first century AD, mentions a certain Joseph, son of Tobias and nephew of the high priest Onias, who travelled to Alexandria, bearing gifts for the king, in order to obtain the post of tax-farmer for the province of Syria-Phoenicia, which he then appears to have held for twenty-two years. With such a position, in Jerusalem he must have exercised power parallel to that of the high priest. Flavius Josephus ends his account by stating that this Joseph, son of Tobias, 'had managed to lead the Jewish people out of a situation of poverty and weakness into a brighter life'. No doubt these improved living conditions were limited to the Hellenised Jewish circles to which the Tobiads belonged. But all the same, this example shows that by the third century, or possibly even earlier, leaders of native groups did have access to more or less important positions that brought them closer to the Graeco-Macedonians.

Nevertheless, it should be stressed that no more than a minority would be involved in such cases. Even if Alexander really did dream of uniting his subjects and erasing the difference between the

Greeks and the Barbarians, as has been claimed, his successors soon reverted to tradition and behaved as conquerors in their dealings with their eastern subjects. All the same, in the long run the development of urban life in the Greek manner and the expansion of trade were bound to influence the eastern societies. The question of the extent to which this influence affected cultural life constitutes the last aspect of Alexander's legacy, and it is now time to tackle this.

CHAPTER 15

The Hellenisation of the East, and its limits

The dominant position of the Hellenes in the eastern states that emerged from Alexander's conquest was bound to produce consequences at the cultural level. Let us now attempt to evaluate them, avoiding the exaggerations into which this question sometimes leads commentators: on the one hand, they tend to overplay a civilising vision of the Greek culture's effect on less evolved peoples; on the other, to suggest that, when it came into contact with the East, that Greek culture was contaminated.

ALEXANDRIA

There can be no doubt that the heart of what, ever since Droysen, has been called Hellenistic civilisation was Alexandria, the city that Alexander founded during his brief stay in Egypt. As has been suggested above, it is unlikely that the conqueror could from the start have envisaged the exceptional destiny of the town to which he had given his name. It was just the first of the whole series of Alexandrias that was to mark the passage of his army.

On the other hand, it is reasonable to suppose that his Companion Ptolemy, the son of Lagos, who very soon established his authority over Egypt, was the real founder of the city that was to develop in such a spectacular manner. We know that, although Perdiccas had planned to return Alexander's mortal remains to Aegae, where the tombs of the Macedonian kings were located, Ptolemy managed to get hold of them. There is no need to enter the debate over whether or not he initially installed the king's tomb at

Memphis, then transferred it to Alexandria later. The essential point is that the tomb was in the new town at the moment when Ptolemy, following the example set by Antigonus, in his turn claimed the title of king. Exactly where Alexander's tomb was located is also unclear. Normally, in Greek cities, the founder's tomb was located in the agora; and that may indeed be where Ptolemy had it placed. But Strabo, writing in the first century AD, situated it in the Sema, the funerary monument said to house not only Alexander's remains but also those of the early Ptolemaic rulers, which was to be found in the palace quarter. The hypothesis has been proposed that the conqueror's tomb was relocated during the reign of Ptolemy IV.

The first Ptolemy was himself quite a remarkable figure. He had accompanied Alexander throughout the Asian campaign, and a number of later historians took their inspiration from the account of it that he produced. Arrian was one of these. In his *Life of Alexander*, Plutarch cites him once, among other historians who believed that the meeting between Alexander and the queen of the Amazons was pure invention (*Alex.*, 46, 2). It is not at all surprising that Ptolemy should have had the idea of making his capital a centre of cultural life.

It is believed that he was advised to do so by the Athenian Demetrius of Phaleron, a disciple of Theophrastus, Aristotle's successor as head of the Lyceum. Demetrius of Phaleron had governed Athens for ten years, from 317 to 307, under the protection of Cassander. When Demetrius Poliorcetes, the son of Antigonus, captured the city, Demetrius of Phaleron found refuge first in Thebes, then in Egypt, at Ptolemy's court. It was on the Athenian's advice that a project altogether in line with Aristotle's teaching was undertaken: the construction of the museum, a sanctuary dedicated to the Muses, which would offer hospitality to intellectuals wishing to debate their theories, and a library, where all the great works of Greek culture would be collected, recopied and analysed.

Athens remained the centre for philosophy and was home not only to the Academy and the Lyceum, but also to the new schools that were developing, such as Zeno's Stoa and the Garden of Epicurus. But meanwhile, Alexandria became the major centre for scientific speculations, as can be seen from a list of some of its scholars: Euclid, whose *Elements* for centuries remained the basis for mathematics; Eratosthenes, who was both a cartographer and a mathematician and was in charge of the library; the astronomer Aristarchus of Samos; and many others. Archimedes, who may have had contacts among the Alexandrian scholars, was the only great scholar of the period not to work there; he remained in Syracuse, ensuring its defence against the Romans.

The library, alongside the museum, became an important centre for philological research. The great works of the past were collected there; and new editions of texts and commentaries rapidly swelled the numbers of the volumes that it housed. The Ptolemaic kings strove to acquire already published great works from all over the Greek world, and then proceeded to have copies made of them. An anecdote told by Galen relates that Ptolemy III Euergetes asked the Athenians for 'the books of Sophocles, Euripides, and Aeschylus, in order to make copies of them', but instead of returning the originals, he kept them and sent copies back in their place. No doubt the edition in question was the one which Lycurgus ordered in the thirties of the fourth century BC so that actors could use an 'official' text of the works of the three great tragic poets.

But the library was not limited to the great works of Greek literature. Translations of works stemming from what the great historian Arnaldo Momigliano called 'Alien Wisdom' were also undertaken. Ptolemy II is supposed to have set bilingual scholars to translate many works from every corner of the known world. They included texts from the Iranian world, the works of the Egyptian Manetho, and the first books of the Hebrew Bible.

A text dating from the second century, written by an Alexandrian Jew, namely the letter from Aristaeus to Philocrates, attributes the paternity of this last project to Demetrius of Phaleron. It began to be realised under the first Ptolemy but was not completed until his successor's reign. The text is worth citing.

> Demetrius of Phaleron, set in charge of the king's library, received large sums of money to acquire a collection – complete, if possible – of all the works ever produced in the world. He proceeded to make many purchases and transcriptions, and in this way managed, in so far as was possible, to carry out the king's project. I was present

when he was asked 'How many dozens of volumes are there, exactly?' He replied, 'More than twenty, o king, but I shall, as a matter of urgency, see to what remains to be done to reach five hundred thousand. I have been told that there also exist laws of the Jews that deserve to be transcribed and become part of the library.' 'Well, what is stopping you?', asked the king, 'After all, you have all the means necessary.' Demetrius replied, 'The trouble is that they also have to be translated, for in Judaea they use special characters, as they do in Egyptian writing; and in the same way as the Egyptians, they have a language of a particular type. People think that they use Syriac, but that is not the case; it is an altogether different type of language.' When the king had found out about the whole matter, he ordered that a letter be sent to the High Priest of the Jews, so that all the above-mentioned projects could be executed.

This text is clearly a reconstruction. The Jews make their appearance in Greek literature only with Hecataeus of Abdera, in the last decades of the fourth century. He presents Moses as a law-giver in the Greek style. As for the Jews' monotheism, he regards it as a kind of philosophy. Did Demetrius of Phaleron really know as much about the Jews, their language and their writing as the text of Aristaeus' letter suggests? We have no evidence to support the hypothesis. However, we do know that a translation of the Pentateuch was not undertaken until the reign of Ptolemy II. What, for Demetrius, was simply interest in a foreign 'philosophy', for Ptolemy was no doubt a response to a prosaic necessity. He needed to know about the laws of a community which, whether located in Judaea or in Alexandria, was a part of his kingdom. The story of the seventy-two sages gathering in Alexandria may be the stuff of legend, but a Greek translation of the Bible must have facilitated the diffusion of the sacred text among the Hellenised Jewish diaspora, even if that was not its initial purpose.

The example of the Septuagint thus testifies to the fundamental role that Alexandria played in the diffusion of not only Greek culture but also the culture of the peoples that Alexander's conquest had integrated into the Hellenistic world.

The other Hellenistic capitals, Antioch in the Seleucid kingdom, and Pergamum, once the Attalid kingdom became established, also contributed to this diffusion of the Greek culture. There, as in Ptolemaic Egypt, the role played by royal power was fundamental. The kings attracted writers, scholars and artists to their courts, and their generosity was competitive. This was a different world from that of the Greek cities, although those cities certainly did play an intermediary role in the diffusion of Greek culture. Quite clearly, however, this culture remained confined to a minority, the urbanised Greek or Hellenised bourgeoisie that Rostovtzeff believed to be such a characteristic feature of the Hellenistic period. All the same, the account of the Greek translation of the Hebrew Bible given in the *Letter of Aristaeus* also shows that, despite the diffusion of Hellenism, religious particularities survived and countered attempts at syncretism with all the force of ancestral traditions.

RELIGIOUS LIFE IN THE WORLD THAT EMERGED FROM THE CONQUEST

The limits of Hellenisation are most visible at the level of religion. First we must bear in mind the nature of Greek religion. It consisted of a body of rituals that implied neither personal commitment nor proselytism. In Greek cities, religious life was included within the framework of social and political practices. Piety consisted primarily in observance of these practices. It is true that throughout the fourth-century Greek world manifestations of popular religiosity subsisted, particularly in rural areas. Elsewhere the great deities of the Olympian pantheon continued to be honoured by monuments many of which were of a grandiose nature, particularly in the Greek cities of Asia (the Artemision of Ephesus provides a good example); and the great panhellenic sanctuaries sometimes still drew crowds of the faithful. But some forms of piety seemed to imply a more personal commitment. The word 'mysticism' is frequently applied to these. Most involved the mystery cults, such as that of the Eleusinian goddesses Demeter and Corè (Persephone), and also Dionysiac worship.

In Athens, the cult of these deities figured in the civic calendar:

the Great Dionysia, in particular, were as spectacular as ever. It was, moreover, in the fourth century that the theatre of Dionysus was refurbished. However, Euripides' last work, the *Bacchae*, reveals other forms taken by the cult of Dionysus, forms more sinister and less civic. Women were particularly involved here. It was they who took part in these orgies, in a state of trance that induced ecstasy, a kind of communion with the god. Other religious currents such as Orphism were also regaining popularity, possibly because they catered for the anxieties of societies that were frequently shaken by violent internal strife. The promise of a blessed Beyond, where the soul would be delivered from the prison constituted by the body, was the reward for an ascetic life that rejected the eating of meat and blood sacrifice.

However, we must remain circumspect with regard to the influence that these beliefs and practices may have exerted over the popular masses. We should be equally prudent on the score of the evidence that Alexander's behaviour offers with regard to his adhesion to this type of mysticism. We have already mentioned the matter of the Dionysiac ceremonies that punctuated the last moments of the conquest, but these were marked above all by processions, sacrifices and dramatic performances, all in the purest classical tradition.

Nevertheless, there can be no doubt that Dionysiac worship became widely diffused throughout the Hellenistic world, particularly in Ptolemaic Egypt. The Ptolemies had integrated this god among their ancestors. In 271, a festival designed to strengthen the royal cult, the Ptolemeiaia, was introduced, and this included a Dionysiac procession. It was also in Alexandrian circles that there arose the myth of Alexander as a new Dionysus, and that Dionysiac mythology took to exalting the figure of the first conqueror of India.

Egypt was, in any case, a place where the diffusion of Dionysiac worship was particularly favoured, for the myth of Dionysus became fused with that of the Egyptian god Osiris. This Egyptian god, like Dionysus, had been put to death. Their common destiny was bound to encourage the identification of the two deities.

But Dionysus was also revered outside Egypt. He was a complex deity, at once civic and marginal, a veritable 'boundary-crosser' who, through drunkenness or ecstasy, could liberate the soul from the prison of the body and brought promises of an eternal felicity. He was particularly suited to become an object of veneration in this changing world of the eastern Mediterranean, in the aftermath of Alexander's death.

Demeter was in a similar position. Like Dionysus, she was linked with the cycle of vegetation. Also like Dionysus, she had contacts with the underworld ruled by Hades, the husband of Demeter's daughter, Corè. In Eleusis, she presided over the initiatory ceremonies known as the famous Mysteries. This initiation, like Dionysiac ecstasy, albeit in a far more institutionalised form, guaranteed eternal happiness. In the world that emerged from the conquest, the Eleusinian religion also became widely diffused. One suburb of Alexandria was called Eleusis, and mysteries took place there.

But we should remember that those most concerned in these religious manifestations were the Hellenes themselves. What encouraged these people cut off from their native lands to adhere to the cult of Dionysus was the hope of salvation that deities such as he held out. We should also remember that the epithet 'Soter', 'saviour', was added to the name of the first Ptolemy.

The new forms taken by some Greek cults naturally enough made them factors in the diffusion of Hellenism in the world that emerged from the conquest. To what extent did these cults penetrate indigenous circles? Did the Greek gods clash with the eastern ones?

To answer those questions, we must take two important factors into account. On the one hand, as we have seen, the occupation of the states of the ancient East by Greeks, whether as administrators or as colonists, had affected the ancient social structures relatively little. The mostly rural populations had preserved their way of life and, with it, their ancient beliefs. Furthermore, the eastern deities – or at least the major ones – were already known to the Greeks and since the late fifth century, at least, had won over a number of Greek devotees. One such, in Athens, was the Thracian goddess Bendis, in honour of whom a nocturnal procession took place in Piraeus. (At the beginning of Plato's *Republic*, we learn that Socrates and his friends have just taken part in it.) Another was Isis, whose cult had been introduced to Athens by a decree that authorised the Egyptian merchants who frequented the port of Piraeus to build a sanctuary for the goddess. A number of other eastern deities were also venerated in Greece: Sabazius, Cybele, Adonis and Attis.

Private associations were formed to ensure the perpetuation of these cults. They brought together citizens and foreigners, men and women, free men and slaves. So Athens, the island cities and the Greek cities of Asia Minor were, long before Alexander's adventure, all places where contact existed between Greek religion and the religions of the East. Greek and eastern gods were quickly assimilated. After the conquest they became familiar generally, not without a certain confusion, for a single eastern deity sometimes became muddled with several Greek deities, and vice versa. Aphrodite, for instance, was assimilated both to the Syrian goddess Atargatis and to the Phoenician Astarte, Isis was confused with Demeter, Osiris – as we have seen – with Dionysus, and the god of Tyre, Melqart, with Heracles.

But the most curious of all these examples is Sarapis, a god generally believed to have been a creation of Ptolemy I, who aimed thereby to gather Greeks and Egyptians together around a single deity. The very name of the god seems to result from a contraction of Osiris and Apis (the sacred bull of Memphis). Sarapis was particularly revered in Alexandria, where his principal sanctuary, the Sarapeion, was located. The cult of Sarapis rapidly spread throughout the Mediterranean world. He was represented as a Greek god, bearded and majestic, as befitted a sovereign. His cult was not confined to Hellenes, and he was frequently associated with Isis. In Alexandria, Sarapis was to some extent an 'official' deity who protected the Ptolemaic rulers. Elsewhere, when he was associated with Isis, the cult addressed to the pair of them was organised by private associations. Meanwhile, in many Greek towns, the cult of Sarapis became part of the civic religion.

A RESISTANCE TO SYNCRETISM:
THE EXAMPLE OF JUDAISM [1]

Again, and as the example of Sarapis confirms, such phenomena of syncretism were essentially a feature of urban centres. Elsewhere, in the countryside, eastern religions resisted Hellenisation. That resistance was generally sustained by the local clergy. Unfortunately, however, we have very little information on the situation. In Egypt, resistance became manifest only in the third century. In the Seleucid Empire, likewise, resistance appears in the third and second centuries. The movement of resistance which is the best documented, for the reasons given above, is that of the Jews.

The case of the Jews is rather special in that two different groups can be seen to have faced up to the problem of Hellenisation: those in Judaea, dominated by a priestly aristocracy intent upon safeguarding religious orthodoxy; and those of the Jewish diaspora, that is to say the Jewish communities scattered throughout the eastern world. This diaspora antedated Alexander's conquest, for it went right back to the period of exile. When the Temple of Jerusalem was rebuilt, with the help of the Achaemenid kings, not all those in exile had returned. A large community remained in Babylon, which certainly kept in contact with Judaea, but had developed its own reading of the sacred text. Around the end of the fifth century, the prophet Esdras, from Babylon, had received royal orders to codify the Torah, the Mosaic Law that provided the juridical and ritual norm for all Jews. Later, as we have noted above, the foundation of Alexandria attracted a strong wave of Jewish emigration to the new city. The Jews, resident foreigners, do not appear, at least initially, to have gathered in any particular quarter. So they were soon in contact with the local population. Alexandria seems to have been home to Hellenised circles anxious to tell the Greeks about their Jewish history and laws. As early as the third century, a number of factors indicate the existence of a Jewish historiography written in Greek.

---

[1] At the time of my writing the present chapter, Maurice Sartre's book, *D'Alexandre à Zénobie. Histoire du Levant antique, IVe siècle av. J. C. – IIIe siècle ap. J.-C.*, Paris, Fayard, 2001, had not yet appeared, so I had had no chance to read the particularly rich pages that the author devotes to the question of Hellenistic Judaism (pp. 305–70).

Given that two kinds of Jewish groups existed, at once connected yet distinct, on the one hand, the Judaean communities, on the other, the communities of the Jewish diaspora, it is not surprising that two forms of Jewish piety developed. In Judaea, respect for the law was reinforced by the presence of the Temple and the authority of the priests. In the communities of the diaspora, religious life, lacking the sacrificial rites that were the prerogative of the Temple, was essentially reduced to the Law and meditating upon it, as in the time of the exile.

Did Hellenism influence Judaism and, if so, which of those two forms of religious practice did it affect? A recent work by Edouard Will and Claude Orrieux tried to answer that question:

> The answer seems to us to be more complex than it might
> at first sight appear. Scriptural and ritual rigour tolerated
> revolutionary innovations never set down in writing (which
> suggests that the promoters of Hellenisation were the high
> priests and those who surrounded them), while an attachment
> to oral jurisprudence, which systematically made good the
> gaps in the written law, multiplied the obstacles to
> Hellenisation but nevertheless did not rule out innovations in
> the spiritual sphere.
>
> (*Ioudaïsmos–Hellenismos*, p. 225)

It was these traditionalist 'legalists' who encouraged the popular movement of the Maccabees against the priestly aristocracy. And when the Hasmoneans, in their turn, succumbed to the attractions of Hellenism and created a Hellenistic-type state, they found themselves opposed by those same 'legalists' who, by the end of this period, were known as Pharisees. But that is another story.

At the end of this rapid analysis of the forms taken by Hellenisation in the East, what conclusions should we draw? The first and least challengeable is the diffusion of the Greek language, the *koinè* that was to remain the 'official' language even after Rome took over the Mediterranean East. To be sure, the peasant masses for the most part remained attached to their own local dialects. But Greek became the language of the urban populations for Greeks and Hellenised natives alike.

The second conclusion is that the most spectacular indication of the diffusion of Hellenism is the great wave of urban development. Tourists today visiting Turkey, Syria and Jordan are struck by the scale of the ancient towns whose ruins testify to the Hellenistic civilisation in this part of the Mediterranean world. In this respect, Egypt remains somewhat apart, for there the traces of the civilisation of the early pharaohs are even more impressive than the ruins left by their successors, the Ptolemies. Perhaps the excavations now being carried out in Alexandria will make it possible to modify that judgement.

Really, the strongest evidence for the penetration of Hellenism in the East is provided by the very place held by Alexandria, not only at the cultural level – with the influence exerted by its museum and library and the role that the latter played in the diffusion of classical Greek culture – but also at the economic level, as the principal trading centre in the Mediterranean.

Alexander's brief reign did not produce a vast territorial state, as the conquered territories were split up so quickly. But it does, without a doubt, mark a turning point in the history of the eastern Mediterranean. Although it was divided politically, the Mediterranean East was certainly united culturally. Even if many layers of essentially rural populations remained unaffected by that unified culture, the face of the civilisation born from the conquest is certainly marked by a real originality that was to endure for centuries. It was within the framework of that civilisation that the mythical figure of Alexander was to be born and to develop.

PART V

Alexander the Mythical Hero

In the preceding pages, we have tried to gauge the historical impact that Alexander's reign made upon the evolution of the Mediterranean world of antiquity. The conquest of Asia, which he completed in just a few years, undeniably constitutes an important fact. But the goals of the king of Macedon, the meaning that he meant to confer upon some of his actions relating to his Iranian subjects, and even the results of his conquest are, as we have seen, complex and often contradictory. Their complex and contradictory nature stems not purely from Alexander's personality, but also from the very character of the 'sources' through which we must try to comprehend them.

As has been emphasised above, those sources were themselves reconstructions put together by writers, historians and biographers living in a world by then unified under Rome's domination. That is a factor that cannot be ignored and that prompts one to ponder upon the very construction of Alexander's image over the decades that followed his death. In particular, we need to understand why the accounts produced in his lifetime or in the years immediately following his death – that written by Callisthenes, which was left unfinished when its author disappeared, and those by Ptolemy, Aristoboulus, Clitarchus and others, dimly echoed by the writers who made use of them several centuries later – never came down to us. The situation seems paradoxical, and we should try to pick out the reasons why it was not until the Roman period that people began to produce histories of Alexander, or at least to devote to him a whole important section in a historical work intended to be universal, as Diodorus did. Paul Goukowsky, who has edited books XVII and XVIII of Diodorus' work, has produced an important study of the origins of the myth of Alexander. I will try to summarise the principal points in his demonstration, in order to gain a better understanding of the renewal of interest in Alexander in the first century BC.

We certainly need to throw more light on the nature of the only sources that have come down to us. But at the same time, we also need to understand how and why, down the centuries, they have nurtured the image of the figure who was to occupy such a place in the imaginary representations of the most diverse civilisations in both the East and the West, and who, over the last two centuries, was also to become the subject of scholarly controversies not entirely innocent of ulterior motives. To study all these questions comprehensively would be an immense task, impossible to be contained within the limits of the present work. Indeed, a whole lifetime would not suffice to complete it. We must be content to make a number of discontinuous approaches based on research into this or that period of history, endeavouring only to gain from the example of Alexander a slightly better understanding of the manner in which historical memory functions.

CHAPTER 16

The image of Alexander in the ancient world

As can be imagined, Alexander's sudden death took his entourage by surprise. We have already discussed the events which took place in Babylon and the compromise which resulted. That compromise was very soon to be brought into question. In the conflicts that were to set the *diadochi* one against another, the image of Alexander was, of course, used by them all. From the very first, it was by claiming to have received from the dying Alexander a ring that made him 'the executor of his last will and testament' that Perdiccas obtained control of the situation. Assembling the principal army leaders around Alexander's mortal remains, Perdiccas distributed functions and satrapies to them. It was also at this point that it was decided to transfer the king's body not to Aegae in Macedon, but to the Siwa Oasis, where it would be close to his 'father'. For this purpose, a carriage richly decorated with paintings portraying Alexander's victories and apotheosis was constructed. Diodorus has left us a vivid description of the Oriental luxury of this vehicle. But we also know that this transport, which was bound to pass through Egypt, presented Ptolemy with the opportunity to seize the royal remains, which he thereupon had buried initially at Memphis, then moved to Alexandria, where the tomb was the focus of processions and funeral Games. By doing so, the master of Egypt placed himself under the protection of the 'god', Alexander. The coins that he had struck by the Alexandrian mint bore all the insignia of that 'deification': the horns of Ammon, the aegis and the diadem. Alexander's effigy now replaced that of Heracles on the upper side of the coins.

Another of the *diadochi*, Eumenes, the former chancellor, also

167

provides an example of the way in which use was made of the dead Alexander. During his struggle against Antigonus, Eumenes would hold council meetings in his tent, where a vacant throne was placed, symbolising the presence of the king. In his *Life of Eumenes*, Plutarch explains that he hoped in this way to ensure the obedience of his soldiers and prevent them from rallying to Antigonus:

> He said . . . that Alexander had appeared to him in a dream, had shown him a tent arrayed in royal fashion, with a throne standing in it, and had then said that, if they held their councils and transacted their business there, he himself would be present and would assist them in every plan and enterprise which they undertook in his name.
>
> (*Eum.*, 13, 5–6)

Little by little, however, as a certain equilibrium became established between the *diadochi*, the memory of Alexander ceased to be referred to as a matter of course. The disappearance of the young Alexander IV and the acceptance of that, soon followed by the *diadochi* declaring themselves kings, showed that the new masters of what used to be Alexander's empire had given up the idea of reconstituting it and, in so doing, desisted from laying claim to his patronage. From the reign of Antigonus Gonatas, that was certainly true of the Antigonids and also, to a lesser degree, of the Seleucids. Only the Ptolemies, in particular the first two, were keen to place themselves under his protection and, later, the Ptolemies took their places beside the remains of Alexander in the famous Alexandrian *sema*, the royal tomb. It was likewise in Alexandria that, from the seventies of the third century onwards, Alexander was identified with Dionysus in the Ptolemeiaia festival, which featured a Dionysiac procession.

Alexandria was also the place where there was to develop a historiography of Alexander, which we know of only through its use by later historians. Ptolemy himself was one of the first of those historians. He had taken part in the campaign and had written an account of it. This account must have been based on his own memories and possibly – it is sometimes suggested – on a diary kept by Callisthenes; but its main purpose was to emphasise the role that

Ptolemy himself had played at Alexander's side. It was deliberately centred on military actions and made no attempt to interpret his king's goals. As Paul Goukowsky observes, 'the Ptolemaic founder wrote an uncritical history of a conqueror with no weaknesses' (*Essai*, I, p. 144). This 'realistic' and 'moderate' Alexander was to win over Arrian (as we shall see).

The other important Alexander historian was Clitarchus. As Paul Goukowsky notes, Clitarchus, unlike Ptolemy, 'recounts not the history of a king, but the high deeds of a hero' (*Essai*, I, p. 139). He does not hesitate to introduce into his account legendary episodes such as Alexander's meeting with the queen of the Amazons. Alexander is presented as a predestined figure who, right from the start of the expedition, envisaged conquering the whole known world.

Clitarchus was writing in Alexandria, and his *History of Alexander* was probably contemporary with Ptolemy's account. It seems reasonable to suppose that Ptolemy, while adopting the objective tone of a historian intent on drawing attention to the military actions in which he himself had taken part, at the same time encouraged the diffusion of an image of Alexander which was to make a far greater impact in the Hellenistic world and which, besides, could only reinforce his own legitimacy as compared to the other *diadochi*. If Clitarchus was indeed the principal source for Diodorus, it is worth noting that the Sicilian left a complimentary portrait of the first Ptolemy: 'Men, because of his graciousness and nobility of heart, came together eagerly from all sides to Alexandria and gladly enrolled for the campaign, although the army of the kings was about to fight against that of Ptolemy' (XVIII, 28, 5).

Clitarchus' oeuvre, which was probably likewise the principal source for Quintus Curtius and Justin/Pompeius Trogus, was to be diffused extraordinarily widely. We can do no better than borrow Paul Goukowsky's conclusion:

This monumental work, enriched with authentic facts, but sublimated by a talented artist, established an image of Alexander which, for all it was challenged by scholars and the literate elite, would haunt the Roman generals of the first century BC and continue to inspire all the authors of literary compilations of the late Hellenistic period and the Empire.

(Essai, I, p. 141)

Who were those argumentative scholars and literary men? We do not really know, as most of the texts by these authors have disappeared. It seems that at first it was above all in the philosophical schools that this idealised image of Alexander was challenged, in particular by the Peripatetics and the Stoics. From that moment on, the tradition concerning Alexander split into two resolutely opposed currents, which were then perpetuated down the centuries: on the one hand, the image of a magnificent conqueror, a philosopher king, dreaming of a fusion of races and a universal civilisation; on the other, that of a brutal, violent character, incapable of self-control and an unscrupulous drunkard. Of course the two are sometimes merged. Plutarch, for example, presents a young king full of excellent qualities who gradually, under eastern influences, turns into an implacable despot.

The late Republic and the first two centuries of the Roman Empire constitute an essential moment for the duality of Alexander's image: an essential moment not only because it enables us for the first time to glimpse manifestations of identification with the Macedonian king but perhaps even more because it was the world unified by Rome that produced the works that are our principal sources for the history of Alexander – sources which, as we can now see, were themselves a product of the evolution of Alexander's image during the Hellenistic period.

Problems of identification arose as early as the second century BC, precisely at the time when Rome became mistress of Macedon. Scipio Africanus, the conqueror of Carthage, may have been seen as a new Alexander. And that was certainly the case with Pompey, who became known as Magnus, Pompey the Great. Following his victories in Asia, he celebrated his triumph, in 61, with a degree of pageantry reminiscent of Alexander:

> Pompey himself was borne in a chariot . . . wearing, it is said, a cloak of Alexander the Great [which] seems to have been found among the possessions of Mithridates that the

inhabitants of Cos had received from Cleopatra. His purpose in wearing this exotic garment was, so to speak, to personify Alexander, whose title he bore.

(Appian, *Mithridates*, 115)

But Pompey's opponent, Caesar, evoked comparison with Alexander even more. Plutarch, who associated the two men in his *Parallel Lives*, records a telling anecdote:

In Spain, when he was at leisure and was reading from a history of Alexander, he was lost in thought for a long time, and then burst into tears. His friends were astonished and asked the reason for his tears. 'Do you not think', said he, 'it is a matter for sorrow that while Alexander, at my age, was already king of so many peoples, I have as yet achieved no brilliant success?'

(*Caesar*, 11, 5–6)

It is striking because it not only represents the Roman general dreaming of matching the greatness of the conqueror of Asia, but also records the fact that he was 'reading from the history of Alexander'. Mark Antony may have been less likely to be reading such a work, but there can be no doubt that, as master of the East and wedded to the last Ptolemaic queen, he too must have dreamed of taking over the conqueror's glory. It was certainly not by chance that one of the sons he fathered on Cleopatra was called Alexander. However, it is more surprising to find Octavian-Augustus, the man who posed as the restorer of the *mos maiorum*, the ancestral traditions, also identifying with the Macedonian king. According to Suetonius, after the capture of Alexandria, 'he had the sarcophagus and body of Alexander the Great brought forth from its shrine, and after gazing upon it, showed his respect by placing upon it a golden crown and strewing it with flowers' (*Aug.*, XVIII). He also had an effigy of Alexander carved on his personal seal. Among his successors, Caligula (again according to Suetonius) fancied himself clad in the armour of Alexander, which he had removed from the latter's tomb (*Cal.*, LII). Other emperors, too, identified with Alexander: Trajan, on his return from the Parthian War, claimed in a letter to the Senate that he had travelled even further than Alexander.

But while victorious generals and conquerors liked to regard themselves as reincarnations of the Macedonian king, or at least encouraged comparisons with him, it was also during the last centuries of the Republic and the first two centuries of the empire that criticisms formulated in the philosophical schools were finding a favourable reception. The positive image elaborated in Alexandrian circles was now opposed by a negative one, that of a brutal despot who had destroyed Thebes and Persepolis and felt no qualms about getting rid of his close followers, Parmenion, Philotas, Cleitus and Callisthenes, either in cold blood or resorting to a parody of a trial, or in a drunken rage: here was a Greek who had not hesitated to adopt eastern ways.

The historiography of Alexander that has come down to us and that dates from the two centuries that separate the work of Diodorus from that of Arrian reflects both the idealised image of the conqueror and the more or less violent critiques of some of his behaviour. Pompeius Trogus, a Gaul from the province of Narbonensis, who lived at the time of Augustus, wrote a work from which we possess only the summary by Justin, which appears in his *Philippic Histories*. Alexander, to whom four books are devoted, is, right from the start, presented as an immoderate figure. In the parallel that Justin draws between Philip and his son, the flaws of the latter are far greater than those of the former. A neat formula sums up the difference: 'The one wished to reign with his friends, the other reigned over them' (IX, 6, 17). In order to have a divine birth attributed to him, Alexander did not hesitate to intimidate the priests of Ammon and dictate the replies that he wished to hear (XI, 11, 6). Once master of the Persian empire, 'he began to treat his men not as a king, but as an enemy' (XII, 5, 1). Even the glory of his victories was tarnished by the darkness of his cruelty (XII, 5, 5). Justin, reporting Trogus, nevertheless rounds off the passage devoted to Alexander with praise for the Macedonian king who was 'endowed with super-human genius' (XII, 16, 1).

Diodorus' Alexander is closer to the idealised image elaborated by Clitarchus, who, as we have seen, was the principal source for the Sicilian historian. In fact, as Paul Goukowsky remarks in his preface to book XVII, Diodorus' admiration is so slavish as to render the figure of Alexander rather trite. Diodorus' portrait shows only the stereotyped virtues that turn the conqueror into the image of a perfect sovereign. To be sure, he is bound to mention Alexander's reprehensible actions – the destruction of Thebes, the assassination of Parmenion, the murder of Cleitus. But he tries to explain, if not justify, them.

The image of Alexander produced by the Roman Quintus Curtius is quite close to that painted by Diodorus. Quintus Curtius Rufus was a contemporary of Claudius. It is thought that he used the same main source as Diodorus, namely Clitarchus, although the researches of some commentators show that he also had recourse to other sources. But his image of Alexander is as idealised as that of Diodorus. And even if Quintus Curtius does recognise some of Alexander's weaknesses, he – strangely enough – blames the Greeks for them: 'And this [the adoration of which Alexander was the object] was not the fault of the Macedonians – for none of them could endure to impair any jot of his native customs – but of the Greeks, who had debased their profession of the liberal arts by evil habits' (VIII, 5, 7). One of those 'evil habits' was love that was contrary to 'natural' desire, but this Alexander resisted (X, 5). So in the end Quintus Curtius' praise of Alexander is without reservations.

As we have seen, this same idealised image partially reappears in Plutarch. But Plutarch made no claims to be a historian, and although his two treatises *On the Fortune of Alexander* do paint a picture of a philosopher king, in his *Life* he is more critical and tries to show how Alexander's character evolved. Plutarch was a Greek and, as he compared Alexander with Caesar in his *Parallel Lives*, he intended to show his Roman readers that the Greeks, now subject to the rule of Rome, had also had their heroes. Strikingly enough, whereas most of the *Lives* end with a comparison of Greek to Roman, in the case of the Alexander–Caesar pair there is no such comparison. It is as if Plutarch, for once, could leave his readers to draw their own conclusions.

It was likewise a Greek, Arrian of Nicomedia, who in the second century AD wrote a history of the conquest which, ever since the book published by the Baron of Sainte-Croix in 1755, has been considered the most exact account of the campaign and the goals that Alexander set himself. Arrian is supposed, in particular, to have used not only the accounts of Ptolemy and Aristoboulus, the best-informed witnesses, but also the famous *ephemerides* (day book), believed to have been a diary kept during the conquest, probably by Eumenes of Cardia. Plutarch alludes to this work in connection with Alexander's death. But nowadays scholars are more sceptical about the transmission of this journal, which, they believe, related only to the last year of Alexander's reign. We have already commented on the dubious objectivity of Ptolemy's memoirs.

It is the very dryness of Arrian's account, the many figures provided, and its deliberately 'Thucydidean' tone that have led many commentators to value it more highly than what the nineteenth-century German scholars called 'the Vulgate', that is to say the account by Clitarchus, which was followed by Diodorus and Quintus Curtius. Today, the tendency is to take more notice of the complementary information that the latter two writers provide so as to supplement the not always reliable statements made by Arrian. But above all, as Pierre Vidal-Naquet has shown in his long postface to Pierre Savinel's translation of Arrian (1984), whatever Arrian's sources may have been – and they were all of Alexandrian origin – the imaginary also has a part to play in his account. Even the descriptions of battles are 'ideological constructions'. So Arrian is no more an objective witness than the authors said to be 'of the Vulgate'. Like them, he describes an important point in time when a new form of monarchical power emerged, which the Roman world inherited. Alexander was the hero of that transformation. To a certain extent he heralded the unity of the world that would be established by Rome. Alexander's historians, living and writing in that Roman world, whether they were Greeks, like Diodorus, Plutarch and Arrian, or Romans like Quintus Curtius and Justin/Trogus, regarded the figure of the Macedonian king as the founder of that new world.

But while the historians accepted what had happened as an ineluctable evolution, the 'intellectuals', or philosophers, rejected it as having destroyed the republican liberty that had existed earlier, and regarded Alexander simply as a despot. Seneca, in his *Letters to Lucilius*, produces a particularly negative image of the situation:

Alexander was hounded into misfortune and dispatched to unknown countries by a mad desire to lay waste other men's territory. Do you believe that the man was in his senses who could begin by devastating Greece, the land where he received his education? One who snatched away the dearest guerdon of each nation, bidding the Spartans be slaves and the Athenians hold their tongues? Not content with the ruin of all the states which Philip had either conquered or bribed into bondage, he overthrew various commonwealths in various places and carried his weapons all over the world; his cruelty was tired, but it never ceased – like a wild beast that tears to pieces more than its hunger demands.

(*Letters to Lucilius*, XV, 94, 62)

Elsewhere (*De beneficiis*, I, 13, 1–3), Seneca declares that ever since his childhood Alexander was nothing but 'a robber and a plunderer of nations, a scourge alike to his friends and to his foes'. And in *De ira* (III, 17, 1–2), he describes Alexander 'who in the midst of a feast with his own hand stabbed Cleitus, his dearest friend, with whom he had grown up, because he withheld his flattery and was reluctant to transform himself from a Macedonian and a free man into a Persian slave'.

Lucan, in his great poem *Pharsalia*, likewise deplores the despotic transformation of Alexander's power. Describing Caesar's visit to the king's tomb, he cannot contain his indignation: 'There lies the mad son of Macedonian Philip, that fortunate freebooter, cut off by death that avenged the world.' And later, he continues in the same vein:

He left his own obscure realm of Macedonia, he spurned Athens which his father had conquered; driven by the impulse of destiny, he rushed through the peoples of Asia, mowing down mankind; he drove his sword home in the breast of every nation; he defiled distant rivers, the Euphrates and the Ganges, with Persian and Indian blood; he was a pestilence to the earth, a thunderbolt that struck all peoples alike, a comet of disaster to mankind.

(X, 1–52)

At the end of the Hellenistic period and in the Roman world, there were certainly two contradictory images of Alexander. And both contrived to develop under the late Empire, even among the Church Fathers. At this point rapid reference must be made to a work that explains the standing of Alexander in the medieval world: the famous *Alexander Romance* (we shall return to it at greater length in the next chapter). This text is attributed to Callisthenes, but was subsequently often reworked. It was probably produced in Alexandria and it presents a jumble of facts, some of which are authentic, others purely legendary, which is reminiscent of the *Odyssey* and eastern tales. Let us focus on the episode in which Alexander arrives in Jerusalem. This was clearly a legend that had made its appearance in the circles of Hellenised Jews in Alexandria during the Hellenistic period. It recurs in Flavius Josephus' would-be historical account (*Jewish Antiquities*, XI, 327–33). But in the *Alexander Romance*, the story takes on a new dimension, in that it suggests the king's adherence to the religion of the one God. It opens with the dispatch of a Jewish embassy to the Macedonians. Dazzled by the courage of Alexander's soldiers, on its return this embassy advised the Jews to surrender to the king:

> Their priests, wearing their priestly robes, went forward to meet Alexander, accompanied by the entire people. Seeing them advancing, Alexander was alarmed by their appearance and ordered them to halt and return to their city. But beckoning forward one of the priests, he said to him: 'Your appearance is truly divine! So tell me what god you honour, for among the gods of my country I have never seen priests so finely arrayed.' The priest replied, 'We serve a single god, who created the heavens, the earth, and all that it contains, but no man has the power to behold him.' At this, Alexander declared, 'As the servants of the true god, go in peace, go, for your god shall be mine and my peace will accompany you. There is not the slightest risk that I shall march against you, as I have against other peoples, because you are consecrated to serve the living god.'
>
> (II, 24)

Later, after founding Alexandria, Alexander again proclaims that 'there is but one true God, invisible, and ever elusive, borne by the seraphim and glorified by the thrice-holy Name' (II, 28).

This Alexander, 'converted' to the faith of the true god, was to be adopted by the Biblical religions of the Middle Ages.

CHAPTER 17

The medieval Alexander

It was possibly in the medieval period that the spectacular development of the myth of Alexander peaked. The story of the Macedonian king's conversion to the religion of the one God is clearly not unconnected with his presence in not only the Christian West and East but also the Muslim world. As for the Jewish tradition, that is explained easily enough by the Alexandrian context in which this myth of the hero emerged. But it was undoubtedly the *Alexander Romance*, along with its translations and adaptations in the last years of the Roman Empire and in the medieval period, that were the principal sources for the construction of an image of Alexander which repeats the contrasts that we have just noted above, and an ambiguity that results in his being represented sometimes as a most perfect knight, sometimes, at the other extreme, as the very incarnation of the Antichrist.

Within the confines of the present work, it is clearly not possible to review all the medieval images of Alexander. But on the basis of a wide range of research studies that have stimulated various colloquia and publications, let us try to follow the various stages in their development down to the dawn of the modern period, when a swing back towards antiquity resulted in the *Romance*'s being eclipsed by the accounts produced by the historians, first Quintus Curtius, then Plutarch, Diodorus and Arrian. We shall be concentrating mostly on the western world, in particular France, partly because it is easier to gain access to the texts, but also because the myth of Alexander seems to have been particularly fully elaborated here.

Our starting point is the *Alexander Romance*, a text that has come down to us through a variety of manuscripts, the most complete of which are located in Paris, and through papyri which preserve the more ancient parts of it, in particular the fictitious correspondence between Darius and Alexander. As Gilles Bonnoure and Blandine Serret, the most recent French editors of the *Roman d'Alexandre*, observe, the text takes the form of 'a nebula of texts and variants elaborated between the fourth and the sixteenth centuries' around the *Romance*, a nebula 'which for us constitutes a dizzying "black hole"' (Paris, 1992, p. xvi).

According to these editors, the most solid evidence on which to base a dating of this work is that provided by its Latin adaptation by Julius Valerius in the late third century AD. This implies the existence of an earlier edition in the Greek language, which probably combined into a single whole a number of traditions. Some of these dated from the decades immediately following the conqueror's death, while others, of more recent date, were elaborated by Alexandrian authors in the course of the three centuries of the Hellenistic period and the first centuries of the Roman Empire. Hence the importance of Egypt and certain Egyptian legends, in particular in the text as reconstituted with its variants.

Egypt is thrust to the fore right at the start of the *Romance*, since the author declares that Alexander was not the son of Philip but, as the best Egyptian sages maintained, the son of Nectanebo (I, 1, 3). This was the name of one of the last Egyptian pharaohs, who in the fourth century tried to throw off the Persian yoke, appealing to Greek *strategoi* for help in this endeavour. The author of the *Romance* represents him as a kind of magician who, having failed to save Egypt from a Barbarian invasion, chose to flee . . . to Macedon. There, he convinced Queen Olympias that she was about to be united with the god Ammon, then himself came to her bed, in disguise: 'Nectanebo . . . prepared the softest fleece of a ram, together with the horns from its head, and a staff and a white robe; and he made a cloak from the skin of a serpent that was soft and limp' (I. 7. 1; English translation, p. 28). Then he entered the queen's chamber, 'got up on to the bed and mated with her'. He told her, 'Long may you live, my lady, for you are pregnant with a boy child who shall be your avenger and become the world-conquering king of the whole civilised universe' (I, 7, 2; English translation, p. 28).

Philip accepted his wife's story of the divine cause of her pregnancy, and when the child was born, during a violent storm, he regarded this as a divine sign, acknowledged the boy as his heir, and named him Alexander. When he was 12 years old, Alexander killed his real father, believing him to be a simple astrologer. Even when Olympias, who had not been duped by Nectanebo's trickery, told him that this was his true father, Alexander soon got over having killed him. A number of episodes in his youth then follow, bringing the reader up to Philip's death. Now that he was king, Alexander made preparations for the expedition to Asia. Its first stage (the conquest of Phrygia, Lycia and Pamphylia) was interrupted by a trip to the West (Sicily and Italy), from which he returned by way of Africa and the Siwa Oasis. Here Alexander consulted the oracle of Ammon and was told, 'Young Alexander, you are my son' (I, 30, 4; English translation, p. 47). Alexander then asked the god to tell him where to found a town bearing his own name. The god's reply reflects the various sources used by the author of the *Romance*, for it refers to several different myths featuring – once again – a pair of ram's horns, this time attributed to Phoebus (Apollo) and Proteus, the Old Man of the Sea. It was when Alexander noticed the little island of Pharos that he decided to build the future Alexandria on the mainland opposite. Soon the town was rising before his eyes.

The war in Asia was then resumed, beginning with the siege of Tyre. This was followed by an exchange of letters with Darius, which led up to the battle of Issus. At this point the story of the Asian conqueror is again interrupted. Alexander returns to Europe, where he lays siege to Thebes, then destroys it, after which he returns to Asia. It is impossible to follow the imaginary itinerary now followed by Alexander, who meantime resumes an exchange of letters with Darius, while the latter is also corresponding with the Indian king Porus. On his deathbed, Darius gives his daughter Roxane to Alexander in marriage. Following the wedding ceremony in Darius' palace, Alexander pens a long letter addressed to his mother and Aristotle, in which he relates the extraordinary adventures that have marked his campaign and describes the no less astonishing peoples he has encountered. One cannot help but think of the account of his travels that Odysseus gives to the court of King Alcinous. Alexander's travels take him to lands populated by extraordinary beings, giants, cannibals, men without heads who can nevertheless 'talk with their tongues like men' (II, 37; English translation, p. 115), and eventually he reaches regions 'where the sun does not rise. These were called the lands of the Blessed.' In the course of these adventures, he has no qualms about descending to the sea-floor, enclosed in a glass vessel, or rising into the sky in a little gondola drawn by two huge birds lured on by a piece of horse-liver stuck on the tip of the spear that Alexander holds out before them. But he returns to earth after an angel appears to him, pointing out a tiny circle far below. It is the earth, surrounded by a snake, the sea. The angel then asks him to limit his conquests to this earth. Alexander concludes his letter as follows: 'So, turning around, as was the will of divine Providence, I returned to the earth, seven days' march away from the expedition. I felt completely cadaverous and half dead. But there I found a satrap who was in my service and, taking three hundred of his horsemen, I rejoined the expedition. Thereafter I never again attempted the impossible' (II, 41, 13). This episode in Alexander's adventures was frequently to reappear in medieval literature, where it was presented as proof of the limits of human knowledge, or sometimes as evidence of Alexander's lack of moderation, or *hubris*.

The third part of the *Romance* tells of the Indian expedition, the highlight of which is the 'Homeric' duel between Porus and Alexander. It is an unequal contest, for the Indian king is five cubits tall, Alexander only three (2.20 metres as against 1.32 metres!). But luck is on the side of the Macedonian king, who, seizing his chance when Porus is momentarily distracted, deals him a blow with his sword, leaving him for dead (III, 4, 3). This victory rallies his Macedonian soldiers to him when they were on the point of abandoning him. He goes on to meet with brahmins and converses with their leader Dandamis. The *Romance* then tells of his meeting with Queen Candace, whose son Candaulus Alexander saves, passing himself off as Antigonus, the chief of his bodyguard. The description of Candace's palace evokes all the splendours of the East. Next, Alexander journeys through the land of the Amazons. It is again in a letter to his mother Olympias that he recounts his last adventures in a series of places, each one more amazing than the last, such as an island with a town comprising twelve towers 'made of gold and emeralds', where he meets men with the heads of dogs or bulls, or with six arms, and birds that speak Greek.

At last Alexander returns to Babylon, where he dies, poisoned on the orders of Antipater. His body is sent to Memphis, then on to Alexandria. This 'central' story is fleshed out by other episodes, borrowed from a variety of sources. One concerns Alexander's visit to Jerusalem, mentioned above, another a curious debate before the Athenian assembly after the fall of Thebes.

Reading the *Romance* and its variants, the reader is struck by a number of features: the haphazard nature of the whole and the disregard for the chronology established by the ancient historians, from whom this account nevertheless borrows; but above all the interjection of magical elements that refer back both to Homeric epic and to Egyptian legends, and the importance of the exchange of letters that makes it possible for Alexander himself to tell the story.

It is not hard to see how such an account, translated first into Latin, then into Aramaic, Persian, Arabic and the European languages, captured the imagination of the people of the Middle Ages. In the West, the principal sources of the poems and prose works devoted to Alexander were, in the first instance, the Latin translation by Julius Valerius, of which a shortened version appeared in the ninth century (the Metz *Epitome*), then the translation produced in the tenth century for Archduke John III of Naples by the archpriest Leo and preserved under the title *Historia de Proeliis*.

In France, this literature began to circulate around the twelfth century. The *Roman d'Alexandre* by Alexandre de Paris is a long poem of 16,000 dodecasyllabic lines (later to be known as Alexandrines). Gauthier de Châtillon's *Alexandreide* dates from the same period. This is a Latin poem in ten books, written between 1178 and 1182 and dedicated to William, Archbishop of Rheims. Gauthier de Châtillon drew his inspiration from not only Julius Valerius' Latin translation but also the account by Quintus Curtius. Both these texts express deep admiration for Alexander, accepting the hero's 'bastard' birth and ignoring both the negative episodes and the uncertainty surrounding his conversion to the religion of the one true God. The same admiration for this figure, who seems a perfect illustration of a Christian knight, is also to be found in the Spanish *Libro de Alexandre* and the *Roman de toute chevalerie*, an Anglo-Norman poem by Thomas of Kent.

It is not possible to cite all the works that fall within this current of literature that moderns label 'courtly' or 'chivalric'. Although the proportion of magical elements is considerable, many of them also had a political objective. They were designed to present rulers with the image of an ideal king. We need not resort to the over-schematic typology of the English historian George Carey (*The Medieval Alexander*, Cambridge, 1956), who set out the works devoted to Alexander under four headings (philosophical, theological, collections of *exempla*, and romances and poems designed to entertain rather than instruct), but it does seem possible to distinguish two periods in the creation of this medieval image of Alexander in the West.

In the first, the eleventh and twelfth centuries, authors seem chiefly concerned to present a chivalric model. Later, as the philosophy of Aristotle became better known, thanks to the Arabic translations of his works, a philosophical and political dimension to Alexander was introduced. This is the case, in particular, of *L'Histoire du bon roy Alexandre* by Jean Wauquelin, composed around 1448 for Jean de Bourgogne, the Count of Etampes. Here, Alexander embodies a new monarchical ideal, a combination of wisdom and temporal power symbolised by the Alexander–Aristotle pairing. Jean Wauquelin's work, which is a mixture of an adventure story and a 'mirror of a prince', was well suited to satisfy the preoccupations of the Burgundian court. A study of the libraries of Burgundy undertaken by Christiane Reynud (in *Alexandre le Grand dans les littératures occidentales et proche-orientales*, Nanterre, 1999) reveals the interest that Philip the Good and his son Charles the Bold took in the adventures of the Macedonian king. In fact, it was for Charles the Bold that the work of Quintus Curtius was first translated into French, in 1468, by the Portuguese Vasco of Lucena. The translation was subsequently reprinted six times between 1500 and 1555.

At about the same time, with the rediscovery of the Greek Alexander historians, the image of the king of Macedon was to become more complex and more ambiguous. The magical elements soon disappeared, in particular the episodes of the descent to the sea-floor and the ascent into the heavens, both of which Vasco of Lucena considered to be 'palpable lies'. The figure of Nectanebo,

Alexander's presumed father in the *Romance* and the diabolical magician of a number of other medieval romances, also disappears. At last Alexander reverts to being the pagan prince who was a pupil of the philosophers who were rediscovered at the end of the Middle Ages.

It may be interesting to conclude this rapid overview of the medieval image of Alexander in the Christian West by citing Montaigne's remarks at the end of the sixteenth century. In book II of the *Essays*, chapter 26, he describes Alexander as one of the three 'most excellent' of men, the others being Homer and Epaminondas. In particular, he praises 'so many eminent virtues that existed in him: justice, temperance, liberality, loyalty to his word, love for those near him, humanity to the conquered', and while recognising that 'it is impossible to carry on such great operations within the rules of justice', which is why Alexander was forced into some reprehensible actions, he nevertheless concludes by acknowledging

> the superiority of his knowledge and capacity, the duration
> and grandeur of his glory, pure, stainless and exempt from
> rivalry; and that, even a long time after his death, it was a
> religious belief to think that medallions with his image
> brought good fortune to those who wore them; and that
> more kings and princes have written of his deeds than other
> historians have written of any other king or prince whatever;
> and that, even at the present day, the Mohammedans, who
> despise all other histories, accept and honour his alone, by
> special prerogative.

This conveniently provides a bridge to lead us to consider some aspects of the medieval Arab Alexander. It is not surprising that the image of Alexander was first reused in the East, particularly in the Arab world, between the eighth and the tenth centuries. Here, as elsewhere, Alexander presents two faces, one positive, the other negative, as F. de Polignac ('Alexandre dans la littérature arabe. L'Orient face à l'hellénisme', *Arabica*, XXIX, 3, 1982) shows in his study of Alexander's image in Masoudi's work, *The Golden Meadows*. The author draws his inspiration from the Pseudo-Callisthenes.

But he does face up to the contradictions. In the chapters on the history of the Persians, Alexander is a usurper, whereas in the passages devoted to the history of the Greek kings, he is a protector of sages. The descent to the sea-bed is associated with the foundation of Alexandria, which thus becomes an 'initiatory threshold' (de Polignac, in *Alexandre le Grand dans les littératures occidentales et proches-orientales*). Finally, in Arab literature, Alexander is also assimilated to Dul Qarnayn, the two-horned man who travelled the world to reach its outer limits in both the eastern and the western Mediterranean, and constructed a wall intended to protect humanity from the impure peoples, Gog and Magog of Biblical fame. This image of the two-horned instrument of God's will also appears in the Koran. Without rejecting the assimilation to Ammon, the god with ram's horns, de Polignac sees it rather as the image of an inspired hero, and invokes the influence of Babylonian Judaism, pointing out that Moses was also described as 'two-horned' ('L'homme aux deux cornes. Une image d'Alexandre du symbolisme grec à l'apocalypse musulmane', *MEFRA*, 96, 1984, pp. 29–51).

De Polignac also draws attention to the incomplete nature of Alexander's achievements according to the Arabic tradition. Despite the divine inspiration behind his mission, he himself never becomes a prophet, unlike the figure who is sometimes introduced as his companion, al-Khidr. He thus comes up against limits that prevent him from attaining to Revelation, as much when he rises into the heavens and when he descends to the bottom of the oceans as when he reaches the edges of the world. Clearly we cannot follow up every aspect of this image of Alexander in Arab thought, as revealed by de Polignac's very rich research. To return to the theme of the ambiguity of Alexander's medieval image, let us simply note a Persian poem dating from the thirteenth century, *The Romance of Alexander* by Nezami. This author portrays Alexander as a pupil of the great philosophers of antiquity, which include Aristotle but also the Indian sages, the famous brahmins of the Indian tradition. At once a conqueror, a philosopher and a prophet, Alexander is the ideal sovereign, according to the model elaborated by the Arab philosopher al-Farabi. This philosophical emphasis can be explained by the impact being made at this time by the translations of the great works of Greek philosophy, with which the name of Averroes remains associated.

But Alexander the philosopher was soon to disappear from Arab literature. What remained was the ambiguous image of a king presented now as a model, now as a persecutor. But in an Arab world increasingly prey to internal conflicts and retreating, in the West, before the reconquest by the Christians, and in the East in the face of the Ottoman threat, this figure was mentioned more and more infrequently.

A similar pattern can be traced in the evolution of the image of Alexander in the works of Judaism. We need not return to the origins of this image: positive in Alexandrian circles and in the part of Judaea under Ptolemaic domination, but negative from the reign of Antiochus IV and the uprising of the Maccabees onwards. In apocalyptic literature (the Book of Daniel), Alexander is the instrument of God; in Flavius Josephus' account, he is welcomed to Jerusalem; in the Jewish version of the *Romance*, he is converted to the faith of the one true God. Then, in the Babylonian Talmud, Alexander becomes the interlocutor of sages, 'Israelite brahmins' (F. de Polignac), that is to say the elders of the Babylonian community. The Fall of the Temple in 70, the failure of the revolt of Bar Kochba in 135, and the transformation of Jerusalem into a Roman colony all resulted in the increasing dispersion of the Jews. A religious centre still remained in. Javneh, near Jaffa, but the principal home of Judaism was now Sassanid Babylonia. Here, the Talmud was produced, a commentary on the Torah which collected together a corpus of juridical regulations, interspersed with many digressions. Some of these relate to conversations between Alexander and the elders. They reproduce some of the themes tackled in the *Romance*. For instance, Alexander asks the Brahmins, 'Which is more vast, the earth or the sea?', to which they reply, 'The earth, because the sea itself is contained by the earth' (*Romance*, III, 6, 4). In the Talmud (VI, 5), the question is slightly different, as is the reply, but the relationship between the interlocutors is similar: 'He asked them, "Is it better to live on the earth or on the sea?" "On the earth, for those who venture on the sea regain their peace of mind only when they disembark on solid land."' Here is another type of question, and it evokes a significantly different reply. 'He then asked, "What came first, the night or the day?" They said, "The night, for that which is born begins to grow in the darkness of the entrails, then comes into the light to join the day"' (*Romance*, III, 6, 7). In the Talmud, the passage runs as follows: 'He asked them, "What was created first, the light or the darkness?" He was told, "That question cannot be resolved." Why did they not tell him that the darkness was created first, since it is written, "And the earth was without form, and void" [Genesis, I, 2]? And God said "Let there be light", and there was light?' (Genesis, I, 3).

Other questions, of a different kind, tackle the question of royal authority. In particular, the Talmud ends with an account of an adventure of which several other versions exist. Alexander, determined to find the way through Africa, reaches the entrance to paradise. He asks for the door to be opened, but is told, 'This is the gate of the Lord through which the righteous shall pass' (Psalms, 118, 20). Then Alexander, pointing out that he is king, asks to be given something important.

He was given an eyeball. He weighed it against all his gold and silver, but put together they did not weigh as much as the eyeball. 'What is happening?' Alexander asked the rabbis. 'This is the eye of a human being, which is never filled.' 'How do you know the human eye is never filled?' 'Cover it with a little dust, and it will become lighter, for it is said: the resting place of the dead and the abyss are insatiable; likewise the eyes of a man.'

In another version, Alexander comes to the outskirts of a town on the banks of the river Ganges. A doorless wall stands before him. Some of the king's companions find a little window, and knock on it. An old man appears and hands them a stone. Alexander carries it back to Babylon. There, an old Jewish sage reveals to him the meaning of this stone whose weight can never be balanced against heaps of silver and gold but which, covered by dust, grows lighter. The meaning of both anecdotes is the same: although God may be favouring Alexander's plans, he is also telling him that there is one limit that he can never overcome: death, which will put an end to his power.

There are other stories and anecdotes in the Jewish tradition that are reminiscent of this image of Alexander: the presence of the bones of the prophet Jeremiah in the foundations of Alexandria, the protection offered to the ten tribes, the construction of a wall to contain God's enemies, Gog and Magog, a tale also to be found in the Arab myth of Alexander, as we have seen.

In the Talmud, unlike in the Jewish version of the *Romance*, Alexander is not a devotee of the religion of the one God. Rather, he is a man of power whom God uses as an instrument for his own designs, at the same time warning him of the limits and the incomplete nature of the power that he believes to be invested in himself.

Like the Alexander of Arab literature, the Alexander of the Jewish tradition was later to be affected by the influence of Greek philosophy, through the Arab translations, and would once again be seen as a philosopher king.

This brief summary does not claim to give an account of all the aspects of the myth of Alexander during the medieval period. The rediscovery of the Greek historians, who were beginning to be translated into Latin and then into the European languages, was soon to confer a new dimension upon the myth of Alexander, a dimension more political than theological or philosophical, and much less romantic. Let us limit ourselves to following this development in the France of the seventeenth and eighteenth centuries, where an absolute monarchical power had developed reminiscent of that of the Macedonian king.

CHAPTER 18

The image of Alexander in seventeenth- and eighteenth-century France

In the fifteenth century, the Alexander historians were rediscovered, and from then on the hero of the *Romance* tended to give way to the historical figure. Within the confines of the present work we cannot attempt to tackle the problem of the evolution of the image of Alexander from the Renaissance onward, throughout the Christian world. Again we shall limit ourselves to France, on which a fairly recent book has provided valuable information (*L'Ecole des princes ou Alexandre disgracié*, by C. Grell and C. Michel, Paris, 1988).

The first French translation of Quintus Curtius dates from 1468, and Amyot's translation of Plutarch appeared in the mid-sixteenth century. Amyot also produced a translation of Diodorus in 1585. Arrian was not translated until 1646. We can be certain that the dominant image of Alexander in the France of the seventeenth and eighteenth centuries was first and foremost that of the victorious warrior and absolute monarch. The siege of the Protestant stronghold of La Rochelle (1627–8) by Richelieu was compared to the siege of Tyre. Although the colourless Louis XIII could hardly be identified with Alexander, the Great Condé, the victor of Rocroi, was another matter. But after the Fronde, it was obviously Louis XIV who became the new Alexander. The painter Le Brun was commissioned to produce a whole series of pictures representing episodes taken from the career of Alexander. Other painters also developed the theme. The moments chosen illustrate either the king's generosity (*The Queens of Persia at Alexander's feet: Darius' Tent*) or his heroic warrior feats (*The Crossing of the Granicus, The Battle of Arbela, The Entry into Babylon*).

In the theatre too, the French king was identified with the Macedonian conqueror, as many dramatic works testify, among them Racine's *Alexandre*. The first performance was given in the theatre of the Palais-Royal on 4 December 1665, and the play went on to be a huge success when Racine transferred it to the players of the Hotel de Bourgogne, the rivals of the Palais-Royal company. In 1666 the text was published, preceded by an address to the king and a preface. The address to the king drew a parallel between Alexander and Louis XIV, 'a king whose fame stretches as far as that of this conqueror, and before which it is fair to say that all the peoples of the world fall silent, just as the ancient texts say of Alexander'. In his preface, Racine justified the title he had given his play, despite the fact that Alexander makes a late entrance, and Porus, the Indian king, 'seems greater than Alexander'. It is true that, although the play ends with the 'generosity' of Alexander, who restores Porus' states to him, the long tirades pronounced by the Indian king and Queen Axiane, with whom he is in love, express some quite severe criticisms of the conqueror. To Taxile, who advises him to negotiate with Alexander, the Indian king replies:

> Peace! How could you accept it from his hand? What? When
> we have seen him disturb the happy calm of our lands with
> the most horrible wars and, sword in hand, invade our states
> to attack kings who did nothing to offend him; when we have
> seen him pillage whole provinces and choke our rivers with
> the blood of our subjects, and when heaven may be preparing
> to abandon him to us, I should wait for this tyrant to deign to
> pardon us?
>
> (lines 140–8)

The tirade that Axiane addresses to Alexander the conqueror is in much the same strain:

> But, Sire, is it not enough that for you everything is possible?
> What more can you want, after casting so many kings into
> chains and, with impunity, making the whole universe groan,
> capturing so many towns and strewing the banks of the
> Hydaspes with so many corpses? . . . No, however much you

flatter yourself that you are kind, you are nothing but a tyrant.

(lines 1074–85)

Racine had read Plutarch and also Quintus Curtius and Justin, from whom he borrows the character Cléophile, making her the sister of Taxile (Quintus Curtius, VIII, 10, and Justin, XII, 7–9). Racine was not unaware of the criticisms which, even in antiquity, part of the tradition levelled at Alexander. It is interesting to see how, despite his disclaimers, he plays on the double aspects of Alexander's image, aspects that were more and more recognised from the mid-seventeenth century onward. Royal absolutism was beginning to be questioned increasingly at this time, and Alexander's image was accordingly being 'depreciated', as Grell and Michel put it. Even if his warrior valour was not called into question, emphasis was laid on the dramatic evolution of his character and the corruption of his original qualities. In the eighteenth century, Alexander became the symbol of rulers who persecuted the *philosophes*: attention was drawn to the Callisthenes affair and to the murder of Cleitus. On the eve of the Revolution, Mably's judgement of Alexander was unequivocal:

What is the point of conquests whose sole goal is to ravage the earth? Is there a sufficiently odious description for a conqueror who always looks ahead, never casting a glance behind him, and who, marching on with the din and impetuosity of a river in spate, rushes ahead and eventually disappears, leaving behind him nothing but ruins? What did Alexander hope for? Did he not sense that conquests so swift, so extensive and so disproportionate to the Macedonian forces could not last? If he could not perceive so obvious a truth, if he never worked out the bases and aims of his father's policies, the understanding of this hero must have been remarkably limited. If, on the other hand, he was well aware of all this, yet still could not moderate his aspirations, he was nothing but a madman worthy of the hatred of all men.

(*Observations sur l'histoire de la Grèce et des causes de la prospérité et des malheurs des Grecs*, 1766)

However, that condemnation was not unanimous. In the seventeenth and eighteenth centuries, both in France and elsewhere, Alexander remained an exceptional figure in many domains: in painting, in the theatre and in the writings of the *philosophes*. Of the many texts that Grell and Michel cite in the appendix to their book, let me pick out three particularly telling examples. The first is an extract from Rollin's *Histoire ancienne*. Following the prophecies of the Book of Daniel, he regards Alexander's conquests as an expression of the will of God. Nevertheless, if the greatness of the Macedonian king is undeniable, so is the fact that the conqueror's image degenerates as he advances further and further into Asia, and adopts eastern customs. What a shame he did not remain true to his original qualities:

Up to this point, was there anything lacking to Alexander's fame? His warrior valour was dazzling. Kindness, clemency, moderation and wisdom crowned all his feats, shining with such glory that their merit was infinitely enhanced. Suppose that in this state, to safeguard his glory and his victories, Alexander had called a halt, set a brake on his own ambitions and, in the same manner that he had toppled Darius, now replaced him on his throne. Suppose he had made Asia Minor, inhabited virtually throughout by Greeks, free and liberated from Persia, then declared himself the protector of all the towns and states of Greece, assuring them of their liberty and allowing them to live in accordance with their own laws. And after all that, suppose he had returned to Macedonia and there, content with the legitimate boundaries of his empire, derived all his glory and joy from making it a happy land of abundance, allowing law and justice to flourish, honouring virtue, and winning the love of his subjects. And suppose that, finally, having – through the terror of his military might and even more through the fame of his virtues – won the admiration of the entire universe, he had found himself somehow the arbiter of all peoples, exerting over all hearts a sway far more stable and honourable than that which is based on fear . . . : supposing all that, would there ever have been a prince greater, more glorious and more deserving of respect than Alexander?

(Histoire ancienne, VI, pp. 690–1)

By rewriting history in this way, Rollin restored Alexander to the image that had been elaborated by one part of posterity.

The second text comes from Montesquieu's *L'Esprit des lois*. The author here draws attention to Alexander's behaviour towards those he vanquished:

Not only did he allow peoples to keep their own mores, he also left them their own civic laws, and in many cases even the kings and governors that he had found in place. He set Macedonians at the head of his troops and local people at the head of governments, preferring to run the risk of a few individual cases of treachery (which did sometimes occur) rather than general revolts. He respected the ancient traditions and all the local monuments to the glory and pride of these peoples. The kings of the Persians had destroyed the temples of the Greeks, the Babylonians and the Egyptians. He restored them. There were not many nations that submitted to him on whose altars he did not make sacrifices. It seemed that he conquered them only in order to become the particular monarch of each of those nations and the first citizen in every town. The Romans conquered so as to destroy everything. He wanted to conquer so as to preserve everything. In whatever country he overran, his first thoughts and plans were always to do something that might increase its prosperity and power.

He committed two bad deeds: he burned down Persepolis and he killed Cleitus. He made those deeds famous by his repentance, so his criminal actions were forgotten and his respect for virtue was remembered, and those bad deeds were regarded as misfortunes rather than personal crimes. Posterity perceived the beauty of his soul alongside his lack of control and his weaknesses, and felt that he was to be pitied and it was impossible to hate him any longer.

(L'Esprit des lois, XIII, 14)

Montesquieu's is a moderate judgement. He does not conceal Alexander's weaknesses, but assesses them fairly, the better to exalt the quality which, in Montesquieu's eyes, was the most essential of all: his respect for the peoples he conquered.

Voltaire's judgement is less nuanced. In his *Essai sur les moeurs*, written a few years after *L'Esprit des lois*, the fact that Alexander encouraged an extraordinary development in trade is what counts the most in his favour:

> Alexander, in the course of a very short life and in the midst of his conquests, built Alexandria and Skandera, refounded Samarkand, which subsequently became the seat of Tamerlane's empire, and built towns almost in India. He founded Greek colonies beyond the Oxus, sent back to Greece observations of Babylon, and transformed the trade of Asia, Europe and Africa, making Alexandria its world centre. That it seems to me is why Alexander was greater than Tamerlane, Genghis, and any other conqueror that one might want to set in comparison alongside him.
>
> (cited by Grell and Michel, *L'Ecole des princes*, p. 189)

In the 'Alexander' entry in his *Questions sur l'Encyclopédie*, Voltaire remarks, 'It is no longer permissible to say anything about Alexander that is not new and that does not destroy the historical stories, both physical and moral, that have disfigured the history of the only great man ever seen among the conquerors of Asia.' And further on, after addressing the question of the deification of Alexander and the contradictory evidence relating to the death of Callisthenes, he concludes, 'All that is really certain is that Alexander, at the age of 24, had conquered Persia in three battles; that his genius was as great as his valour; that he changed the face of Asia, of Greece, of Egypt, and also that of world trade' (ibid., pp. 198–200).

Those positive verdicts from the two great eighteenth-century *philosophes* require us to modify the idea that Alexander's image underwent a depreciation in France. The list of dramatic works about him confirms this, for virtually all of them stress Alexander's generosity and clemency, as Racine did.

What is new from the last decades of the eighteenth century

onward is that the sources of the history of Alexander began to attract considerable criticism. In 1775 a rather bizarre figure, Guillaume Emmanuel Joseph Guilhem de Clermont-Lodève, the Baron of Sainte-Croix, published a work entitled *Examen critique des anciens historiens d'Alexandre*. In this work, he makes no bones about questioning the statements of Arrian, Plutarch and Quintus Curtius relating to both Alexander's behaviour towards the Persians and his personal mores. In particular, Sainte-Croix attacks Montesquieu for 'claiming that Alexander adopted the customs of the Persians so as not to upset them by making them adopt the customs of the Greeks'. He adds,

> Arrian also justified those changes (VII, 29), but I myself cannot applaud them. To adopt the customs of the vanquished is to insult the glory of the victor; it is to destroy the happy distinction that encourages the warlike enthusiasm that carries one to conquest. The luxury to which the customs of the Asiatics led would have inevitably undermined the courage of the Macedonian soldiers by stifling the noble ardour that flares up when the soul reacts to objects that affect it forcefully. Alexander can surely not have been unaware of this common truth.

Sainte-Croix reproaches Plutarch for presenting Alexander as a man in control of his desires, in particular when he rejects the two young boys offered to him by Philoxenus, as 'illicit objects proscribed by nature'. He similarly attacks Quintus Curtius for concealing Alexander's relations with the eunuch Bagoas and for claiming 'that the Macedonian monarch never indulged in any pleasure that was not within the bounds of nature' (cited by Grell and Michel, *L'Ecole des princes*, p. 200).

We shall be returning to the matter of Alexander's real or supposed homosexuality. But it is worth noting that both his defenders (here, Plutarch and Quintus Curtius) and his severe critic (Sainte-Croix) are at one in considering homosexuality to be 'against nature'.

Needless to say, the revolutionary period did not make a hero of Alexander. He could not be set up as a model, for he was the very image of a cruel despot. However, even if the monarch was disparaged, the conqueror still had the power to fascinate generals hungry for glory. It was clearly not simply by chance that Bonaparte surrounded himself with scholars when he embarked on his Egyptian campaign, although it was Rome, rather than Alexander, that served as a model for Napoleon.

By the beginning of the nineteenth century, antiquity was no longer 'the fashion'. The day of history had dawned.

CHAPTER 19

The historians and Alexander's image

As we have seen, in the late eighteenth century the sources for the history of Alexander began to be submitted to critical examination. This was symptomatic of one of the aspects of the historical methodology of the time that was adopted, above all, in Germany: *Quellenforschung*, or research into sources. It was also in Germany that, in 1833, Johann Gustav Droysen produced the first *History of Alexander* based on a minute examination of the source material. Furthermore, this history was viewed in a Hegelian perspective and set within the context of the general evolutionary movement of societies. This young German scholar considered his work on Alexander to constitute the first part of a *History of the Hellenistic World*, an expression more or less 'invented' by Droysen. The third to the first centuries BC, long regarded as centuries of 'decline' for Greek civilisation, were now re-evaluated in so far as they represented Hellenism's 'regeneration' of the eastern world. And that 'regeneration' was itself a product of Alexander's determination to unite the conquerors and the conquered: 'If Alexander had been content to conquer Asia in order to give it to the Hellenes and Macedonians, and if he had allowed them to reduce the Asiatic populations to slavery, the Hellenes and Macedonians would have become Asiatics in the worst sense of the term, all the faster' (*Alexandre le Grand*, Brussels, 1991, p. 458).

What Droysen meant by 'Asiatics in the worst sense of the term' was slaves subject to a despot. For although he believed the conquest had revealed how 'shaky, mildewed, and flawed' the Asiatic world was, that world had produced ancient civilisations that could not but enrich the knowledge of its conquerors.

Alexander's principal merit was to have understood this and to have made it possible for such a fusion to come about, even if he was unable to see the process through to completion. The foundation of new towns, the opening up of roads and the circulation of coined money all favoured such a fusion, the crucial elements of which were 'the ardent vitality of Greece, which aspired to find a body, and the inert masses of Asia, who aspired to find a soul' (p. 463). The fusion was to 'stimulate art, science, and religion, and give an unexpected impetus to the intellectual and moral life of this period' (p. 464).

As Droysen saw it, possibly the most important consequences lay at the religious level:

> Even if we accept that the deities, myths and cults of paganism constituted a live and direct expression of the ethnic and historical diversity of the Mediterranean peoples, we must also recognise that they presented an almost insurmountable obstacle to the work of unification upon which Alexander had embarked. The unity that he wished to establish had first to be embodied by himself. As always, he went straight to the heart of the problem, welcoming into his immediate entourage, on an equal footing, the Lycian seer Aristander, the Hindu ascetic Calanus, and the Persian magus Austhanes, and offering prizes and sacrifices to the deities of the Egyptians, the Persians, the Babylonians, the Baal of the Syrians, and the Jehovah of the Jews.
>
> (p. 467)

By so doing, he paved the way for the triumph of the single god:

> People for the first time glimpsed the possibility that all these populations were, in more or less appropriate ways, honouring a single deity; they were all, in a more or less profound way, seeking to express the same intuition of the supernatural, the Absolute, and the Sovereign Good, and the differences between the names, attributes, and functions of their respective deities were merely external, ephemeral, and illusory phenomena.
>
> (p. 468)

The German historiography of the nineteenth century was to be deeply influenced by Droysen, aided and abetted by the force of circumstances just when a strong push for German unity was being made. It was, to be sure, Philip's Macedon – identified with Prussia – rather than Alexander's empire that was regarded as a model. But Alexander's universalist dreams also chimed with Romantic Germany. Elsewhere, in England and in France, with George Grote and Victor Duruy, there was a growing recognition of the formation of what Nicole Loraux and Pierre Vidal-Naquet have called 'bourgeoise Athens'. But in Germany, Alexander's achievement, when set in opposition to a decadent Asiatic world and a degenerate Greece, tended increasingly to symbolise the superiority of the Nordic peoples (in this instance the Macedonians) over the Mediterranean peoples; and the person of Alexander the conqueror was exalted as a model leader.

In 1975, at the colloquium devoted to Alexander organised by the Fondation Hardt, Professor Badian of Harvard launched a carefully constructed attack against the echoes of that historiography that were to be found, from 1933 onward, in the works of historians such as Helmut Berve and his pupil Fritz Schachermeyr. In particular, Badian cited the latter's *Indogermanen und Orient*, published in 1944, in which Alexander is taken to task on the grounds that he, a representative of the 'pure, Nordic race', committed a 'biological sacrilege' by encouraging a mixture of the races and abandoning historical traditions. Schachermeyr was later to repudiate his 1944 book, and remains one of the greatest historians of Alexander, an Alexander represented as a 'Nietzschean superman'.

At about the same time, William Tarn published his *Alexander the Great* in Cambridge. This British historian, who was far more pragmatic, represented Alexander as a rational man who never believed in his divine origin. He undertook the conquest of Asia with the aim of bringing the advantages of the Greek civilisation to the peoples of the East. In this sense, Tarn carried on Droysen's line on Alexander. Alexander was an idealist who dreamed of uniting the human race. But Badian, again, detected in Tarn a perfect example of a Victorian gentleman, particularly with regard to the matter of Alexander's sexuality. Tarn represented Alexander as faithful solely to his legitimate wife, never indulging in relations with mistresses, let alone with pretty boys. This Alexander resorted to violence only when forced to do so, as in the cases of Parmenion and Cleitus. It was an idealised image, partly inspired by Plutarch, which deliberately blotted out every aspect of Alexander's achievement and every action of his that belied that image.

Tarn's *Alexander the Great* was to be translated into many languages and, for several decades, dominated the historiography of the conqueror, particularly in textbooks and encyclopedias. However, those decades were also the years of 'decolonisation' and the collapse of the empires established in the course of the nineteenth century, foremost among them those of Britain and France. Now Alexander's expedition took on a new look. It was no longer the realisation of a Utopian and universalist dream, but quite simply a colonialist operation. The consequences of the conquest of the eastern world by the Graeco-Macedonians could now be analysed around the model of the acculturation of those colonised. That, in part, is what Edouard Will and Claude Orrieux do in their fine book, *Ioudaïsmos–Hellenismos*, mentioned above, in which the model of that acculturation helps them to illuminate the problem of the Hellenisation of the Jews. Badian evoked a similar attitude in his contribution to the colloquium at the Fondation Hardt, when he remarked that writing the history of Alexander would now involve not only renouncing the image of the charismatic leader but furthermore adopting the point of view of the conquered as much as that of the conquerors.

In recent years, more books on Alexander have been published. But it seems that nowadays any idea of a comprehensive interpretation of this figure has been rejected. Without necessarily opting for minimalism, authors try to stick to such 'facts' as can be established by comparing the literary sources, without favouring any one tradition over the rest and, above all, by replacing those sources within their cultural context, as Pierre Vidal-Naquet does in his postface to Pierre Savinel's translation of Arrian. Furthermore, they endeavour where possible to take account of the evidence provided by archaeology, epigraphy and numismatics. They refrain from passing value judgements on the man, and try instead to weigh up the consequences of his brief reign, in particular with regard to the evolution of the concept of royalty and the creation of a new form of monarchy in the states that emerged from Alexander's conquest.

They attempt to trace the origins of the mythical figure of the conqueror (Paul Goukowsky). Above all, as recent works attest, it is towards the new world born from the conquest that the latest researches are devoted.

However, if historians have given up attempting to fathom Alexander's real intentions or judging the man's qualities, novelists have stepped in to replace them. The authors of modern novels devoted to Alexander belong to a long tradition. In concluding this rapid survey of the myth of Alexander, let us now try to follow the evolution of that tradition by considering a couple of examples.

CHAPTER 20

From the *Alexander Romance* to novels about Alexander

In the twentieth century and outside the field of historical scholarship, what becomes of the romantic hero whose image we have tried to trace down the centuries? To reply to that question, let me limit myself to what I believe to be two telling examples. The first is a novel by Klaus Mann, the son of Thomas Mann, first published in 1929. The second is an Italian novel, French and English translations of which have recently appeared in paperback editions aimed at a vast public.

Klaus Mann's novel, *Alexander. Roman der Utopie*, translated into French, with a preface by Jean Cocteau, in 1931, is chiefly inspired by the account of the Pseudo-Callisthenes but also bears the stamp of its time, the years following World War I. It is presented as both a historical novel and a kind of personal confession. In his autobiography, *Der Wendepunkt* (*The Turning Point*), Klaus Mann notes the reasons why he undertook this novel: 'What attracted me to my new hero was the almost criminal insistence of his dream, the immoderation of his adventure' – the dream of unifying the world and, by eliminating its conflicts, making it happy. That project of unifying the world had also featured in both the ancient historians and the *Alexander Romance*.

However, although that Utopian dimension does indeed lie at the heart of Klaus Mann's book, as its subtitle underlines, the reader is bound to be struck by another factor that is particularly revealing of the author's personality: namely, the sublimated vision of homosexuality. This finds expression early on in the book, in the loving friendship that links Alexander to Kleitos (Cleitus) and Hephestion (Hephaistion), and also in the attraction Aristotle felt for the adolescent Alexander. It is expressed even more forcefully in Mann's interpretation of Pausanias' murder of Philip: Pausanias seeks revenge for Philip's violation of Kleitos, with whom Pausanias is himself in love. But this sublimated homosexuality is above all expressed in the insistent description of the physical charms of the young boys who surround Alexander and those of Alexander himself.

Pausanias is described as 'a superb creature with an insolent, totally effeminate beauty. His mouth, whether pouting or expansively smiling, drove men and women alike mad; so too did the teasing or painfully sentimental gaze of his grey eyes shaded by long, delicate lashes. Above his soft, sweetly rounded brow, as pale as ivory, his glossy, smooth, chestnut-coloured hair curled thickly.' In similar vein, after landing in Asia, Alexander's young companions are busy training. 'Their naked bodies had been exercised and bronzed in the gymnasium. Naked, they moved with an even greater freedom than when clothed in their leather tunics. They would stretch, laughing, then suddenly fall upon one another and wrestle.'

Alexander would walk about with 'his arms intertwined with those of Hephestion' under the ironical and jealous eye of Kleitos. 'His greatest desire was simply to be a young man among other young men, and to participate in their company, which seemed to him more splendid and healthy than any union between a man and a woman.' Kleitos' death comes about in the context of these amorous relationships. Kleitos has rejected Alexander, forcing him to make do with the passive love of the weak Hephestion in whose arms he takes refuge, weeping for three whole days for the one he loved in vain.

Even more telling is the account of Alexander's wedding night with Roxane. Despite all her attempts to arouse her husband's desire, Alexander is unable to make love to her and, in despair, evokes the memory of Kleitos: 'Alas, the one whom I would have loved to clasp in my arms is the one I killed.'

This Roxane, like a number of the other women in the novel, is portrayed as a sinister figure. 'Her nose was like a weapon and beneath her painted, many-coloured lids, her gaze was calculating, that of a bird of prey. She behaved towards the king in a crushingly polite manner, her every movement ceremonious – the way she walked, the way she inclined her face, her complicated coiffure, and the manner in which her hard lips shaped words of meticulous malice.' In the end, it is with Bagoas, presented here not as a eunuch but as a very young hermaphrodite, that the king finds release for his senses.

This presence of homosexuality can certainly be explained by the importance of pederastic relations in ancient Greece. This is not the place to enter into an analysis of the phenomenon. But it is quite clear that the relation between the *erastès*, a mature man, and the *eromenos*, an adolescent, was of an initiatory nature and did not imply a definitive choice of sexuality from which women were excluded. Klaus Mann's Alexander is not simply a young ephebe. And in his links with his companions, we may discern a Platonic influence. But all the same, the choice of a particular kind of sexuality is definitely made, and it is also the choice made by the book's author. It was not by chance that Klaus Mann wrote two other biographies, one devoted to Tchaikovsky, the other to Ludwig II of Bavaria.

But this aspect of the novel should not make us forget the other meaning that Klaus Mann gives to Alexander's adventure: the dream of a Utopia which is destroyed because power corrupts. Mann conceals none of the episodes of violence and excess, nor the crimes that were committed. As the story unfolds, the hero turns into 'the Macedonian despot, tormenter of the Greeks'. Falling increasingly under eastern influence, he is seduced by the discourse of the Brahmins and also by Queen Candace. Their physical relationship marks the beginning of his disintegration. For although he feels a real 'joy' in the queen's arms, it is only thanks to a kind of imposture. He pretends to be Hephestion, thereby doubly betraying his dearest friend (a small alteration is made here to the *Romance* of the Pseudo-Callisthenes, in which Alexander adopts the identity of Antigonus). And just as he is beginning to experience 'a sensation of beatitude', he is forced to flee when one of Candace's sons bursts in, intent upon killing him. After this, Alexander is determined never again to give way to such feelings, and becomes harder than ever. 'The further he advanced in his empire, the more threatening his look became. He was no longer recognisable. In the past he had shown himself to be violent, but this calm cruelty that his face expressed was something new.' He was also becoming increasingly orientalised, even to the point of refusing to receive his Greek-speaking subjects. In Mann's novel, as in the accounts of the ancient historians, it is this orientalisation that explains his rift with the Macedonians in the army. But here this rupture takes on an even more dramatic character in that it even affects Hephestion. It is because the king has refused to listen to Hephestion that the death of his friend provokes such a mad frenzy in Alexander:

> The king launched himself on to the corpse. He was howling, frothing at the mouth. People had to restrain him, but he fought them off, his eyes bloodshot. You could never have believed that a mortal could produce such cries. They expressed neither mourning nor any suffering of a human nature, but a sense of abandonment, a despair that is not that of a human being but can only be known by despairing gods.

From this point on, the tyrant's mask hides a terrible anguish that Alexander can only dull by dint of frenetic activity: 'He lived amid his projects and his immoderate plans, hardly sleeping at night and working without let-up. Meanwhile, he offered up sacrifices and received diviners' (and slept, deeply drugged, alongside Bagoas).

Then comes the episode of the last battle, followed within a few days by his death, in the arms of an angel to whom Alexander has confessed his sins and whose parting words are, 'You will return in another form.' Alexander's response is, 'To establish the kingdom, my angel? To establish the kingdom?' It is an ending that looks forward to a resurrection, possibly of Dionysus but also, and perhaps even more, the resurrection of Christ.

This novel by Klaus Mann enlists one's sympathy on several scores. It certainly reveals the impact that the image of Alexander made on a young writer who was soon forced into exile by the advent of Nazism. The Alexander of Valerio Massimo Manfredi, a contemporary Italian writer, whom we shall now, at the end of this survey, consider, is a very different figure. This long novel, in three volumes, translated into French under the title *Alexandre le Grand*

(Paris, Plon, 1999; Pocket, 2001) and into English as *Alexander the Great* (Pan Macmillan, 2001–2) has reached a large readership in France, Italy and the United Kingdom. It does not follow the tradition of the Pseudo-Callisthenes, although the author acknowledges that he 'occasionally' consulted him. Valerio Manfredi endorses the interpretations of all four principal historians, Diodorus, Quintus Curtius, Plutarch and Arrian, without, however, seeking to reconcile them. He is a novelist, not a historian. The choices that he makes are primarily of a 'narrative' nature, and in the author's note to the last volume of his novel, he states clearly that 'it is not the task of a novel to unravel problems that have been widely debated in the historical literature'. He is accordingly essentially faithful to the sources, which, as we know, are themselves reconstructions and are, moreover, regarded with circumspection by scholars. At the same time, his language is 'relatively contemporary'. For example, he translates *strategos* as 'general', which is not at all shocking but makes his repeated use of the terms *hetairoi* and *pezhetairoi* rather surprising. His concern to communicate in the modern idiom is expressed, in the first instance, by his use of terms to render personal relations that are unexpected in a 'royal' context; Alexander calls Philip 'Father' and Olympias 'Mother'.

The overall composition of the novel also reflects a conscious choice. The first volume ends with the departure for Asia, so is chiefly concerned with Alexander's childhood and education. Only a hundred pages or so are devoted to the first two years of his reign. Similarly, the second volume ends with the founding of Alexandria. Only the third volume deals with the campaigns to which the ancients paid the most attention: the end of the war against Darius, the conquest of his royal capitals, the difficult operations carried out in the upper satrapies, and finally India and the return journey. The novel is remarkable for two features: one is the virtual absence of magical elements, in accordance with author's declared desire 'to tell one of the greatest adventures of all time in a realistic and engaging fashion'; the other is the attention paid to describing the most famous sieges (Miletus, Halicarnassus, Tyre) as precisely as possible, and also the battle of Issus, for which the author claims to have carried out 'a field visit'.

The image that Valerio Manfredi creates of his hero is close enough to that of Plutarch's *Life of Alexander*, that is to say it is, all in all, positive. Alexander is a spirited and proud young man, and in consequence clashes with his father. But when Philip is struck down by Pausanias, Alexander is deeply shocked. 'He held him while the blood flowed strong and red, wetting his clothes, his arms and his hands. "Father!" he shouted as the sobs came, and he held him tight. "Father, no!" and Philip felt his son's burning tears on his bloodless cheeks.'

This Alexander tenderly loves his mother and his sister Cleopatra. He has nothing in common with Klaus Mann's hero, who is so attracted by the bodies of boys. A young slave-girl initiates him to physical love. Later he develops a passionate love for Barsine, the widow of his opponent Memnon. After her tragic death, he marries Darius' daughter Stateira, whom he loves with great tenderness. But it is with Roxane that Alexander discovers real love: 'Then Alexander understood that he had never really loved anyone up to that point, that he had lived through affairs of deep and intense passion, of burning desire, of affection, of admiration, but never love. This was love.'

But, obviously enough, Alexander is not just a great lover. He is a remarkable tactician, a man of great courage, who exposes himself to danger in every battle, narrowly escaping death on several occasions, a skilful politician who knows how to conciliate his enemies, and also a sage who loves to talk with the Indian Calanus. Finally, he dreams of putting an end to the old antagonism between the Greeks and the Persians and, before his soldiers, he justifies the marriages organised between Macedonians and Iranian women in Susa: 'This is the only way we can create a future for our conquests, to wipe out the rancour, the hatred, the desire for revenge – a single homeland, a single king, a single people. That is my plan and this is also my will.'

But despite his admiration for his hero, Valerio Manfredi cannot ignore the reprehensible actions that the tradition attributed to Alexander: the fate of Thebes, the burning of Persepolis, the trial of Philotas, the assassinations of Parmenion and Cleitus, and the death of Callisthenes. In the case of Thebes, Manfredi echoes the tradition according to which the decision was taken by the council of the League of Corinth 'by a large majority, and although

Alexander himself was against it, he could not oppose it because he had proclaimed that he would respect the Council's motion'.

The burning of Persepolis is justified not only by the orgiastic night that precedes it, which involves the young courtesan Thais, but also by the fact that just before entering the city Alexander encounters a miserable group of horribly mutilated men, Greeks taken prisoner by the Persians in the course of the various campaigns. When old Parmenion reproaches Alexander for the destruction of this great work of art, Alexander's reply is as follows:

> I will answer you. I will tell you why I did this. I permitted the sack of Persepolis because in this way the Greeks know that I am the real avenger, I am the one they can identify with, the only one who has succeeded in bringing a centuries-old duel to an end. And I wanted it to be a young Athenian woman who torched the palace of Darius and Xerxes.

Philotas is guilty of not reporting a plot that he knew of. But it is the army assembly that condemns him, and Alexander, who is bound to accept the verdict, is none the less shattered by the death of his childhood friend. And when he decides to have Parmenion assassinated, he does so shedding hot tears, first inviting his closest friend to strike him down for it: 'If you think that I have gone beyond every reasonable limit, if you believe that what I am about to do is the action of a heinous tyrant, then kill me.'

This novel destined for a vast readership thus purveys a resolutely positive image of Alexander. We may wonder what prompted the author to create such an image. Was it simply a desire to tell a fine story which, even if it has a sad ending, is of a kind to capture the imagination of a public nurtured on spectacular films? In any great adventure, the hero, despite his weaknesses, must be a man one would wish to resemble, a good son and a good husband but also an exceptional being. This one 'dies at the age of thirty-three [*sic*], having changed the course of History and realised his dream of conquering the world', to quote the blurb of one of the foreign-language paperback editions.

I chose those two novels to conclude this quest for the mythical image of Alexander because I think they demonstrate the ambiguity of both that image and what people have tried to make it express, down the ages. On the basis of the very same sources, Alexander has been portrayed now as a Utopian dreamer, now as a cruel despot, now as a covert seducer of women or a lover of young men, now as a chivalrous hero, now as a brutal drunkard, and also as a philosopher, a Jew, a Muslim and a Christian, if not as Christ himself, who died at the same age.

Faced with such a figure, the historian swept up in the whirl of this kaleidoscope eventually wonders whether his or her work has any value at all. I shall conclude by attempting an answer to that question.

Conclusion

Now, at the end of this biography, is it possible to decide on a reply to the question of what, if any, is the validity of such a work as this?

Alexander the man will always remain a stranger to us, since we can see him only through the eyes of others. At the most, all we can discern are his unquestionable physical qualities of courage and endurance, an immoderate ambition that led him to press on beyond the original aims of the Asian expedition, a keen sense of opportunity that was manifest at not only the military but also the political level, as when he took those whom he had conquered first into the administration of his conquered lands and, later, into their defence.

However, that said, and if we leave aside the psychological dimension that is so dear to novelists but that a historian must approach only with extreme caution, the essential question remains: did Alexander really change the course of history?

Nowadays it is fashionable to stress the continuity of classical Greece, as essentially expressed by the city (polis), right down to the end of the third century. Thanks, in particular, to the testimony of epigraphy, there can be no doubt that the Greek cities of Europe and even those along the west coast of Asia Minor continued to live as in the past, holding assemblies, electing magistrates and honouring benefactors.

Nor did their social structures undergo any important modifications either in the old Greek world or in the eastern territories. So far as we can judge, the same goes for the economic domain. Even the diffusion of coined money, which was limited to particular regions, did not really upset traditional commercial practices.

Finally, as we have seen, although the use of Greek certainly spread, particularly in urban centres, local dialects were resistant. It was only the firm grasp of the Roman administration that imposed linguistic unity on the eastern part of the empire.

And yet... that fragile unity, which was called into question immediately following Alexander's death, did leave some profound traces. First and foremost, it imposed a new form of political power in the eastern basin of the Mediterranean: personal monarchy. This was very different from earlier forms of monarchical power, even if it more or less integrated those. Its difference was based on two principles: on the one hand, the right of the spear, military victory; on the other, the 'royal' qualities of the monarch. Alexander's adventure certainly contributed to the elaboration of this personal monarchy, even if it was his successors who gave it its definitive form. It was probably Ptolemy, son of Lagos, the first king of Hellenistic Egypt, who laid the foundations for it. It was he who, by gaining possession of Alexander's mortal remains, helped to create the Alexander myth. It was also he who, by completing the seizure of the country's resources that was initiated by the Greek Cleomenes of Naucratis, turned Alexandria into not only the preeminent Mediterranean port but also the main centre of Greek intellectual life. In this capacity, it was capable of rivalling even Athens, now that the latter had lost all real independence, forced as it was to accept the presence of a Macedonian garrison in Piraeus and obliged to seek support from one or other of the *diadochi* in order to recover at least a semblance of liberty.

First Ptolemaic Egypt, then Seleucid Syria became the crucible that produced cultural syncretisms which are impossible to ignore and without which it would be hard to understand the ideological and religious ferment of the end of the first millennium AD.

It may be objected that none of the above became manifest until well after Alexander's death. And it is true that, during his brief reign, occupied for virtually the whole time with military operations, nothing really solid could be constructed. But what developed after his death and after the quarrels that set his Companions in opposition to one another was of his making, precisely in the sense that it was his image, the representation given of his actions and his ambitions, that constituted the founding element of what is known as Hellenistic civilisation.

In the last section of this book, in which we have followed up a few lines of research (which it would be interesting to pursue in greater depth), we have seen how important the figure of Alexander became over the centuries. And even if that figure is, to a large extent if not totally, a mythical one, that does not in any way alter the fact that, like any myth, it played a role that no historian can ignore.

It is not a matter of again raising the famous problem of the place and role of individuals in history. To respond negatively by, for instance, quite rightly contrasting the internal developments of societies over the long term with the action of individuals, however prestigious, and then dismissing biography as a genre worthy of the attention of historians, is to fail to appreciate the importance of the mythical dimension. What is true, in that respect, of Alexander is also true of Louis XIV, Napoleon and de Gaulle, to take but three French examples, although of course the historians who write about those three 'heroes' have at their disposal sources of documentation far more extensive than those available to a historian of Alexander. I am aware that my remarks imply breaking with an important tradition. But at the same time they are in tune with a movement that has introduced a new approach to history, one that takes the imaginary into account, along with its place in the evolution of societies.

Alexander's principal
Companions

Antigonus Monophthalmus (the One-eyed) Son of a Macedonian noble, he accompanied Alexander to Asia. In 333, he became the satrap of Phrygia and thereafter his role was that of an administrator rather than a military leader. After Alexander's death, his importance was first established as overall *strategos* (general) in Asia. In this capacity, he led a victorious campaign against Eumenes, the ally in Asia of Polyperchon. His power prompted the other *diadochi* (successors) to form a coalition against him. But, with the aid of his son Demetrius, he strengthened his authority in the Aegean. In 306, he was the first to have himself acclaimed king by his army. He died at Ipsus in 301, bequeathing to Demetrius ambitions still intact, but a diminished empire.

Antipater A Companion to Philip. After the assassination of his father, Alexander, now king, entrusted him with the government of Macedon and with the task of keeping the Greeks under surveillance. He worked hard to maintain links with the League of Corinth, particularly during the war against the Spartan king Agis III, who had managed to form a coalition against Macedon. Antipater defeated this coalition at Megalopolis in 331. Following Alexander's death, he was faced by an uprising on the part of some of the Greeks, led by Athens. Under siege in the fortress of Lamia, in Thessaly, he was relieved by reinforcements sent from Asia and forced the Athenians to accept the presence of a Macedonian garrison in Piraeus and also to adopt an oligarchic regime. After the disappearance of Craterus and Perdiccas, who, immediately following Alexander's death, had shared the guardianship of the two 'kings', Philip

Arrhidaeus and the infant Alexander IV, Antipater was made regent at the conference of Triparadeisus. His death in 319 signalled a resumption of hostilities among the successors.

Callisthenes Callisthenes of Olynthus, Aristotle's nephew, accompanied Alexander to Asia. He undertook to write an account of the conquest. But he could not bring himself to support Alexander's adoption of certain Persian customs. It is uncertain whether he was assassinated on the king's orders or whether he died in prison. His work is known only through the references that later historians make to it. The famous *Alexander Romance* was later attributed to him.

Cassander The son of Antipater. He opposed his father's decision to entrust the regency to Polyperchon and remained solidly established in the Aegean. He managed to seize possession of Macedon and tried to contain the ambitions of Antigonus by forming a coalition against him, which included all the other successors. He too assumed the title of king after 306 and took part in the war that ended with Antigonus' defeat and death at Ipsus (301). However, Cassander was unable to prevent Demetrius from retaining solid support in Greece. His death in 287 set off a new round of wars for the possession of Macedon, wars that came to an end only with the accession of Demetrius' son, Antigonas Gonatas, in 276.

Craterus One of Alexander's generals. He took part in all three great battles in the conquest of Asia. After Parmenion's execution, he received a high command. In 324, Alexander made him responsible for leading the veterans back to Europe. He was thus able to help Antipater to overcome the Greeks who had revolted after Alexander's death was announced. Later, Craterus took part in the war against Perdiccas and Eumenes, and was killed in battle in 321, fighting against the latter.

Demetrius of Phaleron An Athenian philosopher of the Peripatetic school who, in 317, was entrusted by Cassander with the government of Athens, which he then headed for ten years, trying to establish a moderate regime inspired by his master Theophrastus. When Antigonus' son Demetrius captured Athens in 307, Demetrius of Phaleron fled first to Thebes, then to Ptolemy in Alexandria. There, he inspired the two great institutions that were to make Alexandria famous: the museum and the library. Nothing remains of his extensive works except a few fragments preserved by later writers.

Demetrius Poliorcetes The son of Antigonus. He was involved with his father's operations from an early age, and supported his efforts to retain a large portion of Alexander's empire. The naval victory that he won over Ptolemy's fleet in the seas off Cyprus in 306 enabled his father to assume the title of king and to associate Demetrius with his power. In Athens, which he took in 307 and where he resided over several periods, he was the object of a cult that assimilated him to a god. He was famous as a 'besieger of towns' (*poliorcetes*), but nevertheless failed when faced with Rhodes. After Antigonus' death at Ipsus, and having lost his father's Asiatic empire, he retained his authority in Greece and the islands. In 294, he managed to seize Macedon. But he was ejected by Lysimachus and Pyrrhus, the king of Epirus, who then divided Macedon between them. Demetrius set off for Asia, with the idea of winning back Antigonus' empire, but he was taken prisoner by Seleucus and died in 283.

Eumenes of Cardia This Greek, a native of the Thracian Chersonese, accompanied Alexander to Asia and became his secretary. From 330 onward, he was responsible for the royal chancellery. After Alexander's death, on the occasion of the distribution of lands, in Babylon, he was allotted the satrapy of Cappadocia. He remained loyal to Alexander's heirs and clashed with Antigonus, who managed first to confine him to the upper satrapies, then won over his army. Abandoned by his soldiers, Eumenes was condemned to death and was executed in 316.

Harpalus A Macedonian noble and childhood friend of Alexander's, accompanied him on the Asiatic expedition. In 331 he was put in charge of the management of the royal treasury. He may have misappropriated funds while Alexander was campaigning in India. At any rate, at the news of the king's return he fled from Babylon with a force of mercenaries and part of the treasure for which he was responsible. He took refuge in Athens, of which he was an honorary citizen. At first he was rejected, possibly at the instigation of Demosthenes, then was eventually imprisoned. Part of the money that he had brought with him was deposited on the Acropolis. With the aid of accomplices, he managed to escape. But the disappearance of half of the 700 talents deposited in the treasury of Athena led to an enquiry conducted by the Areopagus and charges laid against Demosthenes and several other orators, who were accused of siphoning off this money. Demosthenes, who was sentenced to the payment of a large fine, fled into exile and only returned to Athens at the news of Alexander's death. As for Harpalus, he took refuge in Crete, where he was assassinated in 321.

Hephaistion This Macedonian noble, a childhood friend of Alexander's, was at his side throughout the Asiatic campaign. After 330, he was given an important post of command, with the title of chiliarch or vizier (borrowed from the Iranian hierarchy). His sudden death in 324 was a severe blow to Alexander, who ordered a grandiose funeral for him and raised him to the status of hero, instituting a festival in his honour.

Lysimachus This Companion of Alexander's, of Thessalian origin, was the head of his bodyguard. At the distribution of territories organised in Babylon, after Alexander's death, he received Thrace and part of the Hellespont region. He took part in the war of the successors against Antigonus and in 306 himself took the title of king. Having consolidated his power in the northern Aegean, in 285 he succeeded in becoming the master of Macedon, putting Demetrius to flight. But his split with Seleucus proved fatal, and he died after being defeated at Couroupedion, in 281. His kingdom did not survive him.

Nearchus A native of Crete and a faithful Companion of Alexander, who entrusted him with the command of the fleet on the return from India, all the way from the Indus delta to the mouth of the Tigris. He left a description of India, which was used by both Strabo and Arrian. After the death of Alexander, he transferred to the service of Antigonus and Demetrius. He died in 312.

Parmenion A Macedonian general who served with distinction under Philip. It was no doubt in obedience to Philip's orders that he crossed into Asia in 336. But in the face of the opposition of the Persian forces, he was only able to secure a few strongholds. When Alexander crossed to Asia, Parmenion became his second-in-command of the army. It was despite his prudent advice that Alexander engaged in the Battle of the Granicus. Parmenion nevertheless retained his position of command. But the rift between him and the king became increasingly serious and when he appeared to be implicated in the 'plot' of his son Philotas, he was summarily executed, without trial, at Ecbatana.

Perdiccas As one of Alexander's Companions, he fought at his side throughout the campaign. After the death of Hephaistion and Craterus's departure for Europe, during the last months of Alexander's life, he held a privileged and intimate position. The king's death brought him to prominence. After the compromise thrashed out in Babylon, he became the 'protector' of the kings. But his triumph was short-lived. In 321, when attempting to invade Egypt, he was assassinated by the Macedonian soldiers in his own army.

Philotas One of Parmenion's sons, who took part in Alexander's campaign. His personal ambition and possibly also his refusal to accept the king's orientalisation following the death of Darius caused him, if not to take part in a conspiracy organised within the army, at least not to report it. When denounced, he was brought before the army, condemned and executed.

Polyperchon A Macedonian noble who had taken part in Alexander's campaigns but did not attract much attention during the military operations. Only after the death of Antipater, in 319, did he come to play a political role. He opposed Cassander, in the guise of a defender of Greek liberties, and tried in vain to gain control of Macedon. Eventually he entered the service of Antigonus. It is not known precisely when he died.

Ptolemy As one of Alexander's Companions, he took an active part in the whole campaign and wrote an account of it that was later used by Clitarchus and most of the other historians, Arrian in particular. When Ptolemy had become the master of Egypt, after Alexander's death, he took possession of the king's mortal remains and deposited them first in Memphis, then in Alexandria. Unlike the other successors, he had no designs on Macedon, preferring to strengthen his positions in Egypt, Syria and the islands. In 305 he assumed the title of king (calling himself Ptolemy I Soter), and made Alexandria his capital. There, on the advice of Demetrius of Phaleron, he founded the museum and the library. With the aim of bringing his Greek and Egyptian subjects together, he instituted the cult of the god Sarapis. He died in 285, having taken care to hand on his power to his son Ptolemy II Philadelphus.

Seleucus He accompanied Alexander to Asia, but without performing any outstanding deeds. In 321, when Alexander's empire was divided up at Triparadeisus, he was allotted the satrapy of Babylonia. For a while he was ejected from his Asiatic positions, but then managed not only to recapture but even to increase them, by acquiring Susiania and Media. In 305, he, like the other successors, took the title of king. After the battle of Ipsus, he obtained Cilicia and part of Syria. He thus controlled an immense territory, in which he proceeded to found many towns. Having become the master of Asia and following his victory over Lysimachus at Couroupedion, he briefly considered reconstructing Alexander's empire for his own advantage by seizing Macedon. But in 281 he was assassinated, before putting this plan into action. He had already ensured his succession by sharing his power with Antiochus, his son by his Bactrian wife Apamea, whom he had married in Susa in 324.

Chronology

338	Philip II of Macedon's victory over Athens and its allies at Chaeronea.
337	Formation of the League of Corinth
336	Assassination of Philip. Accession of Alexander in Macedon and of Darius III Codomannus in Persia.
335	The revolt and destruction of Thebes.
334	Alexander lands in Asia. Battle of the Granicus.
333	Battle of Issus.
332	Capture of Tyre and Gaza.
331	Alexander's visit to Egypt. Foundation of Alexandria. Battle of Gaugamela. Defeat of the Spartan king Agis III at Megalopolis.
330	Capture of the royal capitals. Persepolis sacked. Death of Darius.
329	The crossing of the Hindu Kush. Execution of Bessus.
328	Campaign in Sogdiana.
326	Victory over the Indian king Porus.
325	Descent of the Indus Valley to the sea. The crossing of the Gedrosia desert.
324	The Susa 'weddings'. Nicanor's embassy to Olympia.
323	Death of Alexander. The Babylon dispensation. Beginning of the Lamian War.
322–321	The defeat of the Athenians at Crannon. The Conference of Triparadeisus and a new distribution of satrapies.
319	Death of Antipater.
316	Assassination of Philip Arrhidaeus and Olympias.
310	Assassination of Alexander IV and Roxane.
306–305	The successors all assume the title of king.

301	Battle of Ipsus. Death of Antigonus.
297	Death of Cassander.
294	Demetrius Poliorcetes seizes Macedon.
281	Battle of Couroupedion. Accession of Antiochus I in Syria and Ptolemy II Philadelphus in Egypt.
276	Antigonus Gonatas seizes Macedon.

The succession of the Achaemenid kings

Cyrus I, *c.* 640–600
Cambyses I, *c.* 600–558
Cyrus the Great, *c.* 558–528
Cambyses II, 528–522
Darius I, 521–486
Xerxes I, 486–465
Artaxerxes I, 465–424
Darius II the Bastard, 424–405
Artaxerxes II Mnemnon, 404–358
Artaxerxes III Ochos, 358–338
Artaxerxes IV, 338–336
Darius III Codomannus, 336–330

Bibliography

SOURCES[1]

Epigraphic and numismatic

Heisserer, A. J., *Alexander the Great and the Greeks. The Epigraphic Evidence*,
Norman, OK, University of Oklahoma Press, 1980.
Oikonomides, A. N., *The Coins of Alexander the Great. An Introductory Guide*,
Chicago, Ares, 1981.

Archaeological

Most important is the publication of the excavations of DAFA (Délégation
archéologique française en Afghanistan) in *Mémoires*, XIX (on Bactria); XXI,
XXVI–XXXI (on Ai Khanoum), Paris, 1964–92.

Literary

As we have seen, these are the sources that pose the most problems. I have
consulted the following editions:

Arrian, *Histoire d'Alexandre. L'Anabase d'Alexandre le Grand*, translated from the
Greek by P. Savinel, followed by 'Flavius Arrien entre deux mondes' by P.
Vidal-Naquet, Paris, Editions de Minuit, 1984. For the Greek text: Arrian,
Anabasis of Alexander, vol. I, books 1–4, and vol. II, books 5–7, with a preface
by P. A. Brunt, Loeb Classical Library, Harvard University Press and William
Heinemann, Cambridge, MA, and London, 1976, 1983.
Diodorus, books XVII and XVIII, text edited and translated into French by P.
Goukowsky, Paris, Belles Lettres, 1976 and 1978. English translation: *Diodorus
of Sicily*, book XVII, translated by C. Bradford Welles, Loeb Classical Library,
Harvard University Press and William Heinemann, Cambridge, MA, and
London, 1963.
Justin, *Abrégé des Histoires philippiques de Trogue Pompée*, vol. I, French
translation by E. Chambry, Paris, Classiques Garnier, 1936.
Plutarch, *Lives*, vol. IX: *Alexandre–César*, text edited and translated by R.
Flacelière and E. Chambry, Paris, Belles Lettres, 1998. English translation:

[1] We now have at our disposal a valuable work, *Les Historiens d'Alexandre*, Paris, Belles
Lettres, coll. 'Fragments', 2001.

Parallel Lives, vol. VII, translated by Bernadotte Perrin, Loeb Classical Library, Harvard University Press and William Heinemann, Cambridge, MA, and London, 1919.

—, *Oeuvres morales*, vol. V, 1, text edited and translated into French by F. Frazier and C. Froidefond, Paris, Belles Lettres, 1988. English translation, *Moralia*, vol. IV, translated by Frank C. Babbit, Loeb Classical Library, Harvard University Press and William Heinemann, Cambridge, MA, and London, 1936.

Pseudo-Callisthenes, *Le Roman d'Alexandre. La vie et les hauts faits d'Alexandre de Macédoine*, translated into French with a commentary by G. Bonnoure and B. Serret, Paris, Belles Lettres, 1992. English translation, *The Romance of Alexander the Great*, translated by A. M. Wolohojian, New York and London, Columbia University Press, 1969.

Quintus Curtius, *Histoires*, text edited and translated by H. Bardon, 2 vols, Paris, Belles Lettres, 1961–5. English translation: vol. I, books 1–5, vol. II, books 6–10, translated by John C. Rolfe, Loeb Classical Library, Harvard University Press and William Heinemann, Cambridge, MA, and London, 1946.

Many commentaries have been written on these literary sources. The earliest is that by Guillaume Emmanuel Joseph Guilhem de Clermont-Lodève, Baron of Sainte-Croix, *Examen critique des anciens historiens d'Alexandre*, Paris, 1775, 2nd edn, 1804. More recent works include:

L'Alessandro di Giustino (ed. L. Braccesi), Rome, l'Erma di Bretschneider, 1993.

Atkinson, J. E., *A Commentary on Q. Curtius Rufus Historiae Alexandri Magni*, books III and IV, London, Studies in Classical Philology, 1980.

Centanni, M., *Il Romanzo di Alessandro*, Turin, Einaudi, 1991.

Hammond, N. G. L., *Three Historians of Alexander the Great: The So-called Vulgate Authors, Diodorus, Justin, and Curtius*, Cambridge, Cambridge University Press, 1983.

—, *Sources for Alexander the Great: An Analysis of Plutarch, Lives, and Arrian, Anabasis Alexandrou*, Cambridge, Cambridge University Press, 1993.

Merkelbach, R., *Die Quellen des griechischen Alexander-Romans*, Munich, Zetemata 9, 1954.

Pédech, P., *Historiens compagnons d'Alexandre*, Paris, 1984.

Prandi, L., 'L'Alessandro di Plutarco', in L. Van der Stockt (ed.), *Rhetorical Theory and Praxis in Plutarch*, Louvain Namur, 2000.

Stadter, P. A., *Arrian of Nicomedia*, Chapel Hill, NC, University of North Carolina Press, 1980.

GENERAL WORKS

Bosworth, A. B., *Conquest and Empire. The Reign of Alexander the Great*, Cambridge, Cambridge University Press, 1988.

—, 'Alexander the Great. Part I: The events of the reign. Part II: Greece and the conquered countries', *The Cambridge Ancient History. VI: The Fourth Century BC*, Cambridge, Cambridge University Press, 1994.

Briant, P., *De la Grèce à l'Orient. Alexandre le Grand*, Paris, Gallimard, 1987.

Droysen, J. G., *Alexandre le Grand*, French translation by J. Benoist-Méchin, Paris, 1934, 2nd edn, Brussels, Complexe, 1991.

Goukowsky, P., 'Alexandre et la conquête de l'Orient', in E. Will, C. Mossé and P. Goukowsky, *Le monde grec et l'Orient, II: Le IVe siècle et l'époque hellénistique*, Paris, PUF, 3rd edn, 1993.

Green, P., *Alexander of Macedon (356–323 BC). A Historical Biography*, Berkeley and Los Angeles, University of California Press, 1991.

Hamilton, J. R., *Alexander the Great*, London, Hutchinson, 1973.

Hammond, N. G. L., *Alexander the Great. King, Commander and Statesman*, Bristol, Bristol Classical Press, 2nd edn, 1989.

Lane Fox, R., *The Search for Alexander*, Boston, Little, Brown, 1980.

O'Brien, J. M., *Alexander the Great. The Invisible Enemy*, London, Routledge, 1992.

Radet, G., *Alexandre le Grand*, Paris, Paul Geuthner, 1931.

Schachermeyr, F., *Alexander der Grosse. Das problem seines Persönlichkeit und seines Wirkens*, Vienna, Österreichischen Akademie der Wissenschaften, 1973.

Seibert, J., *Alexander der Grosse*, Darmstadt, Erträge der Forschung, 10, 1972.

Tarn, W. W., *Alexander the Great. I: Narrative. II. Sources and Studies*, Cambridge, Cambridge University Press, 1948.

Wilcken, U., *Alexandre le Grand*, French translation, Paris, Payot, 1933. English translation, with introduction by E. N. Borza, New York, Norton, 1967.

Will, W., *Alexander der Grosse*, Stuttgart, 1986.

Wirth, G., *Studien zur Alexandergeschichte*, Darmstadt, 1985.

THE WORLD BORN FROM THE CONQUEST

Aymard, A., 'L'institution monarchique' and 'Sur l'assemblée macédonienne', *Etudes d'histoire ancienne*, Paris, PUF, 1967, pp. 123–35 and 143–63.

Cabanes, P., *Le Monde en partage, de la mort d'Alexandre à la paix d'Apamée (323–188)*, Paris, Seuil, 1996.

Rostovtzeff, M., *Histoire économique et sociale du monde hellénistique*, French translation, Paris, Robert Laffont, 1989. English original, *The Social and Economic History of the Hellenistic World*, Oxford, Oxford University Press, rev. edn, 1953.

Sartre, M., *D'Alexandre à Zénobie. Histoire du Levant antique, IVe siècle av. J.-C. – IIIe siècle ap. J.-C.*, Paris, Fayard, 2001.

Will, E., *Histoire politique du monde hellénistique*, vol. I, Nancy, 2nd edn, 1979.

—, 'Le monde hellénistique', in E. Will, C. Mossé and P. Goukowsky, *Le monde grec et l'Orient, II. Le IVe siècle et l'époque hellénistique*, Paris, PUF, 3rd edn, 1993.

Will, E. and Orrieux, C., *Ioudaïsmos–Hellenismos, essai sur le judaïsme judéen à l'époque hellénistique*, Nancy, Presses Universitaires de Nancy, 1986.

THE MYTH OF ALEXANDER

On the origins, the essential book is P. Goukowsky's *Essai sur les origines du mythe d'Alexandre. I. Les Origines. II. Alexandre et Dionysos*, Nancy, Université de Nancy, 1978–81. Here are a few collective works:

Alessandro Magno tra Storia e Mito (ed. Marta Sordi), Milan, Jaca Books, 1984.
Alessandro Magno. Storia e Mito (ed. T. Quirico), Rome, Fondazione Memmo, 1995–6.
Alexandre le Grand dans les littératures occidentales et proche-orientales (Proceedings of the Paris colloquium, 27–9 Novenber 1997), Université de Paris-X, Nanterre, 1999.
Alexandre le Grand. Image et réalité, Fondation Hardt pour l'étude de l'Antiquité classique, vol. XXII, Geneva, 1976.
Carey, G., *The Medieval Alexander* (ed. D. J. A. Ross), Cambridge, Cambridge University Press, 1956.
Frugoni, G., *La Fortuna di Alessandro Magno dell'Antichità al Medioevo*, Florence, La Nuova Italia, 1978.
Grell, C. and Michel, C., *L'Ecole des princes ou Alexandre disgracié*, with a fore-word by P. Vidal-Naquet, Paris, Belles Lettres, 1988.
Meyer, P., *Alexandre le Grand dans la littérature française du Moyen Age*, Paris, 1882.

On the image of Alexander in the Arab tradition, see two articles by F. de Polignac: 'Alexandre dans la littérature arabe. L'Orient face à l'hellénisme', *Arabica*, XXIX, 3, 1982, pp. 296–306, and 'L'homme aux deux cornes. Une image d'Alexandre du symbolisme grec à l'apocalypse musulmane', *MEFRA*, 96, 1984, pp. 29–51.

On the image of Alexander in the Jewish tradition, apart from the remarks of P. Vidal-Naquet in the foreword to the book by C. Grell and C. Michel, see two old articles by I. Lévi, 'La légende d'Alexandre dans le Talmud', *Revue des études juives*, 2, 1881, pp. 293–300, and 'La légende d'Alexandre dans le Talmud et le Midrash', *Revue des études juives*, 7, 1888, pp. 78–93; also J. P. Rothschild, 'Alexandre hébreu ou Micromégas', *Mélanges de l'Ecole française de Rome. Moyen Age*, vol. CXII, 2000–1, pp. 27–42.

Finally, the image of Alexander in two novels:
Manfredi, V., *Alexandre le Grand*, 3 vols, Paris, Plon, 1999; Pocket, 2001. English translation, London, Pan Macmillan, 2001–2.
Mann, K., *Alexander. Roman der Utopie*, Munich, 1929; French translation, Paris, 1931; more recent translation by P. F. Kaempf, Paris, Solin, 1989.

Supplementary bibliography

Paul Cartledge

SOURCES

General

Heckel, W. and Yardley, J. C., *Alexander the Great. Historical Sources in Translation*, Oxford, 2003.

Epigraphic, numismatic, archaeological

Camp, J. M., *The Archaeology of Athens*, New Haven, CT, 2001, pp. 142–60.
Price, M. J., *The Coinage in the Name of Alexander the Great and Philip Arrhidaeus*, 2 vols, Zurich and London, 1991.
Stamatopoulou, M. and Yeroulanou, M. (eds), *Excavating Classical Culture. Recent Archaeological Discoveries in Greece*, Oxford, 2002. This includes: A. Kottaridi, 'Discovering Aegae'; A. Lilimpaki-Akamati, 'Recent discoveries in Pella'; M. Tsibidou-Avloniti, 'Excavating a painted Macedonian tomb near Thessaloniki'; and D. Pandermalis, 'New discoveries at Dion'.

Literary (in chronological order)

Ptolemy

Bosworth, *Alexander and the East* (below), pp. 31–65.

Polybius

Billows, R. A., 'Polybius and Alexander historiography', in Bosworth and Baynham, *Alexander the Great in Fact and Fiction* (below), pp. 286–306.

Curtius

Baynham, E., *Alexander the Great. The Unique History of Quintus Curtius Rufus*, Ann Arbor, 1998.

Plutarch

Mossman, J., 'Tragedy and epic in Plutarch's Alexander' (1988), repr. in B. Scardigli (ed.), *Essays on Plutarch's Lives*, Oxford, 1995, pp. 209–28.

229

Arrian

Bosworth, A. B., *A Historical Commentary on Arrian's History of Alexander*, vol. I: books 1–3, Oxford, 1980; vol. II: books 4–5, Oxford, 1995.
Bosworth, A. B., *From Arrian to Alexander*, Oxford, 1988.

GENERAL WORKS

Bosworth, A. B., *Alexander and the East. The Tragedy of Triumph*, Oxford, 1996.
Briant, P., *Alexander the Great. The Heroic Ideal*, London, 1996. French original 1987.
Carney, E., *Women and Monarchy in Macedonia*, Norman, OK, 2000.
Ellis, J. R., 'Macedon and north-west Greece' and 'Macedonian hegemony created', in *The Cambridge Ancient History*, 2nd edn, vol. VI, Cambridge, Cambridge University Press, 1994.
Fraser, P. M., *Cities of Alexander the Great*, Oxford, 1996.
Hatzopoulos, M. B., *Cultes et rites de passage en Macédoine*, Paris, 1994.
—, *Macedonian Institutions under the Kings*, 2 vols, Athens, 1996.
Heckel, W., *The Last Days and Testament of Alexander the Great*, Stuttgart, 1988.
—., *The Marshals of Alexander's Empire*, London, 1992.
Holt, F. L., *Alexander the Great and Bactria: The Formation of a Greek Frontier in Central Asia*, Leiden, 1988.
Roisman, J. (ed.), *Brill's Companion to Alexander the Great*, Leiden, 2003 (comprehensive bibliography, pp. 365–88).
Worthington, I. *Alexander the Great: Man and God*, London, forthcoming.
—, (ed.), *Alexander the Great. A Reader*, London, 2003.

THE WORLD BORN FROM THE CONQUEST

Bosworth, A. B., *The Legacy of Alexander. Politics, Warfare, and Propaganda under the Successors*, Oxford, 1993.
Habicht, C., *Athens from Alexander to Antony*, Cambridge, MA, 1997.
Ogden, D., *Polygamy, Prostitutes and Death. The Hellenistic Dynasties*, London, 1999.
Shipley, G., *The Greek World after Alexander, 323–30 BC*, London, 2000.
Stewart, A. F., *Faces of Power: Alexander's Image and Hellenistic Politics*, California and Oxford, 1993.
True, M. and Hamma, K. (eds), *Alexandria and Alexandrianism*, Malibu, 1996.

THE MYTH OF ALEXANDER

Bosworth, A. B. and Baynham, E. (eds), *Alexander the Great in Fact and Fiction*, Oxford, 2000.
Carlsen, J. et al., *Alexander the Great. Reality and Myth*, Rome, 1993.
Cohen, A., *The Alexander Mosaic. Stories of Victory and Defeat*, Cambridge, 1997.
Roisman, J. (ed.), *Alexander the Great: Ancient and Modern Perspectives*, Lexington, MA, and Toronto, 1995.
Spencer, D., *The Roman Alexander*, Exeter, 2002.

Translator's note

I have used the following translations for the quotations from these ancient and other texts (in other cases the translations are my own from the author's French).

ANCIENT TEXTS

All from the Loeb Classical Library, Harvard University Press and William Heinemann, Cambridge, MA, and London:

Aeschines, *Against Ctesiphon*, translated by C. D. Adams, 1919.
Appian, *The Mithridatic Wars*, translated by Horace White, 1912.
Aristotle, *Rhetoric*, translated by John Henry Freese, 1926.
—, *Politics*, translated by H. Rackham, 1932.
Diodorus of Sicily, *Library of History*, translated by C. Bradford Welles, 1963.
Herodotus, *Histories*, translated by A. D. Godley, 1920–5.
Isocrates, *To Nicocles*, translated by George Norlin, 1928.
Lucan, *Pharsalia*, translated by J. D. Duff, 1913.
Plato, *Republic*, translated by Paul Shorey, 1930–5.
—, *Statesman*, translated by Harold N. Fowler, 1925.
Plutarch, *Lives (Alexander, Caesar, Eumenes)*, translated by Bernadotte Perrin, 1914–26.
—, *Moralia (The Fortune of Alexander, I and II)*, translated by Frank C. Babbit, 1927–69.
Quintus Curtius, *History of Alexander*, translated by John C. Rolfe, 1946.
Seneca, *De Beneficiis*, translated by John W. Basore, 1935.
—, *De Ira*, translated by John W. Basore, 1970.
—, *Letters to Lucilius*, translated by Richard M. Gummere, 1920.
Suetonius, *Life of Augustus*, translated by J. C. Rolfe, 1914.
Thucydides, *History of the Peloponnesian War*, translated by Charles Forster Smith, 1919–23.
Xenophon, *Cyropaedia*, translated by Walter Miller, 1914.
—, *Memorabilia*, translated by E. C. Marchant, 1923.
—, *Oeconomicus*, translated by E. C. Marchant, 1923.

OTHER TEXTS

Montaigne, *Essays*, translated by G. B. Ives, New York, Limited Editions Club, 1946.

Pseudo-Callisthenes, *The Romance of Alexander*, translated (from the Armenian) by A. M. Wolohojian, New York and London, Columbia University Press, 1969.

Index